Thinking Again About Marriage

Thinking Again About Marriage: Key Theological Questions

Edited by
John P. Bradbury
and Susannah Cornwall

scm press

© The Contributors 2016

Published in 2016 by SCM Press
Editorial office
3rd Floor, Invicta House,
108–114 Golden Lane,
London EC1Y 0TG, UK

SCM Press is an imprint of Hymns Ancient & Modern Ltd
(a registered charity)
13A Hellesdon Park Road, Norwich,
Norfolk NR6 5DR, UK
www.scmpress.co.uk

British Library Cataloguing in Publication data

A catalogue record for this book is available
from the British Library

978 0 334 05369 9

Typeset by Regent Typesetting
Printed and bound by CPI Group (UK) Ltd, Croydon

Contents

Acknowledgements   vii

About the Authors   ix

1   Introduction: Thinking Again About Marriage in
    Changing Time   1
    Susannah Cornwall and John P. Bradbury

2   Marriage, Gender and Doctrine   14
    Mike Higton

3   Thinking About Marriage: What Can We Learn from
    Christian History?   29
    Charlotte Methuen

4   Thinking About Marriage with Scripture   44
    Ben Fulford

5   Taking Time Over Marriage: Tradition, History and
    Time in Recent Debates   62
    Frances Clemson

6   A Perfect Crown: Towards a Liturgical Theology of
    Marriage   82
    Julie Gittoes

7   Faithfulness to our Sexuate Bodies: The Vocations of
    Generativity and Sex   101
    Susannah Cornwall

8   An Ascetical Critique of the Concept of 'Gender
    Complementarity'   121
    Raphael Cadenhead

9 Called to Become ... A Vocational Theology of
   Marriage   135
   John P. Bradbury

10 Reproduction and The Body's Grace   152
   Brett Gray

11 Marriage and English Law   167
   Augur Pearce

12 Afterword: Setting Marriage in Context   191
   Rachel Muers

Bibliography   203
Index of Biblical References   213
Index of Names and Subjects   216

Acknowledgements

This book has been a real team effort, and as editors we'd like to thank, first and foremost, all of the contributors. They are friends as well as colleagues, and we are especially grateful to Brett Gray, whose Facebook wall hosted the original conversation that became the genesis for the book. We are also grateful to Westminster College, Cambridge, who made it possible for most of the contributors to meet in person on two occasions to work on ideas. We'd also like to thank other friends and colleagues who were involved in conversations along the way, including Steve Holmes and Jon Morgan.

On the technical side, our thanks go to Natalie Watson, who commissioned the book while she was at SCM Press, and to the rest of the team at SCM for taking it forward. We also owe much gratitude to Emily Chadwick for her hard work in formatting the references and Bibliography.

About the Authors

John Bradbury is Vice-Principal of Westminster College, Cambridge. He is the author of *Perpetually Reforming: A Theology of Church Reform and Renewal* (Bloomsbury, 2013). He is a minister of the United Reformed Church, and ministered in Liverpool for a number of years before taking up his present appointment.

Raphael Cadenhead earned his doctorate in Theology and Religious Studies from the University of Cambridge in 2014. The title of his dissertation is "Corporeality and Desire: A Diachronic Study of Gregory of Nyssa's Ascetical Theology". He is currently working as a statutory social worker in child protection and training in systemic (family) therapy.

Frances Clemson is Lecturer in Theology and Ministry at Durham University. Her research interests include Anglican thought, the nature of theological education, and the relationship between theology and the arts. She is the author of a forthcoming book on the Anglican thinker, novelist, translator and playwright Dorothy L. Sayers.

Susannah Cornwall is Advanced Research Fellow in Theology and Religion at the University of Exeter, and Director of EXCEPT (Exeter Centre for Ethics and Practical Theology). Her books include *Sex and Uncertainty in the Body of Christ* (Routledge, 2010), *Controversies in Queer Theology* (SCM, 2011), and *Theology and Sexuality* (SCM, 2013).

Ben Fulford is Senior Lecturer in Systematic Theology at the University of Chester. He has published *Divine Eloquence and Human Transformation*, on history and the theology of Scripture (Fortress Press, 2013). His research interests include Hans Frei's political theology, the Cappadocians, and the place of fragile goods in the Christian life.

Julie Gittoes is Residentiary Canon at Guildford Cathedral, responsible for developing educational work, including engaging in public dialogue. She is a part-time doctrine tutor for SEITE (South East Institute of Theological Education), and co-editor of *Generous Ecclesiology: Church, World and the Kingdom of God* (SCM, 2013).

Brett Gray is Chaplain and Fellow in Theology at Sidney Sussex College, Cambridge. His recently completed doctorate was on the theology of Rowan Williams. In addition to time spent as a college chaplain, he served for a number of years as a parish priest in the Diocese of St Albans.

Mike Higton is Professor of Theology and Ministry at Durham University, and author of several books including *A Theology of Higher Education* (Oxford, 2012), *Christian Doctrine* (SCM, 2008), *Difficult Gospel: The Theology of Rowan Williams* (SCM, 2004), and, with Rachel Muers, *The Text in Play: Experiments in Reading Scripture* (Cascade, 2012).

Charlotte Methuen is Senior Lecturer in Church History at the University of Glasgow, and a member of the Church of England's Faith and Order Commission. She has a particular research interest in the history of women's ministry and the place of women in the Church.

Rachel Muers is Senior Lecturer in Christian Studies at the University of Leeds. Her publications include *Keeping God's Silence: Towards a Theological Ethics of Communication* (Blackwell, 2004); *Living for the Future: Theological Ethics for Coming Generations* (T&T Clark, 2008); and *Testimony: Quakerism and Theological Ethics* (SCM, 2015).

Augur Pearce pursues public law litigation for the Government Legal Service. He has been a partner with Westminster solicitors and a lecturer at Cardiff University, in both places specializing in law's interaction with religion. He is an Elder in the United Reformed Church, serving on its Law and Polity Advisory Group.

Introduction:
Thinking Again About Marriage in
Changing Times

SUSANNAH CORNWALL AND JOHN BRADBURY

Marriage appears to be on the decline. In England and Wales, 42 per cent of marriages now end in divorce, with couples who have been married for between four and eight years the most likely to divorce (Office for National Statistics 2013a). In 2013, almost half of births in England and Wales were to unmarried parents (Office for National Statistics 2014). So in this context, why have we written yet another book about the Christian theology of marriage? And why should anyone bother to read it? In this opening chapter, we will try to explain why we believe that marriage is worth attending to in Christian theological terms, both for those who are already involved and invested in church contexts, and for those who are interested in what contribution, if any, Christian discourse might make to broader discussions about the nature and purpose of marriage in society.

Marriage, more than most things considered theological goods (i.e. benefits or interests), has usually had a distinctively public character. Since 1753 in England and Wales it has been mandatory that a marriage ceremony be formal and public in nature: the couple's intention to marry must be declared publicly prior to the ceremony (which takes place by mechanisms such as the reading of banns in Anglican churches, and the displaying of notices of intent to marry in register offices). The ceremony must involve witnesses, and declarations that the spouses give their free consent to marry. Marriage practices have their own theological, pastoral and social significance, which is why questions around the language, music and accoutrements that may or may not be used in marriage ceremonies are so important. For example, in England and Wales, at the time of writing, civil marriage ceremonies may not involve any hymns, prayers, or readings from sacred texts.

For couples who want to have an entirely secular ceremony, this is not necessarily a problem (though there has been debate in recent years over whether poems that mention God, or songs with spiritual content, are legitimate or must always be excluded). The secular nature of civil ceremonies may, however, be more of a difficulty for same-sex couples, who are not currently able to marry in many churches. People who have a religious faith but who cannot acknowledge it within their wedding ceremony may feel that the 'guts' of the ceremony have been removed, that a civil ceremony is rather soulless, and that what they would really like is to be able to marry in their place of worship before God.

For, significantly, in a Christian context, marriage takes place during a *service*, an act of worship, which may or may not include the specifically sacramental element of a nuptial mass. (Roman Catholic and Eastern Orthodox Christians consider that marriage is a sacrament in its own right; most Protestants do not.) It is therefore a *liturgical* event in the lives of those who marry – and in the life of a worshipping community. It is simultaneously a *festival* event (that is, a celebratory interruption of the normal routine of the community) and a *quotidian* one (that is, a relatively frequent and expected event in the life of many church communities). Where the average age of a congregation is relatively young, or where the majority of people getting married in a church are already members of the congregation, weddings may be fairly commonplace, even though they are, of course, all unique and still a significant rite of passage for the individuals involved and their family and friends. But demographic shifts mean that the average age of congregations in many denominations is rising,[1] and that fewer younger people are choosing church weddings.[2] Where church weddings do take place, they may well now be between people who are not 'regulars' there but who have other connections to the church (for example, that they live in the parish; that they attended the church as children; or that their parents or grandparents were married there). There may well not be much or any crossover between the wedding guests and the regular congregation. There are therefore questions to be asked about how, if

---

1 The average age of congregations in Church of England churches is 62; as of 2007, 47 per cent of adult attendees at Church of England churches were aged 65 and over (Church Growth Research Programme 2014).

2 The proportion of weddings taking place in religious premises has fallen steadily since the middle of the twentieth century, and more than two-thirds of couples in England and Wales now have civil ceremonies. Over half of ceremonies now take place not in churches or register offices but in other 'approved premises', such as hotels and historic buildings (Office for National Statistics 2013b).

at all, such services fit into the 'everyday' life and pattern of worship of a church, and how far churches should consider weddings an evangelistic or church-growing opportunity.

This book does not focus on same-sex marriage specifically (though we comment on it further later in this Introduction), but there are questions about marriage practices and liturgy for ceremonies involving same-sex couples that are certainly of relevance. For example, to what extent might denominations need to alter the wording of existing marriage liturgies to reflect the situation of same-sex couples? How far might trends towards non-monogamous marriage (particularly, anecdotally, among gay male couples) influence the assumption that other marriages must also entail 'forsaking all others'? However, our broad assumption in this book has been that same-sex marriages need not explicitly be constructed in different terms theologically from heterosexual marriages. We do not, for example, advocate a different kind of legally recognized or covenanted partnership for same-sex couples than for heterosexual ones, or for childless couples than for those with children (though some theologians, notably Robert Song in his 2014 book *Covenant and Calling*, have done so – Song 2014).

Individual Christian denominations have put forward their own responses to questions surrounding marriage (some of which Mike Higton discusses in his chapter in this volume), and these have appeared with increasing frequency since the 1990s. Part of the reason for this has been the move to legalizing civil partnerships and same-sex marriages in some jurisdictions, which has prompted Christians to think again about to what extent they want to endorse and recognize such partnerships, and whether marriage is to be considered, in Christian terms, an institution open only to couples of different sexes. However, although some of the responses that individual churches have made to public debates about marriage repeatedly make explicit and implicit theological claims about marriage, those claims are often not explored in any depth. Other aspects of the debate – issues of biblical interpretation, ecclesial authority or the attempt to maintain unity in the face of potential division – have often taken centre stage; the theology of marriage itself has been somewhat neglected. Some church reports and statements have been rather self-referential, appealing mainly to earlier teachings from the same denomination, and have not seemed to engage with questions such as how far issues of genre and transmission matter when appealing to the Bible, or how shifts in world view and scientific understandings might affect how Christians today relate to their own traditions and Scriptures.

This book is not a summary of existing theological claims about marriage. (Other excellent books of that type already exist; some suggestions for further reading are given at the end of this chapter.) Rather, it aims to guide readers into the *practice* of thinking theologically about marriage. We will explore what is involved in thinking through marriage in the light of the Bible; what it means to draw on the Christian tradition; what it means to attend to the liturgical forms in which marriage is celebrated; and what it means to attend to experience theologically. The book will show how theological thinking about marriage has been bound up with theological thinking about the nature of sex and gender, and with thinking about the place and importance of procreation and fecundity more generally. It will explore the place that marriage can have within broader accounts of Christian life, and develop a theology of marriage as vocation. And we also include chapters that introduce aspects of the history of marriage and aspects of the legal questions surrounding it, in order to provide a wider context for these theological questions.

The book is prompted in part by recent debates about same-sex marriage, but its focus is not limited to those debates, and it will be relevant to audiences who are interested in many other questions about marriage. Those debates have, nevertheless, revealed that there is a striking need for rich, positive theological thinking about the nature of marriage – and the book is written in the conviction that theological thinking can be a useful resource for those debates precisely because it is not wholly determined by them. One of the things we acknowledge throughout the volume is that marriage is not, and has never been, a single, monolithic thing: at different times and across different cultures there have been diverse things called 'marriage', which have varied according to factors such as whether they involve only two people or multiple spouses (polygamous marriages, where one man marries several women, have been particularly common); whether they are understood as private or public arrangements; what the minimum age is for entering into marriage; whether and on what grounds marriages can be ended via divorce; whether marriages can be contracted between family members; and so on. Given that marriage is already multiple, then, it is deliberate and conscious that there are also multiple perspectives on marriage represented throughout this volume. All the authors are Christian theologians but we have different disciplinary and denominational backgrounds. We include a mixture of clergy and lay people; a mixture of sexualities, sexes and genders; a mixture of married and unmarried people, with and without children; and a mixture of ages and career stages.

Acknowledging the multiplicity of marriage is important for other reasons too. For one thing, we are clear throughout the volume that marriage is not something over which Christians, or indeed other people of faith, have a monopoly. Christians may have particular *perspectives* on what they believe marriage signifies theologically, but marriage is not something that only *exists* or makes sense in a faith context. Plenty of people who marry do so with no concern whatsoever for what theologians may or may not understand by what they are doing. And so they should: marriage is public property, an institution in which many people feel invested and want the right to access, regardless of their religious affiliation or otherwise. Marriage in most jurisdictions confers particular legal rights and responsibilities; it is therefore almost always a civil matter as well as (or instead of) a religious one. As authors, then, we are not seeking to tell other people that marriage has to look a particular way or be understood only in a particular way (though, as we will see, there may be special themes that arise as goods frequently and distinctively within *Christian* accounts of what marriage might be). We are also circumspect about the idea that marriage is a 'creation good', something instituted by God at the beginning of creation and understood as basically unchanging. Rather, we are setting out a range of Christian theological reflections on *what it means to think about marriage theologically* – and *whether marriage is something about which it is worth continuing to think at all* – at a time when public and legal definitions of marriage continue to shift. One outcome will, we hope, be to assist the Christian churches in their own ongoing conversations about marriage and the relationship between religious institutions and civil society. But another will be to offer a vision for what Christian theology might offer to broader public debates on marriage. Many Christian responses to questions about marriage seem to start from saying what marriage is *not*: we hope to offer something positive and constructive, drawing on the depth and richness of the Christian tradition, to say what marriage *is* and might have the potential to be.

So what is the state of the conversation to which we hope to contribute? One of the catalysts for putting this book together was the frustrations that some of us felt about the kinds of conversations about marriage that were taking place – or *not* taking place – in the churches. Some of us were upset and discouraged by the fact that Christian responses to prompts such as the UK government's 2012 consultation on same-sex marriage seemed theologically 'thin', and seemed not to acknowledge or draw on the breadth of existing rich theological reflection on marriage, gender, sexuality and relationship that we knew existed. Some of us were bothered by the fact that denominations' official pronouncements on matters of this kind often seemed not to reflect the diversity of belief, practice and experience we knew were present within their memberships. Some of us felt that such pronouncements tended to occur in top-down fashion, and were not reflective of the ongoing conversations taking place at all levels of the denominations. One of the reasons why this book is appearing in 2016, and not in 2012 when our initial conversations took place, is precisely because it has been developed in dialogue. It has grown via a mixture of face-to-face meetings, as well as Skype, Facebook and email exchanges. We have all been convinced that the way good theology is done is in conversation, with an acknowledgement, rather than a stamping-out, of our disagreements and divergences.

Another reason why it has taken longer than it might have done is because of the other, related conversations in which many of us have simultaneously been involved. Some of us have contributed to formal ecclesial and denominational consultations on marriage and sexuality over the last few years; some of us have been involved in teaching and training on these and other issues for the denominations, as well as in universities; some of us have faced these questions directly in the course of ordained ministry. All of us are interested and invested in how theology is worked out and implemented on the ground, in the everyday business and formal resolutions of our churches. Importantly, though, we believe that theology is not only a matter of being informed by churches' internal concerns. We believe that when academic theology is working well, it can be part of what encourages churches to think wider about their assumptions, about their norms, about the goods they want to uphold. And we therefore want to suggest that denominations ought to remain aware of and engaged by what is being done in *other* denominations; by theologians not affiliated to a particular denomination; and in fields such as sociology, history and law that have ongoing relevance for theology too.

So what does it mean to conduct a properly theological exploration of an issue? What makes a claim about marriage meaningful in the light of the sources, norms and practices of Christian theology?

It is, perhaps, harder to give a coherent response to this question than one might at first think. This volume itself exemplifies some of the challenges one encounters in trying to give a coherent account of the sources and norms of theology. In one sense, it is not unusual for a volume to be produced by theologians from a range of diverse church traditions. Theology in the academy, particularly in the British context, is used to this kind of theological dialogue. This is rather different from contexts where confessional theology from one particular tradition might be more common. It is not, however, ecumenical groups of academic theologians who form church policy; it is the specific church institutions themselves that do that. Furthermore, different church traditions work with different sources and norms. The Roman Catholic tradition might speak in terms of Scripture, tradition and the teaching authority of the Magisterium. Anglicanism has classically understood the sources and norms of theology as being Scripture, tradition and reason. The Reformed tradition has classically claimed that the teaching of the Church can only be authoritatively derived *sola scriptura*, from Scripture alone. While the boundaries between these different accounts of theological authority shift, and are in reality porous (particularly in the academy), the differences between them have a significant impact on the outcome of theological conversations about marriage. This is probably particularly so in debates surrounding same-sex marriage.

A good illustration of the way prior theological commitments shape accounts of marriage emerges from the famous debate about natural theology between Karl Barth and Emil Brunner in Brunner's pamphlet 'Nature and Grace' and Barth's riposte, 'Nein!' ('No!') (first published together in *Natural Theology* in 1946). While this might seem an unusual place to go to illustrate the way different theological starting points impact upon accounts of marriage, it actually does so with great clarity. Brunner's essay is a critique of Barth's total rejection of natural theology, the idea that one can in creation come to comprehend something of God's ways with the world. Brunner argues that within both Scripture and the theological tradition, an account is offered of 'ordinances of creation', and 'ordinances of preservation' (Brunner 2002 [1946], p. 30). These are understood as gifts of God in creation for general human flourishing. Brunner identifies two specifically: 'Matrimony and the State, without which no communal life is conceivable, that could in any way be termed human'. In Christian understanding, for Brunner, marriage is 'instituted by the creator'. It is therefore a '"natural" ordinance of the creator because the possibility of and the desire for its realization lies within human nature and because it is realized to some extent by men who are ignorant of the God revealed in Christ' (Brunner 2002 [1946], pp. 29–30). This is an understanding of marriage that ultimately finds its roots in the idea of a natural law, or natural theology. It rests on the assumption that if one thinks rationally about marriage, and one takes account of the physical world, one can accurately discern something of God's intentions for human life.

Karl Barth's response to Brunner's critique, 'Nein!', is sharp and stinging. Barth mounts a spirited defence of the utter primacy of revelation over anything that might be understood to be natural theology or natural law. In doing so he responds directly to Brunner on the question of the idea of the 'ordinances of creation' (Barth 2002 [1946], p. 86). It is worth quoting Barth in full at this point:

> No doubt there are such things as moral and sociological axioms which seem to underlie the various customs, laws and usages of different peoples, and seem to appear in them with some regularity. And there certainly seems to be some connection between these axioms and the instinct and reason which both believers and unbelievers have indeed every reason to allow to function in the life of the community. But what are these axioms? Or who – among us, who are 'sinners through and through'! – decides what they are? If we consulted instinct and reason, what might or might not be called matrimony? Do instinct and reason really tell us what is *the* form of matrimony, which would then have to be acknowledged and proclaimed as a divine ordinance of creation? (Barth 2002 [1946], p. 86; emphasis in original).

For Barth, it is simply impossible to read off creation a theological account of any human institution such as marriage. This leaves open the question of the form of marriage, a question Barth later would develop (in ways that are not necessarily in line with the general views expressed in this volume) in the section of the *Church Dogmatics* on 'man and woman'.[3]

The Barth–Brunner debate was taking place in a very specific context: Germany in 1934. The other example of a 'creation ordinance' that they debate is the state. In the context of the rise of Hitler and National Socialism, one can see how significant the issues at stake were. If God ordained the state, or even, as some National Socialists would claim, a particular form of the state, this made the state inviolable, which would destabilize the possibility of resistance to Hitler's regime. This perhaps serves to illustrate two things that are also significant to our present debate about the theology of marriage: first, that one's theological presuppositions have political consequences; and second (and rather differently), that extreme cases (such as Germany in 1934) make bad law. None of the contributors to this volume would necessarily go all the way with Barth on the question. Indeed, Ben Fulford, in his essay

---

3 Barth fills out his constructive account of marriage rooted in his understanding of revelation in the *Church Dogmatics* (Barth 1961, especially pp. 117–20, 145–75).

about Scripture as the fundamental source and norm of theology, is, in part, concerned with the way Scripture itself opens up the need to take seriously the created life of the world.

The essays in this volume do not set out to engage overtly with debates such as the place of natural theology within the practice of theology. Nonetheless, it is possible to see how some prior theological decisions underpin what the various essays are pointing to. The essays by the two editors provide interesting examples. In her essay on sexuate bodies, Susannah Cornwall draws into her argument intersex bodies. To make this move, it is necessary to have some place for natural theology; it has to be possible for the biological reality of creation to inform or challenge our theological thinking, and therefore in some sense to be a legitimate, authoritative principle in the practice of theology. A strict Barthian would not be able to make this move. Revealed theology might ultimately be able to say something about intersex bodies, but those bodies themselves could not in any way be authoritative in the construction of a theological argument. In contrast, John Bradbury's essay remains fairly close to the exegesis of biblical texts, albeit significantly through the lens offered by the tradition and commentators on the text and with an awareness of created reality in terms of the diversities of the human situation. Placed side by side, these two essays do not offer anything that resembles a 'systematic theology', in part because, methodologically, they proceed in slightly different ways, with slightly different theological presuppositions (which by and large remain unstated) about theological methodology. This illustrates something important about this volume, which is that it is not intended to offer any kind of systematic theological account of marriage. Rather, the essays emerge from their different starting points and different traditions to engage the topic in a rich variety of theological ways. We hope they offer something of a tapestry that will generate further creative thinking about marriage, rather than a last word on the subject.

That marriage is a topic for theology to engage with seems self-evident, although many attempts to engage the theme within different denominations do not always do so theologically, or at least not theologically in the broader understanding of the term. Many of the debates surrounding marriage, particularly same-sex marriage, boil down to different accounts of the nature of the authority of Scripture and the interpretative principles one uses to engage Scripture. This approach makes a sweeping presupposition: that one can read directly from the pages of Scripture about twenty-first-century marriage. This leads all too often to different 'sides' in the debate battling it out over one set of proof texts or another. One thing the contributors to this book share in common is an understanding that, where same-sex marriages are concerned, Scripture neither knows nor speaks of the relationships we understand as same-sex relationships today. Scripture knows of sex acts between people of the same gender, but not the kind of relationships that through their fidelity, longevity and fecund nature typify what we might understand by 'same-sex marriage'. Equally, Scripture does not know of the 'romantic' notion of marriage so common today following the Enlightenment and romanticism. Given this, the question is forced away from debates about particular biblical texts and becomes a fully fledged theological issue. In some ways it is more similar to questions theology asks concerning issues such as global warming or drone warfare. Scripture does not specifically tell us about these things but Scripture, particularly when read in the light of the Christian heritage and thought about rationally, has much to say about them. Ultimately one needs to go through an overt process of 'theologizing' to speak meaningfully about these topics.

One of the features of this volume is the way it seeks to engage explicitly some of the sources and norms of theology (noting, though, our previous caveat about these being different in different traditions). Ben Fulford's chapter therefore seeks to ask how we might read Scripture theologically as the primary norm of Christian theology on a topic that Scripture does not explicitly speak about. Mike Higton asks how far the notion of complementarity is central to doctrines of marriage in a specifically Anglican context. Alongside this, Frances Clemson explores the idea of the relationship between theological tradition as one of the sources of Christian theology, and the tradition that is the 'time taking' of a marriage. Equally, the practice of the life of the Church liturgically is another key resource that theology (particularly, perhaps, Anglican theology) turns to, and that Julie Gittoes explores as the source for the theological understanding of marriage. In these ways this volume begins to sketch a wider theological approach than simply asking after the 'plain sense' reading of Scripture concerning something Scripture is far from plain about. The book also contains 'worked examples' of engaging with the tradition more broadly, in Raphael Cadenhead's examination of gender and asceticism in Gregory of Nyssa, and Brett Gray's exploration of the Augustinian category of 'procreation'. Charlotte Methuen and Augur Pearce guide us through the development of the 'tradition', in the institutional aspects of marriage within the Church and the state. Finally, in her Afterword, Rachel Muers suggests that theological discussions of marriage have the potential to be fruitful and significant in more ways than they are usually allowed to be – precisely because of marriage's commonplace, everyday nature, such that it is 'one place where we cannot avoid making enormous, indeed extraordinary, theological claims about the stuff of ordinary life – and then living, day by day, with and into the claims that we make' (Muers, Chapter 12, this volume).

Even if, statistically, marriage is on the decline, and even if it is no longer considered a necessary prerequisite for living and parenting together, in a theological context it will continue to have importance beyond the lives of the individual couples who choose to marry. First, the Church continues to imbue the metaphor of marriage with theological significance, such that what is said about marriage is not only about actual *marriages* but about, in some sense, how the human beings who comprise the Church understand themselves in relation to God. Second, the Church has often been among those voices that claim marriage is a bedrock for social stability and well-being (which raises hard questions, beyond the remit of this collection, about how far the Church also has a duty to stand against the kinds of social and fiscal conservatism and even exploitation that marriage often seems to uphold – in other words, to resist marriage's more sinister aspects). Third, the Church also continues to seek to colour broader social accounts of what marriage may and may not mean even for those who neither know nor care what it has to say – or who do know and actively reject it. As this book goes to press, debates continue in the established Church of England about how far the Church's authorities may prevent Church of England clergy from entering into marriages with their same-sex partners – even though there is legally nothing to prohibit this and even though, in cases where couples have 'converted' their civil partnerships to marriages, they are considered to have been legally married from the time of their civil partnership.

This latter point also highlights what may seem to be a truism about marriage: aside from its social and theological resonances, it matters very much in an immediate sense *to those who marry*, to those who wish to marry but are prevented from doing so and to those who make up the broader communities in which marriages live and die. Marriages are not just about weddings, but weddings, perhaps, sum up something of the curious mixture of the jollity and gravity, the campy festivity and the bald practicality, of life in community. They testify to the hope that, whatever the statistics say, *this* relationship of commitment and faithfulness will be one that sticks; they speak into the human propensity to make promises even before we have learned how to keep them. And as such, this commitment to shared life, to bear with one another for better or worse, richer or poorer, in sickness and in health, to ask the question whether what is broken can be fixed, echoes those tensions facing all Christians as they work out how to coexist with others with whom they have the profoundest of disagreements.

References

Barth, Karl, 2002 [1946], 'No!', in Emil Brunner and Karl Barth, *Natural Theology: Comprising 'Nature and Grace' by Professor Dr Emil Brunner and the Reply 'No!' by Dr Karl Barth*, London: Geoffrey Bles/Centenary Press, pp. 67–128.

Barth, Karl, 1961, *Church Dogmatics III.4: The Doctrine of Creation*, trans G. W. Bromiley and T. F. Torrance, Edinburgh: T&T Clark.

Brunner, Emil, 2002 [1946], 'Nature and Grace', in Emil Brunner and Karl Barth, *Natural Theology: Comprising 'Nature and Grace' by Professor Dr Emil Brunner and the Reply 'No!' by Dr Karl Barth*, London: Geoffrey Bles/Centenary Press, pp. 15–64.

Church Growth Research Programme, 2014, 'Statistics – Age Profile', www.churchgrowthresearch.org.uk/statistics_age_profile.

Office for National Statistics, 2013a, 'What Percentage of Marriages End in Divorce?', www.ons.gov.uk/ons/rel/vsob1/divorces-in-england-and-wales/2011/sty-what-percentage-of-marriages-end-in-divorce.html.

Office for National Statistics, 2013b, 'Trends in Civil and Religious Marriages, 1966–2011', www.ons.gov.uk/ons/rel/vsob1/marriages-in-england-and-wales-provisional-/2011/sty-marriages.html.

Office for National Statistics, 2014, 'Live Births Within Marriage / Civil Partnership', www.ons.gov.uk/ons/rel/vsob1/birth-summary-tables--england-and-wales/2013/stb-births-in-england-and-wales-2013.html#tab-Live-Births-Within-in-Marriage-Civil-Partnership.

Song, Robert, 2014, *Covenant and Calling: Towards a Theology of Same-Sex Relationships*, London: SCM Press.

Suggestions for further reading

On theologies of marriage

Cahill, Lisa Sowle, 1996, *Sex, Gender, and Christian Ethics*, Cambridge: Cambridge University Press – especially ch. 6, 'Sex, Marriage, and Family in Christian Tradition'.

Coleman, Peter, 2004, *Christian Attitudes to Marriage: From Ancient Times to the Third Millennium*, London: SCM Press.

Jordan, Mark D., 2005, *Blessing Same-Sex Unions: The Perils of Queer Romance and the Confusions of Christian Marriage*, Chicago, IL: University of Chicago Press.

Jordan, Mark D. (ed.), 2006, *Authorizing Marriage? Canon, Tradition, and Critique in the Blessing of Same-Sex Unions*, Princeton, NJ: Princeton University Press.

Roberts, Christopher Chenault, 2007, *Creation and Covenant: The Significance of Sexual Difference in the Moral Theology of Marriage*, New York, NY: T&T Clark International.

Thatcher, Adrian, 1999, *Marriage After Modernity: Christian Marriage in Postmodern Times*, Sheffield: Sheffield Academic Press.

Witte, John Jr, 1997, *From Sacrament to Contract: Marriage, Religion, and Law in the Western Tradition*, Louisville, KY: Westminster John Knox Press.

On the history of marriage

Gillis, John R., 1985, *For Better, For Worse: British Marriages, 1600 to the Present*, Oxford: Oxford University Press.

Jones, Timothy Willem, 2013, *Sexual Politics in the Church of England, 1857–1957*, Oxford: Oxford University Press.

Porter, Muriel, 1996, *Sex, Marriage, and the Church: Patterns of Change*, North Blackburn, Victoria: HarperCollinsReligious.

Stone, Lawrence, 1977, *The Family, Sex and Marriage in England 1500–1800*, London: Weidenfeld & Nicolson.

2

Marriage, Gender and Doctrine

MIKE HIGTON

Introduction

In many of our churches – not least in my own Church of England – we are arguing about marriage, and our arguments go deep. In this chapter, I try to diagnose one of the deep currents of disagreement that lends energy to our arguments, and ask where it might take us.

In the first two sections of the chapter, I will provide an exposition of two recent official reports on marriage from the Church of England. I will highlight the ways their arguments about marriage rely on an account of the essential complementarity between men and women.

In the third section, I will provide a brief critique of this complementarian account of gender, pointing to some problems with the appeals to biology and history that help drive it. The reports make those appeals, however, because they insist that our understanding of marriage should be responsive to the natures we have been given in creation. I therefore turn in the fourth section to suggest an alternative way of thinking about what such responsiveness involves. My alternative way of thinking, I suggest, might lead to a rather different account of marriage's nature and function, because it would be unlikely to continue appealing to the supposed essential complementarity of men and women.

In the final section of the chapter, I take a step back from this discussion and suggest that one of the questions facing the Church, as its members pursue this kind of debate about the nature of marriage, is whether the complementarian account of gender is a core Christian teaching. Must we, now that our disagreements about marriage are forcing us to ask questions about gender with renewed urgency, define complementarianism as a doctrine of the Church?[1]

---

1 My exposition in sections 1 to 4 was first developed in a series of blog posts at mikehigton.org.uk, from 1 March to 25 April 2014. I explore some of the ideas in section 5 further in Higton 2016.

Marriage and Complementarity

I'm going to start with the Church of England's official 'Response to the Government Equalities Office Consultation – "Equal Civil Marriage"' (Church of England 2012). In 2012 the government published a consultation document, seeking views on 'how we can remove the ban on same-sex couples having a civil marriage in a way that works for everyone', while insisting that 'no changes will be made to how religious organizations define and solemnize religious marriages' (Government Equalities Office 2012, p. 1).

The Church of England's formal response makes two moves that are at least partially independent. It argues that the proposed legislation is contrary to the 'intrinsic nature of marriage', and it argues that there will be legal problems with its implementation and in particular with its guarantees about religious marriages. I will focus on the first of these strands (the argument about the intrinsic nature of marriage), because it is in that strand that the centrality to the debate of questions about gender becomes most clear.

The argument of the document can be summarized as follows.

1 There is an essential complementarity between men and women – an 'underlying, objective, distinctiveness' (§10).
2 The essential complementarity of men and women is biologically grounded, even if it is not reducible to capacity for procreation. Procreation certainly matters in the report. It is, according to the report, fundamental to the definition of marriage that the couple be '*open* to bringing children into the world as a fruit of their loving commitment' (§25; my emphasis); it quotes the *Common Worship* liturgy to the effect that marriage is the 'foundation of family life in which children may be born' (§2). More precisely, marriage relies on a 'biological complementarity with the possibility of procreation' (§6); more precisely still, 'This distinctiveness and complementarity are seen *most explicitly* in the biological union of man and woman which potentially brings to the relationship the fruitfulness of procreation' (§10; my emphasis). Procreation does not, however, exhaust the meaning of complementarity: 'And, even where, for reasons of age, biology or simply choice, a marriage does not have issue, the distinctiveness of male and female is part of what gives marriage its unique social meaning' (§10).
3 The acknowledgement and expression of this essential complementarity of the sexes is therefore necessary for the flourishing of

human society. Properly acknowledged, complementarity will be expressed in specific and distinctive contributions from men and women in all social institutions. The report states that 'a society cannot flourish without the specific and distinctive contributions of each gender' (§12). After all, this is a fundamental reason for supporting 'the deeper involvement of women in all social institutions' (§12). This is why gender complementarity has been recognized and expressed in societies down the ages; it is 'enshrined in human institutions throughout history' (Summary). Such recognition and expression serves 'the common good of all in society' (§4) and is of high 'social value' (§12).

4 Acknowledging and expressing this complementarity is central to the purpose of marriage. 'Marriage benefits society in many ways, not only by promoting mutuality and fidelity, but also by acknowledging an underlying biological complementarity which, for many, includes the possibility of procreation' (Summary). This is what the document means when it speaks of the 'intrinsic nature of marriage as the union of a man and a woman' (Summary), and says that 'marriage in general – and not just the marriage of Christians – is, in its nature, a lifelong union of one man with one woman' (§1). The emphasis falls firmly on 'man' and 'woman'. Of course, there are other goods proper to marriage – mutuality and fidelity – but these are not at issue in this debate, nor are they unique to marriage (§9). '[T]he uniqueness of marriage – and a further aspect of its virtuous nature – is that it embodies the underlying, objective, distinctiveness of men and women' (§10).

5 Marriage is the *primary* social institution by which our society acknowledges and expresses this complementarity. 'Marriage has from the beginning of history been *the* way societies have worked out and handled issues of sexual difference. To remove from the definition of marriage this essential complementarity is to lose *any* social institution in which sexual difference is explicitly acknowledged' (§11; my emphases).

6 If marriage ceases to be a way for our society to acknowledge and express this complementarity, our society's capacity to acknowledge and express it at all will therefore be seriously reduced, and society as a whole will be harmed. This is why the report describes the government proposals as constituting an attempt 'to remove the concept of gender from marriage' (Summary). And this is what is meant by the claim that the proposals would 'change the nature of marriage for everyone' (Summary). It is not that the authors of the report think

that the strength of my marriage will be undermined if other people enter into a union of which I disapprove. Rather, they think that marriage as an institution will be less capable of performing one of its most important social functions if it ceases to be clearly defined in gender terms. And this is also what the authors of the report mean when they say that the legislation will involve 'imposing for essentially ideological reasons a new meaning on a term as familiar and fundamental as marriage' (Summary). The ideology in question is, they believe, one in which 'men and women are simply interchangeable individuals' (§12) – which is the only alternative the report imagines to its own account of essential gender complementarity. And all of this is why the report can say that this is not (directly) an issue about the acceptability of homosexual sexual activity, but rather about the fact that 'the inherited understanding of marriage contributes a vast amount to the common good', and that this will be lost, 'for everyone, gay or straight', if 'the meaning of marriage' is changed (§5). 'We believe that redefining marriage to include same-sex relationships will entail a dilution in the meaning of marriage for everyone by excluding the fundamental complementarity of men and women from the social and legal definition of marriage' (§13) and 'the consequences of change will not be beneficial for society as a whole' (§8).

In other words, marriage is presented in the report as the means by which we recognize and express an essential gender complementarity. This complementarity needs to be recognized and expressed not simply for the sake of marriage but for the sake of society as a whole, which will only truly flourish when the specific and distinctive contributions from men and women are given full expression in all parts of its life.

Men and Women in Marriage

In 2013 a follow-up to the Church's response to the government consultation appeared, in the form of a report from the Church of England Faith and Order Commission (FAOC) entitled *Men and Women in Marriage* (Archbishops' Council 2013).[2] It can be read as providing

---

2 I am myself a member of FAOC, and I was a member when the report was proposed, when it was discussed and when it was published. As a member I share responsibility for the report, even if (as is often the way with reports produced by committee) it does not represent my own views. The report was, however, 'commended for study' by the Archbishops in their Foreword, and it has seemed to me that

a more carefully articulated expression of the theology of gender contained in the earlier document.

In the Foreword, the Archbishops say that it aims to provide a 'short summary of the Church of England's understanding of marriage' and, more fully, that

> It sets out to explain the continued importance of and rationale for the doctrine of the Church of England on marriage as set out in The Book of Common Prayer, Canon B30, the *Common Worship* Marriage Service and the teaching document issued by the House in September 1999. (Archbishops' Council 2013, p. v)[3]

That description could be misconstrued, however. The Faith and Order Commission's report did not provide an evenly balanced summary of all the main things that the Church of England has wanted to say about the nature and purpose of marriage, but was an attempt to set out more fully the background in the Church of England's thinking to the specific arguments made in the debate about same-sex marriage. Nearly everything in the report is (as the title says) about the necessity of marriage's taking place between a man and a woman, and about 'how the sexual differentiation of men and women is a gift of God' (§3). Other topics (including such central topics as faithfulness and public commitment) appear only briefly, and only insofar as they relate to that central topic.

Like the original response to the government consultation, then, this is a report about gender. It speaks about the importance of gender difference to marriage, but also about the wider importance of gender in society.

The report is arranged around a very clear central vector. It begins with creation and moves towards culture. That is, it begins with sexual difference as a feature of the natural world (a defining feature of human biology) and then argues that human behaviour (our relationships, our

---

the best way for me to accept my responsibility for it is to take that commendation seriously: to study the report, to ask what agenda it suggests for further deliberation and to pursue that deliberation vigorously.

3 Canon B30, part of the canon law that provides the legal framework for the Church of England, can be found at www.churchofengland.org/about-us/structure/churchlawlegis/canons/section-b.aspx, and the marriage service, part of its authorized liturgy, at www.churchofengland.org/prayer-worship/worship/texts/pastoral/marriage/marriage.aspx. The 1999 teaching document mentioned in the Foreword is *Marriage: A Teaching Document* (House of Bishops 1999).

institutions, our culture) should respect and respond to this feature. The report is, in other words, an exercise in 'natural law' ethics (§9). It is an exercise in describing how our behaviour should be regulated so as to do justice to our (physical, biological, ecological) nature. 'Not everything in the way we live, then, is open to renegotiation', it says. 'We cannot turn our back upon the natural, and especially the biological, terms of human existence' (§10).

This argument begins with a claim made about marriage found in the Church of England's marriage liturgy: that it is 'a gift of God in creation' (§2, 5, 6). Or, in the words of an earlier report (House of Bishops 2005, quoted in §2), marriage is 'a creation ordinance'. In other words, marriage is underpinned by, and gives expression to, a structure of the natural world (§8). And that means that it is underpinned by, and gives expression to, a fact about us as human beings that runs deeper than our politics, our economics and our cultures (§6). It is underpinned by, and gives expression to, something beyond all the relativities of history: the biological fact that we are, naturally, sexed creatures. Our sexual differentiation is cultural as well as biological, but its biological aspect is fundamental, underpinning all its other aspects. This biological aspect is not restricted to (though it certainly includes) our capacity for differentiated involvement in the process of procreation (§3).

Marriage is, according to the report, given to us as a way of acknowledging and expressing this natural differentiation. The report does not use the word 'natural' to describe marriage itself. Rather, marriage is an institution that *responds* to nature. Nevertheless, the report makes it clear that to form lifelong, monogamous, exogamous (that is, not with relatives), male–female relationships, for the sake of reproduction and the nurture of children, is a primary way we can live in accordance with our biological nature.

When discussing the nature of marriage as lifelong, monogamous and exogamous, the report says that 'most developed traditions give these three structural elements a central place in their practices of marriage' (§18), and that the exceptions 'have tended to be of limited scope' and 'hardly amount to a significant challenge to these structural foundations' (§19). The idea here is that history reveals nature. We can look at the patterns of relationship that have prevailed and flourished across multiple human societies, and see in them clues to the underlying natural structure to which they are responding. And the idea underlying *that* is that cultures can only truly flourish if they are shaped in accordance with nature.

The report therefore argues that 'we need a society in which men and women relate well to each other' (§12), where the word 'well' clearly means 'in accordance with the complementarity found in nature'. Marriage is our central means of ensuring that relationships between man and women achieve this goal. It is 'a paradigm of society, facilitating other social forms' (§13). Marriage (in the sense of a lifelong, monogamous, exogamous, male–female relationship, ordered towards procreation and family life) therefore 'enriches society and strengthens community' (§15, quoting the marriage service), and is 'central to the stability and health of human society' (§2, quoting House of Bishops 2005 on civil partnerships).

What are we to make of all this?

Gender, Biology, and History

Let me begin with the positive. The aspects of this theology that I am most readily able to affirm are its insistences that to live well involves responding attentively to our bodiliness, and that we are not bodily in the abstract but always as particular sexed bodies. We receive that particularity, that differentiation, as a gift from God. As *Men and Women in Marriage* says, 'Persons in relation are not interchangeable units, shorn of whatever makes one human being different from another. They are individuals who bring to the relationship unique experiences of being human in community, unique qualities, attributes and histories' (§25).

I do not believe that our options reduce to complementarianism on the one hand (the belief that to respond adequately to our bodiliness primarily means acknowledging and distinguishing the essentially distinct contributions of men and women) or some kind of free-flowing and effectively disembodied individualism on the other (in which the constraints and possibilities yielded by our differently sexed bodies play no appreciable role, and 'men and women are simply interchangeable individuals', as the response to the government consultation says in §12). Nevertheless, the basic point about taking embodied difference seriously is a very important one.

That very affirmation, however, gives rise to serious questions. First of all, it gives rise to questions about *what it is* that we are given in our 'nature' and *how we know* what we have been given. The stress in *Men and Women in Marriage* on the biological underpinnings of marriage suggests that what we are given is fundamentally our biological constitution, and that this can be known by means of natural science. The words 'biology' or 'biological' turn up six times, mixed in with the thirteen occurrences of 'nature' or 'natural', and there's an explicit mention of the way 'the marvellous ordering of the created world' is discovered in 'physics and biology' (§8). This report was intended to communicate the Church's understanding of marriage to a wide public audience, and I think the strongest message conveyed about how we arrive at that understanding is that it is squarely based on the scientific facts of human biology.

Attention to biology can certainly yield the idea that procreation requires the involvement of someone with male reproductive organs and someone with female reproductive organs, and that is certainly not a trivial matter. And yet it is – to say the least – questionable whether attention to biology will underpin the broader claims of the report. After all, attention to the facts of human biology doesn't yield a neat differentiation of male and female characteristics (see further Susannah Cornwall's and Ben Fulford's chapters in this volume); it doesn't yield the idea that all the human beings that God has created can be neatly divided into 'men' and 'women' (see further Raphael Cadenhead's chapter); and it doesn't yield the idea that lifelong, monogamous, exogamous relationships are biologically natural in a way that other patterns of relationship are not. More appears to be being built on biology in the report than it can bear, and biology on its own would seem to push us to rather more complex conclusions than this report allows.

The argument does not, however, rely exclusively upon this appeal to biology. There is also an appeal to history. Both *Men and Women in Marriage* and the earlier document suggest that we can look at the patterns of relationship that have prevailed through history, and see in them clues to the underlying natural structure to which they respond, a structure that is itself beyond the relativities of history.

Yet history both reveals and conceals nature. We are indeed called to respond attentively to our bodiliness, and we are indeed not bodily in the abstract but always as particular sexed bodies. True flourishing does require some such responsiveness, as the reports suggest. Furthermore, we do only know the nature of our bodiliness, including our sexed bodiliness, through the ways we have responded to it through history. That is, we know the constraints that our sexual differentiation imposes upon us and the possibilities that it creates for us only by knowing how it has been registered as constraint and as possibility in specific ways by human beings in our history together.

And yet it is also important to acknowledge that all of those historical responses are inadequate and open to challenge. We can't point to any historical example and say, 'Here is where we see the constraints and possibilities of sexed bodily existence registered truly and completely.' We have become increasingly aware in recent years that our history is in large part a history of the *mis*identification of the constraints and possibilities that our sexed bodily existence yields – whether we have claimed that having a female body obviously means a moral and intellectual incapacity for the serious business of voting, or that girls are naturally interested in pink toys and boys in blue.

The brief reliance in the reports upon the history of our responses to sexed bodily nature suggests that those responses tend very largely to fall into one groove. They are canalized by the shape of the underlying biological landscape over which they are flowing. Yet it is far from clear that the diversity and complexity of our history reduces to the canalized form suggested in the report: that there is one main groove into which marriage has fallen in human history, and that the various exceptions to that groove have been (as *Men and Women in Marriage* says) 'of limited scope'. It is equally clear that where, for large parts of our history, our marriage practices *have* fallen into a groove, that it has seldom been something to celebrate without reserve (as Charlotte Methuen notes in this volume). The grooves into which our practices have fallen have very often been deathly.

The appeals to biology and history in the reports are, therefore, problematic. The problems with them are not simply technical problems, however, of interest only to academic theologians. They have sharp edges that intrude deeply into everyday life. We have, after all, a very, very bad history of appealing to nature and to history when speaking about the proper roles and relations of men and women. We have a toxic, death-dealing history. We have used appeals to the 'obvious' facts of biology and appeals to the 'obvious' lessons of history to oppress and to abuse. And that history is not a tale of long ago and far away; it is all around us still.

We live in a world, and continue to *make* a world, in which we restrict the lives of women and of men by telling them fables about what is naturally appropriate to them thanks to their gender. We continue to build a world in which toxic myths about 'normal' family life are used to exclude and to demean – to underwrite our poisonous profligacy in naming others' relationships as inadequate or dysfunctional or unnatural or malformed. We continue to build a world in which we use our valorization of marriage, as a bond forged from links that are prior to law and culture, to mark out spaces in which violent abuse can hide.

What our problematic history reveals is that our attempts to register and respond to our bodiless are fallible and fraught, and that we are far from done with the process of learning to respond well. We do not yet know what it means to respond truly to our sexual differentiation – but to understand the import of that realization for our thinking about marriage, we need to change the terms of our discussion, and shift from talking about the relationship between biology and history to talking about the relationship between creation and redemption.

Redeeming Creation

Men and Women in Marriage quotes the *Common Worship* marriage service to the effect that 'as man and woman grow together in love and trust, they shall be united with one another in heart, body and mind, as Christ is united with his bride, the Church' (§39), and then expands that to say, 'The encounter of man and woman in marriage affords an image, then, of the knowledge and love of God, to which all humans are summoned, and of the self-giving of the Son of God which makes it possible' (§40). A little earlier it had spoken of marriage's attaining 'a permanence which could speak to the world of God's own love' and of this as a matter of our species' 'spiritual vocation' (§33).

In other words, the report presents marriage as a means by which human beings learn to embody and to communicate God's love, and suggests that marriage can be a sharing in, a participation in, a love that is prior to it: God's own Christlike love. God's love is marriage's context and goal, and that love therefore defines marriage. Marriage is, fundamentally, ordered towards Christlike love.

To run with these ideas, however, might take us in a rather different direction from that marked out by these reports. We are, these ideas suggest, not simply called to live in attentive response to our bodiliness but to live in attentive response to our bodiliness *in the light of God's love for the world in Jesus Christ*. Christian ethics, then, is not simply about conformity to creation but about creaturely participation in redemption. Redemption is the fulfilment of creatureliness, so that the route to *true* response to our created nature is by participation in redemption. Redemption does not abolish or override but brings to fruition our creatureliness. Creation and covenant belong together, because the creator is also the redeemer.

The call to live in response to our created natures is not, therefore, to be thought of primarily as the imposing of a constraint already known or knowable to us without regard to redemption. It is the call to discover together the possibilities of godly growth and transformation that our created natures give us. It is the call to discover the particular forms of flourishing that our bodies make possible, and to discover the particular ways that we, as these particular bodies, can become by the Spirit's work conformed to Christ, and so become particular icons of God's love, communicating that love in a way that no other bodies could.

That transformation might therefore be thought of as a craft, working with the grain of the material at hand to make something beautiful, something that speaks ever more clearly of God's love. It is a transformation that happens under the discipline of the material with which we are working and under the discipline of the word that we are called to let that material speak, the word of Christlike love. But those two disciplines are inextricable: we only discover the *true* nature of the material with which we are working as we discover how it can speak this word. Our 'nature' is not a neutral biological fact: it is the particular possibility that we have been given in creation of communicating the love of God, and we will discover that possibility in it only as we discover how to communicate that love.

A Matter of Doctrine?

My language is meant to suggest that this task of disciplined discovery is an ongoing one. That is, I am deliberately suggesting that we are still in the process of discovering the ways of speaking about and responding to sexual difference to which we are called by the good news of God's love in Jesus Christ. And that means that I am deliberately suggesting that our accounts of and practices of marriage are also properly a matter of ongoing discovery. And by saying all this I am suggesting that the answers to that question are not already clear to us. God has given us marriage, but that gift is one that we are still receiving.

This does not mean that 'anything goes' or that marriage can mean whatever we feel like letting it mean. The process of discovery that I am suggesting is a matter of spiritual discipline, and of growth in holiness. It will be informed by a careful attentiveness to the full complexity of what scientific investigation can show us, but we will not simply be able to read off our answers from the results of such investigation. It will be informed by a careful attentiveness to the full complexity of the history of human practice in this area, even if much of that attentiveness will take the form of the penitent discernment of sinful distortions. Most importantly, however, it will be informed by our attentiveness to what we learn of the love to which we are called from Christ and Christ's witnesses, and by the purification of our distorted loves in prayer and worship.

I have also been suggesting – though I realize that I have done no more than suggest, and that I have certainly not demonstrated my claim – that these explorations will be likely to lead us somewhere different from the complementarian understandings of gender found in these two church reports, and from the gender-focused account of marriage that is built on that foundation. Both of the reports that I have analysed, however, strongly suggest that the Church does not have the freedom to take its exploration of marriage in that direction. As *Men and Women in Marriage* says, 'Not everything in the way we live, then, is open to renegotiation' (§10). Most directly, the Church's response to the government consultation on same-sex marriage claims that its understanding of marriage is 'a matter of doctrine', 'derived from the teaching of Christ himself' (§1), 'derived from the Scriptures' and 'enshrined within [the Church of England's] authorized liturgy' (§2). It strongly suggests, therefore, that the whole complementarian account of gender that it sets out is itself such a 'matter of doctrine'.

One way of construing the debate within the Church of England is as a debate about precisely this claim. Is gender complementarianism a doctrine of the Church? After all, while it is clearly true that the Church of England has consistently assumed that marriage involves a man and a woman, it has not been brought before to face squarely the question of why that is so and whether it has to be so, and it has not been brought before to face squarely the question of the status of the account of gender that the reports believe underpins that assumption about marriage. One could therefore see the debate as pushing for a decision on this matter: a decision on whether these claims about gender (and so about marriage) are properly a matter of doctrine.

To ask this question is not, I suggest, quite the same as asking whether this account of gender is *true*. There are many true things that are not properly doctrines of the Church. The Church might be united in believing that Canterbury is to the south of York, and might rely upon this assumption in numerous documents, and we may be satisfied by every means proper to the investigation of such a claim that it is true. That does not make this claim properly part of the Church's doctrine. To see whether it should be counted as doctrine of the Church, we need to ask not just whether it is true but whether the Church *has* to teach this truth in order to be faithful to its calling to proclaim the gospel in word and deed.

It is not enough to find that a teaching is *present* in tradition or in Scripture; it is not enough to find that a teaching is *consistent* in tradition or in Scripture; it is not even enough to find that a teaching is *pervasive* in tradition or in Scripture. To be given the status of a doctrine of the Church – a formal claim about the proper limits of our explorations – a teaching must satisfy a further condition. It must be *necessary* to support the Church's proclamation of the good news of Jesus Christ. The motto for the process of determining such doctrinal limits could therefore be provided by 1 Corinthians 2.2: 'I decided to know nothing among you except Jesus Christ, and him crucified.'

Consider (to give an unrelated example) Christian disagreements about the doctrine of creation. I do not believe that we are required to teach, as a doctrine of the Church, that the earth was created some thousands of years ago, in a sequence of six days aptly described by the opening chapter of Genesis. This is not because Genesis 1 is poetic in nature, nor because these elements of the Genesis narrative are clearly culturally determined. Rather, these claims about creation cannot be counted as doctrines of the Church because they are not *germane to the gospel*. If we were to claim them as authoritative Christian teachings – as matters of doctrine – then we would have to regard them as authoritative Christian teaching *in addition* to the gospel. We would have to say, in our catechesis, 'Do you believe that, in Jesus, God was reconciling the world to Godself – and do you also believe this other thing: that the earth was created in six days some thousands of years ago?' By contrast, to say 'I believe in God ... creator of heaven and earth' is a doctrine of the Church, because it has been shown to be part of what we need to say if we want to say 'Jesus is Lord' with full seriousness, in the light of Scripture. Jesus is Lord of all the earth because the earth is his; redemption in Christ is the fulfilment of our creaturely natures because we were made in, through and for him.

Similarly therefore, in the Church's debates about marriage the key question in determining the proper limits of our explorations is, 'What is germane to the gospel in what our faith says about gender?' What do we need to say about this topic in order to go on saying 'Jesus is Lord'? I have suggested that our explorations can and should take us beyond complementarian accounts of gender because I can't currently see that those accounts could be anything other than additions to the gospel, were we to take them to be authoritative Christian teachings. That is, if they were to be held out as authoritative for Christians it could only be because we said, in our catechesis, 'You must believe that, in Jesus, God was reconciling the world to Godself – and you must also believe this other thing: that men and women have essentially complementary ways of being.' If that is true, then we cannot and must not regard complementarianism as a matter of doctrine.

Conclusion

The Church of England's debates about marriage (and the debates of other churches too, perhaps) are deeply bound up with patterns of thinking about gender. They are bound up with questions about the proper responsiveness of our habits of thought, speech and action to our embodied sexual differentiation, and about what the good news of redemption in Christ demands of us in this area.

In our debates, questions have been raised forcefully and insistently about an existing answer – the complementarian answer – and defences no less forceful and insistent given. Yet however pervasive that answer is and has been, however deep its roots, however much its supporters can appeal to Scripture and tradition in its defence, it cannot properly be claimed as a necessary teaching of the Church if we have not determined that it is *required* of us by the nature of redemption. That is, now that weighty onslaughts have been launched against it, it can only properly stand as an authoritative limit upon the acceptable exploration and development of our accounts and practices of gender if it can be made clear that to deny it would be to deny the good news of God's gracious love for the world in Jesus Christ.

We are called, as I said above, to the intense and demanding work of discovering together the particular possibilities of godly growth and transformation open to us, the particular ways we can be conformed by the Spirit to Christ to become icons of God's love, as the particular sexually differentiated bodies that we are. Our debates about marriage are, at least in part, debates about what accounts of gender are demanded of us, or permitted to us, in the context of serious commitment to this task.

Despite the length and volume of the arguments about marriage and sexuality in my Church, these questions, about the demands of Christian holiness in the realm of gender, are ones that demand much more intensive attention and debate. We may have been arguing about sexuality and gender for ages, but our arguments still have much deeper to go.

References

Archbishops' Council of the Church of England, 2013, *Men and Women in Marriage: A Document from the Faith and Order Commission Published with the Agreement of the House of Bishops of the Church of England and Approved for Study*, GS Misc 1046, London: Church House Publishing.

Church of England, 2012, 'A Response to the Government Equalities Office Consultation – "Equal Civil Marriage", from the Church of England', www.churchofengland.org/media/1475149/s-s%20marriage.pdf.

Government Equalities Office, 2012, *Equal Civil Marriage: A Consultation*, www.gov.uk/government/uploads/system/uploads/attachment_data/file/133258/consultation-document_1_.pdf.

Higton, Mike, forthcoming 2016, 'Christian Doctrine and the Discipline of Reading Scripture', in Angus Paddison (ed.), *Theologians on Scripture*, London: T&T Clark.

House of Bishops of the Church of England, 1999, *Marriage: A Teaching Document from the House of Bishops of the Church of England*, London: Church House Publishing, www.churchofengland.org/media/45645/marriage.pdf.

House of Bishops of the Church of England, 2005, 'Civil Partnerships – A Pastoral Statement from the House of Bishops of the Church of England', www.churchofengland.org/media-centre/news/2005/07/pr5605.aspx.

3

Thinking About Marriage:
What Can We Learn from
Christian History?*

CHARLOTTE METHUEN

Introduction

Marriage has been much in the news recently. Not just discussion about marriage between two people of the same gender but marriage in general. Short marriages, broken marriages: the British press seems to find them fascinating. Marriage and sexuality are emotive topics because they are so fundamental to who we are. How each of us experiences our own relationships with other people and, if we are married, our own marriage; how we did (or did not) experience the marriage of our parents as small (and indeed not so small) children; the ideals and *mores* of marriage and relationships with which we grew up: all of that, as well as our reading of Scripture, our reading of history and our understandings of authority, comes together to shape our expectations of marriage, our sense of what it is and should be about and thus our responses to (for instance) the legalizing of marriage between two people of the same gender. The definition of marriage matters to us because it touches our own identity but also because as Christians we believe that how we live and how society is structured matter to God.

However, in this debate, as so often, that fundamental belief leads Christians in different directions. Some Christians are adamant that the Christian ideal of marriage is and can only be between one man and one woman, providing the proper context in which children are conceived and raised. Others understand deep committed relationships to be God-given and marriage-like, regardless of whether they are

---

* This article draws on earlier versions that appeared as Methuen 2013a; Methuen 2014.

between a man and a woman, two women or two men.[1] And within those general categories, people have very varied opinions. Some who hold that marriage is properly between one man and one woman mean that Christian marriage is fundamentally a relationship between two people who are equal in the sight of God, while others mean that the proper understanding of Christian marriage is that the woman, while equally beloved to God, is by the created ordinance subordinate to the man. As Christians, our views of marriage are informed by Scripture, but we always read Scripture in a cultural context, and that context has caused Christian views on marriage to shift and change throughout the Church's history. In particular there were significant changes to the ideal of marriage during the nineteenth century, so that, as noted also in a recent reflection on marriage published by the Scottish Episcopal Church, 'We are inheritors of an especially romantic view of marriage which largely took hold in the nineteenth century' (Doctrine Committee of the Scottish Episcopal Church 2012, p. 5). This article offers a brief exploration of some of those changes.

Marriage in the Bible

The Church of England's recent report, *Men and Women in Marriage*, roots its presentation of the theology of marriage in Genesis 1.26–28. Marriage, the report suggests,

> is an expression of the human nature which God has willed for us and which we share. And although marriage may fall short of God's purposes in many ways and be the scene of many human weaknesses, it receives the blessing of God and is included in his judgment that creation is 'very good' (Gen. 1.31). (§6, Archbishops' Council 2013, pp. 2–3)

This passage can also be read, as *Men and Women in Marriage* does, to present the complementarily of male and female as a fundamental aspect of the created order. Read in this way, Genesis offers us a vision of marriage as the means by which male and female human beings are

---

1 In 2013 a YouGov poll commissioned for the Westminster Faith Debate on same-sex marriage found that 'despite the churches' official opposition to gay marriage, British Christians who identify as Anglican, Catholic or Presbyterian are now in favour of allowing same-sex marriage by a small margin.' See Woodhead 2013; Woodhead 2014.

drawn into and share in God's creative purposes. Importantly, as *Men and Women in Marriage* affirms:

> We share with many animal species the sexual differentiation of male and female, serving the tasks of reproduction and the nurture of children, but we do more than share it; we build on it to enhance the bond between the sexes culturally ... To flourish as individuals we need a society in which men and women relate well to each other. (§§11–12 Archbishops' Council 2013, p. 4)

In this reading, Genesis 1 offers a vision of the complementarity of men and women not only in the increase of humankind but in ensuring the well-being and the flourishing of creation. Genesis 1 is taken as a blueprint for modern monogamous marriage rooted in complementarity and perhaps mutuality, focused on the procreation and nurture of children. However, the Old Testament's depiction of marriage is much more complex than this. Old Testament marriage is not always monogamous, as the story of Jacob (Genesis 29) illustrates: Jacob served seven years for Rachel, was tricked into marrying Leah and then served another seven years to marry Rachel. This is clearly a bigamous marriage, and further examples include David and Solomon and their many wives and concubines.

Moreover the Old Testament – and particularly the legal codes in the Pentateuch – tends to view a marriageable woman as the property of her father, to be passed to her husband. Deuteronomy 22.28–29 instructs, for instance, that a man who rapes a young woman who is not engaged to another man shall marry her. Exodus 22.16–17 covers the case when a young woman has been seduced by an older man: he must either marry her or pay her father her bride price. Family honour is at stake in these passages, as is the regulation of inheritance: the marriage of a young woman involves a financial negotiation between the husband and the father. Exodus 21.7–11 lays out a husband's responsibilities to his first wife if he wishes to take a second wife; the interpretation of this passage is no doubt complicated by the fact that it is discussing a daughter who has been sold to be a slave, but it certainly suggests that polygamy was not confined to kings and it further emphasizes the idea that a woman, a daughter, is a commodity. The Wisdom literature offers an image of more interpersonal commitment, and by the post-exilic period, monogamy seems to have become the norm and polygamy uncommon in Judaism. The Old Testament witnesses to shifting conceptions of marriage (F. Martin 2001).

In contrast, the Gospels, Paul and the household codes included in the New Testament all present a monogamous understanding of marriage. However, marriage is not idealized. Jorunn Økland points out that Christians were selective about which aspects of Old Testament law they incorporated into their Scriptures: rules about meat, to some extent, and *porneia* (a term that includes idol worship as well as marital infidelity), and particularly those relating to sex, women and female purity, tended to be retained in the New Testament, while other laws, such as those relating to clothing, were not (Økland 2014). Økland points out, however, that the community of the early Church is primarily defined by language pertaining to the relationships within Christian communities, between brothers and sisters in Christ, rather than about marital relationships: 1 Corinthians 13, for instance, the so-called 'hymn to love', is not about love between a man and a woman in marriage but about relationships between members of the community. Marriage is not definitive for the emerging Christian community: 'The New Testament is about being part of the kingdom of God, and everything else is measured against that standard.' The New Testament texts do not fit easily with modern understandings of marriage and nuclear family. Indeed, Økland suggests that it is difficult to find any family in the New Testament that is presented in such a way that the father would have no difficulty being appointed to a conservative congregation. Marriage is most prominent in the household codes, which suggest that a wife is properly subordinate to her husband, although a husband is also – and probably for this context counterculturally – reminded of his duty to love his wife (Eph. 5.22–25; cf. Col. 3.18—4.1; Titus 2.1–10; 1 Pet. 2.18—3.7). The understanding that the submission of women to men forms the basis for the correct understanding of marriage persists through much of Christian history, and much of the contemporary discussion of headship is based on precisely these texts. Christian understandings of marriage and of the role of women have frequently been – and continue to be – intertwined.[2]

Celibacy and Marriage in the Medieval Western Church

The early Church knew marriage, but marriage was not a Christian institution: Greek, Roman and Jewish marriage practices all influenced developing Christian approaches to and understandings of marriage.

---

2 Consequently the current discussion of marriage has implications for – among other debates – the discussion of the ordination of women.

Writing to the Corinthians, Paul explores marriage as the Christianizing of a pagan institution, and one that he is not entirely sure about, for he thinks it distracts attention from following Christ (1 Cor. 7.1–16). If Christians really must marry, he concedes that they should, but he would much prefer that they did not. Also instructive are his thoughts on those married to non-Christian partners. If the spouse consents, they should stay together, 'For the unbelieving husband is made holy through his wife, and the unbelieving wife is made holy through her husband. Otherwise, your children would be unclean, but as it is, they are holy' (1 Cor. 7.14).[3] None of the marriages of which Paul was writing would have been made through Christian ceremonies: these were marriages contracted under Greek or Roman law, made holy by the presence of a Christian partner. Marriage remained a pagan – or at least civic – institution, and there are several figures in the early Church, particularly Jerome, who were profoundly ambiguous about its merits. Greek and Roman practices as well as Jewish practices influenced developing Christian understandings of marriage, and these different traditions, and the differences of local practice, brought about considerable tensions.[4]

Cally Hammond has explored the way Roman law about marriage served to stabilize the inheritance of property through ensuring legitimate children and thus stabilized society (Hammond 2014). This was an important aspect for Augustine, but he also saw marriage as benefitting the couple concerned. Affection, procreation and sacrament were for Augustine the purposes of marriage: marriage should, he thought, ideally be the sexual expression of friendship (Hammond 2014). This is still an attractive characterization of marriage, but as Hammond points out, it should not be allowed to disguise the fact that today's understanding of marriage centres on its ability to support 'stable, faithful, and loving relationships' and is a long way from Augustine's 'affection, procreation and sacrament'. Indeed, suggests Hammond, the two paradigms are so far apart that it is hard to see how they are continuous with each other.

Augustine's concern for marriage in society is a reminder that he, like Paul, was operating in a context in which marriage was a matter for civic society. Indeed, the contracting of marriage would long remain a legal and civic affair: although there is some evidence for Christian marriage rites – or at least blessings – in the early centuries, these do

---

3 I am grateful to Loveday Alexander for this point.

4 For the tensions between Roman concepts of marriage and emerging Christian practices, see Cooper 2007, pp. 143–98.

not seem to have been common (Crouzel 1982, p. 327). As late as the tenth century, and probably for some people long afterwards, marriages were generally entered into not in church but outside the church door. From around 1200, the Western Church claimed the right to preside over and therefore to 'solemnize' marriages (to use a later and thus anachronistic term), although it was still recognized that it was the couple who actually made the marriage. Legally couples might still marry through mutual agreement without the involvement of a priest, and that marriage would be recognized by the Church (Brink 1982, pp. 332–3).

Nonetheless, theologians reflected on marriage, and a theology of marriage emerged. This drew on exegesis of Ephesians 5.32 and other passages presenting marriage as a model for the relationship between the Church and God, or Christ, but doubtless also reflected the fact that marriage was an important social and societal institution. Christian understandings of marriage came to emphasize the need for both partners to consent freely to the marriage (in opposition to the idea, propagated also sometimes by Augustine, that a Christian wife was purchased by her husband, like a slave; Cooper 2007, p. 43); they also came to define marriage as insoluble except by death (based on Matt. 5.31–32 and Matt. 19.7–9); and, in the Western Church, introduced restrictions on marriage on the basis of consanguinity (blood relations), affinity (in-laws) and spiritual affinity (godparents). By the fourteenth century these restrictions had become a money-spinner for popes and bishops, who extracted large sums from those who wished to circumvent them.[5] As marriage gained religious significance, it came to be understood as a means by which God offered grace, and was included in the definitive list of seven sacraments articulated by the Fourth Lateran Council in 1215 (Brink 1982, pp. 333–4).

However, marriage was not the only form of life recognized for Christians. Paul's letters witness to a certain ambiguity in the assessment of marriage: was it not wiser to remain celibate (1 Cor. 7.8–9)? The tension between the valuing of marriage and the valuing of celibacy, heightened from the fourth century with the increasing focus on Christian asceticism, forms the background for much Christian writing about marriage in late antiquity and in the medieval period (Brown 1989; 2008). Augustine believed that marriage would have existed in paradise but that sexual intercourse would have been a rational process,

5 In the sixteenth century Henry VIII paid handsomely to gain a papal dispensation to marry his deceased brother's wife, Katharine of Aragon, although later he did not succeed in attaining papal consent to annul the marriage.

governed and controlled by reason. The lack of control in sex since the Fall was the means by which Adam's sin was transmitted. Marriage was still necessary and the proper place for sexual intercourse, but it was also the locus of original sin (for Augustine's position, see Bonner 1963, pp. 370–88). Jerome's words to the young Christian virgin Eustochium encouraged her to privilege virginity over 'the drawbacks of marriage, such as pregnancy, the crying of infants, the torture caused by a rival, the cares of household management, and all those fancied blessings which death at last cuts short', although he conceded that women in chaste marriage – that is 'the marriage that is honourable and the bed undefiled' – have 'their own place' (Jerome, letter 22, *To Eustochium*).

The perception that marriage was second-best and, in particular, that the sexual act that made possible the procreation of children was inherently sinful, coloured the understanding of marriage – and indeed of proper discipleship – throughout the medieval period. This may have been difficult for both men and women, but it tends to have been women who wrote about it. St Birgid of Sweden and her husband, Ulf Gudmarsson, were an upper-class couple who were expected by their families to procreate in order to safeguard their inheritance but who believed strongly that their true vocation as Christians was to celibacy.[6] For medieval Christians, marriage was a second-best option, necessary for society. It was recognized to be necessary for the procreation of children, but in the eyes of many theologians this required a living-out of sexuality that was profoundly problematic. Good Christians would keep their marriages as chaste as possible.

The fundamental assumption of inequality between men and women persisted, even when, as in the thought of Thomas Aquinas, an argument for equality was made (McCluskey 2007). Assumptions about the respective place of men and women in marriage were related to Aristotelian–Galenic biological understandings of sexual differentiation that persisted well into the early modern period.[7] These biological differences were held to express themselves in different characteristics of maleness and femaleness: the rational, warm male was opposed to the emotional, cold female.[8] In procreation the creative principle was held to be contributed by the semen – or 'seed' – which took root in

---

6 For the tensions between motherhood and asceticism, see Methuen 2008.

7 Varying interpretations of that biology are offered by Laqueur 1990 and by MacLean 1980.

8 For Aristotle, truly masculine men could be identified by the fact that the heat of their intellect had burned the hair off their heads, causing baldness.

the fertile 'soil' offered by the woman's womb.[9] The active principle was contributed by the male; the female's role was passive: she provided a nurturing body in which the baby could grow.[10] This biological understanding of how procreation worked was extended to define the proper role for men and women: men were active, engaged in public life; women were passive, nurturing, with a focus on the private.

Marriage in the Reformation

The Protestant Reformation accorded marriage a new importance. Luther was deeply critical of the privileging of celibacy, and particularly of the hypocrisy of a Church that required clerical celibacy but turned a blind eye to the living arrangements of priests (except, in many dioceses, to fine them when a child was born). In a sermon on marriage in 1519 he affirmed that 'A woman is created to be a companionable helpmeet to the man in everything, particularly to bear children. And that still holds good, except that since the Fall marriage has been adulterated with wicked lust' (Luther 1519, p. 8). Marriage was necessary for men – particularly clergy – who could not control their natural lusts. In his treatise on *The Estate of Marriage* in 1522 he complained that reason – and, with reason, men – tended to 'turn up her nose' at the physical aspects of caring for a baby (Luther 1522, p. 39). However, Luther thought that both men and women should see the 'insignificant, distasteful, and despised duties' relating to parenthood as gifts of the Spirit (although he allowed that a father who did so might be 'ridicule[d] ... as an effeminate fool'). Nonetheless, while he affirmed that the tasks of caring for the children should be shared by both parents, Luther believed that a woman's true vocation lay in marriage, her companionship with and obedience to her husband, and the bearing and bringing up of children. Women who died in childbirth, he emphasized, were truly following Christ (Luther 1522, p. 40). Sexual desire, he thought, 'was natural and created by God', and was therefore such a fundamental part of marriage that impotence was a reason for divorce (Wiesner-Hanks 2000, p. 63). The obedience of a

---

9 That women and other female mammals produced eggs was not discovered until the late seventeenth century, soon after the identification of spermatozoa in semen (Cobb 2012). However, it took about 150 years for the roles of egg and sperm to become clear, and assumptions about the active nature of men and the passive nature of women also shaped that debate: see E. Martin 1991.

10 This biological understanding is deeply influential for the development of the doctrine of the Trinity, and in particular the relationship between Father and Son.

wife to her husband, and the subordination of women to men, were in Luther's eyes part of the natural order given under the law, to which marriage belonged; the gospel transcended this order, and men and women stood equal before God (Luther 1535b, p. 355; Luther 1535a, p. 69; Methuen 2013b, pp. 88–9).

In 1549 the Book of Common Prayer (BCP) emphasized that marriage 'is not to be enterprised, nor taken in hand, unadvisedly, lightly, or wantonly, to satisfy men's carnal lusts and appetites, like brute beasts that have no understanding: but reverently, discreetly, advisedly, soberly, and in the fear of God'. It listed three 'causes for which matrimony was ordained': the procreation and education of children; as 'a remedy against sin, and to avoid fornication'; and for 'mutual society, help, and comfort' of the couple, 'both in prosperity and adversity'.[11] These three aspects, procreation, the managing of lust, and companionship, shaped early modern understandings of marriage and they continue to shape our understanding today, as can be seen, for instance, from the prefaces to the Church of England marriage service in both the *Alternative Service Book* (1980) and *Common Worship* (2000). The BCP saw the wife as helpmeet, as director of the household and teacher of the children (that is, as *materfamilias* alongside but subordinate to the *paterfamilias*, as the BCP's homily on marriage makes quite clear), and this became the model for the Protestant household. The biblical reading suggested in the BCP marriage service consists of extracts from the household codes in Ephesians, and the view of women as subordinate was buttressed by the model homily.[12] Moreover as Hannah Cleugh has observed, the doctrine of marriage in the English Reformation is presented not only in the Book of Common Prayer but also in the Thirty-Nine Articles and the two Books of Homilies, all of which make assumptions about the proper ordering of households and about relationships between men and women that are very far from a modern Western understanding (Cleugh 2014). Reformation views of marriage were predicated on very different expectations about the relationship between men and women than those often prevalent in Western European or North American society today.

---

11 Book of Common Prayer 1549 (www.justus.anglican.org/resources/bcp/1549/ Marriage_1549.htm), retained in 1552, 1559 and 1662. In the 1928 revisions to the BCP the second aim was rephrased: 'That the natural instincts and affections, implanted by God, should be hallowed and directed aright', www.justus.anglican.org/ resources/bcp/CofE1928/CofE1928_Confirmation&Marriage.htm#Marriage.

12 It is therefore necessary to be cautious about apparently innocuous motions to the Church of England's General Synod to reaffirm the BCP's doctrine of marriage: this doctrine is not defined only by the preface to the service.

Wives and Femininity in the Nineteenth Century

The prospect of dying in childbirth – probably the most common cause of death for adult women until the modern period – must have been one reason why celibacy, whether within the convent or within marriage, was attractive to some women. The closure of convents as a consequence of the Reformation left many women no option other than marriage (see, for instance, Wiesner 2008, pp. 143–57). The wife as helpmeet, as director of the household and teacher of the children became the model for the Protestant household, although this pattern grew out of the kind of family relationships experienced by the middling sort and nobility and cannot have been possible for many working families. As indus-trialization took hold, the difference between the lives of the working poor, in which men and women – and often also children – had to work to survive, and those of the middle and upper classes in which women could remain at home, became more pronounced. The Protestant ideal of the role of the woman in the marriage and the family became more prevalent: it fed into a social ideal that tended (and indeed still tends) to identify women as nurturing and caring – and also as more religious – than men, and as a civilizing influence on them. This was the rhetoric that underpinned the ideal role of women in the nineteenth century but also shaped many of the arguments for women's suffrage, for example: should not the civilizing influence of (middle class) women be able to make itself felt in the running of society?[13]

The eighteenth and nineteenth centuries witnessed significant changes in the legal definition of marriage and in the status of married women (Probert 2009; Perkin 1989). Rebecca Probert observes that in eighteenth-century England the marriage ceremony (even when clandestine) 'had to be conducted by an episcopally ordained minister in order for the parties to enjoy the legal rights of married couples' (Probert 2008, p. 35). Once married, a couple was a legal unit and the woman could not hold property in her right. This situation changed with the Married Women's Property Acts of 1870 and 1882.[14] These and other Acts granted greater equality within marriage by law, and Timothy Willem Jones argues that in the period from 1857 to 1957, despite 'the Church's increasing, sometimes hysterical, opposition to marriage law reform' (Jones 2013, p. 19), there was indeed a 'decline of subordination in Anglican understandings of sex' (2013, p. 9).

---

13 This is a frequent motif in suffragette literature. See, for instance, Aitken 2007, pp. 112–17.

14 The outworking of the 1870 Act has been explored by Combs 2006.

Jeremy Morris concurs that these changes to legislation made marriage more equal and also introduced distinctions between civil and canon law in questions of marriage in English and Scottish law. He concludes: 'We must be wary of absolutizing any particular historical model of marriage and saying "This is how it must be". ... It has long ceased to be true for the majority of British citizens that the Church's doctrine of marriage ... is what constrains their understanding of what they are entering into when they get married' (Morris 2014). However, in some parts of the Church the subordination of women to men continued to be emphasized, and with it the expectation that a woman must accept the behaviour of her husband – even a violent husband. Even now, studies of domestic violence consistently discover cases of women who seek help from their pastors and clergy only to be told that the woman should be obedient to her husband and submit to his ill-treatment, while trying to redeem him through her loving behaviour.[15]

Procreation in an Age of Fertility Treatments

It is clear that marriage has long been associated with procreation, although the *Alternative Service Book* (1980) listed the bearing and nurturing of children as the third aim of marriage, after companionship and the 'delight and tenderness' and 'the joy of their bodily union' (ASB 1980, p. 288). Perhaps this was a recognition of the extent to which, by 1980, contraception and other modern methods of 'managing' fertility had already radically changed the experience of marriage, particularly for women. It might be argued that in Western society sexual intercourse and procreation have over the past half-century become increasingly detached from one another, for although procreation is not – yet – separate from the need to have contributions from both one man and [at least] one woman,[16] conception need not take place through sexual intercourse, and many families exist in which the children are not biologically or genetically the offspring of their nurturing parent(s). Adoptive children and step-families have long been

---

15 See, for instance, Macdonald, 2001. This is the approach advocated by 1 Peter 33.1–2 and what Augustine's mother Monica is said to have done to reform her husband Patricius: Augustine, *Confessions* I.11.17.

16 Research into maternal spindle transfer and pronuclear transfer, which involve the creation of embryos containing nuclear DNA from a man and a woman, plus mitochondrial DNA from another woman, thus avoiding the transfer of mitochondrial disease, raises the possibility of three-parent embryos. This was opposed by the Church of England in spring 2015.

familiar, but increasingly children are born after conception resulting from techniques including IVF, artificial insemination, sperm dona-tion (sometimes anonymous, sometimes not) and surrogacy. Some of the parents of these families are heterosexual couples, or sometimes multiple couples after divorce or separation; some are gay couples, sometimes parenting as two mothers in one relationship and two fathers in another; some are single parents. Recent research indicates that the 'constellation' of the parents makes little difference to the well-being of the children; what matters is the quality of the relation-ship both between the adults of the family and between the adults and the child(ren).[17]

Conclusion

All this is a reminder that neither marriage nor 'Christian marriage' (however that is defined) has ever been a static institution. Moreover marriage has often been an institution that has not fostered women's flourishing. Christian conceptions of marriage have transmitted par-ticular views of the role of women and about relationships between men and women that continue to shape expectations of women today.[18] This is one reason why it is difficult for me to affirm marriage unequiv-ocally as one of the 'goods' of creation: it is a human institution, rooted in the social context in which it is lived and subject to the norms and expectations of that context. Perhaps one of the flaws of our current conception of marriage is precisely the emphasis on 'one man and one woman', which seems consistently to be bring with it particular expect-ations about the role of women and men that tend to reach far beyond the question of who is biologically capable of bearing children. Against this background, extending the definition of marriage to include same-sex couples might in fact be a redemptive step, enabling the institution of marriage to transcend the profound inequalities that have too often shaped it.

17 http://pediatrics.aappublications.org/content/early/2013/03/18/peds.2013-0377. However, some of the complexities of the experiences of these children can be observed from recent court cases in the UK (known sperm donors requesting and being granted access to their biological children; see Taylor 2013) and in Germany (children of 'anonymous' sperm donors claiming the right to know the names of their fathers; see, for instance, the case of 'Stina': www.spenderkinder.de/Main/Stina). These are parallel to developments around adoption in the 1980s.

18 In the churches, language of the complementarity of the roles of men and women and the subordination of women to men underlies many of the arguments against the ordination of women.

References

Aitken, Jo, 2007, '"The Horrors of Matrimony among the Masses": Feminist Representations of Wife Beating in England and Australia, 1870–1914', *Journal of Women's History* 19, 2007, pp. 107–31.

Archbishops' Council of the Church of England, 2000, *Common Worship: Pastoral Services*, London: Church House Publishing.

Archbishops' Council of the Church of England, 2013, *Men and Women in Marriage: A Document from the Faith and Order Commission Published with the Agreement of the House of Bishops of the Church of England and Approved for Study*, GS Misc 1046, London: Church House Publishing.

Augustine, *Confessions* I.11.17, trans. and ed. Albert C. Outler, London: SCM Press, 1955, p. 21, online at www.ccel.org/ccel/augustine/confessions.pdf.

Bonner, Gerald, 1963, *St Augustine of Hippo: Life and Controversies*, Norwich: Canterbury Press.

Book of Common Prayer 1549, www.justus.anglican.org/resources/bcp/1549/Marriage_1549.htm.

Book of Common Prayer 1928, www.justus.anglican.org/resources/bcp/CofE1928/CofE1928_Confirmation&Marriage.htm#Marriage.

Brink, Leendert, 1982, 'Ehe/Eherecht/Eheschliessung VI: Mittelalter', in Gerhard Krause and Gerhard Müller (eds), *Theologische Realenzyklopädie*, vol. 9, Berlin: De Gruyter, pp. 330–6.

Brown, Peter, 2008, *The Body and Society: Men, Women, and Sexual Renunciation in Early Christianity*, new edn, New York, NY: Columbia University Press.

Central Board of Finance of the Church of England, 1980, *Alternative Service Book*, London: Church House Publishing.

Cleugh, Hannah, 2014, 'Marriage, the Reformation and the BCP', paper given at the Affirming Catholicism conference 'Thinking About Marriage? Theological and Historical Perspectives', on 25 January 2014; available at www.youtube.com/watch?v=jCs7S3FMuls.

Cobb, M., 2012, 'An Amazing 10 Years: The Discovery of Egg and Sperm in the 17th Century', *Reproduction in Domestic Animals* 47, suppl. 4, pp. 2–6.

Combs, Mary Beth, 2006, 'Cui bono? The 1870 British Married Women's Property Act, Bargaining Power, and the Distribution of Resources Within Marriage', *Feminist Economics* 12.1–2, pp. 51–83.

Cooper, Kate, 2007, *The Fall of the Roman Household*, Cambridge: Cambridge University Press.

Crouzel, Henri, 1982, 'Ehe/Eherecht/Ehescheidung V: Alte Kirche', in Gerhard Krause and Gerhard Müller (eds), *Theologische Realenzyklopädie*, vol. 9, Berlin: De Gruyter, pp. 325–30.

Doctrine Committee of the Scottish Episcopal Church, 2012, *Marriage and Human Intimacy: Perspectives on Same-Sex Relationships and the Life of the Church*, Grosvenor Essay No 8, Edinburgh: General Synod Office.

Hammond, Cally, 2014, 'Augustine and Early Church Understandings of Marriage', paper given at the Affirming Catholicism conference 'Thinking About Marriage? Theological and Historical Perspectives' on 25 January 2014, available at www.youtube.com/watch?v=suD2iFiKtZQ.

Jerome, letter 22: *To Eustochium*, 2, www.fordham.edu/halsall/basis/jerome-letter22.asp.

Jones, Timothy Willem, 2013, *Sexual Politics in the Church of England, 1857–1957*, Oxford: Oxford University Press.

Laqueur, Thomas, 1990, *Making Sex: Body and Gender from the Greeks to Freud*, Cambridge, MA: Harvard University Press.

Luther, Martin, 1519 (1966), 'A Sermon on the Estate of Marriage', in Jaroslav Pelikan (ed.), *Luther's Works*, vol. 44: *The Christian in Society I*, Minneapolis, MN: Fortress Press, pp. 7–14.

Luther, Martin, 1522 (1962), 'The Estate of Marriage', in Jaroslav Pelikan (ed.), *Luther's Works*, vol. 45: *The Christian in Society II*, Minneapolis, MN: Fortress Press, pp. 13–51.

Luther, Martin, 1535a (1958), 'Lectures on Genesis' (part 1), in Jaroslav Pelikan (ed.), *Luther's Works*, vol. 1: *Lectures on Genesis Chapters 1–5*, ed., Minneapolis, MN: Fortress Press.

Luther, Martin, 1535b (1963), 'Lectures on Galatians, 1535' (part 1), in Jaroslav Pelikan (ed.), *Luther's Works*, vol. 26: *Lectures on Galatians, 1535, Chapters 1–4*, Minneapolis, MN: Fortress Press.

Macdonald, Lesley Orr, 2001, *Out of the Shadows: Christianity and Violence against Women in Scotland*, Edinburgh: Centre for Theology and Public Issues.

MacLean, Ian, 1980, *The Renaissance Notion of Woman*, Cambridge: Cambridge University Press.

Martin, Emily, 1991, 'The Egg and the Sperm: How Science Has Constructed a Romance Based on Stereotypical Male–Female Roles', *Signs: Journal of Women in Culture and Society* 16.3, pp. 485–501.

Martin, Francis, 2001, 'Marriage in the Old Testament and Intertestamental Periods', in Glenn W. Olson (ed.), *Christian Marriage: A Historical Study*, New York, NY: Crossroad, pp. 1–49.

McCluskey, Colleen, 2007, 'An Unequal Relationship between Equals: Thomas Aquinas on Marriage', *History of Philosophy Quarterly* 24.1, pp. 1–18.

Methuen, Charlotte, 2008, '"Denke an dein Kind, das ohne dich nicht leben kann!" Mütter in der Nachfolge Christi', in Annette Esser and Andrea Günther (eds), *Kinder haben – KindSein – Geboren sein*, Königstein: Ulrike Helmer Verlag, pp. 47–60.

Methuen, Charlotte, 2013a, 'Marriage: One Man and One Woman?', www.opendemocracy.net/ourkingdom/charlotte-methuen/marriage-one-man-and-one-woman.

Methuen, Charlotte, 2013b, '"And your Daughters shall Prophesy!" Reforming Women and the Construction of Authority', *Archiv für Reformationsgeschichte* 104.1, pp. 82–109.

Methuen, Charlotte, 2014, 'Thinking About Marriage: An Excursion Through Christian History', *Modern Believing* 55.2, pp. 149–62.

Morris, Jeremy, 2014, 'Marriage and the Church of England in the Nineteenth Century', paper given at the Affirming Catholicism conference 'Thinking About Marriage? Theological and historical perspectives' on 25 January 2014, available at www.youtube.com/watch?v=RE5NRB_W5MY.

Økland, Jorunn, 2014, 'Paul, Marriage and the New Testament', paper given at the Affirming Catholicism conference 'Thinking About Marriage? Theological and Historical Perspectives' on 25 January 2014, available at www.youtube.com/watch?v=eh8Zv-A2Ti4.

Perkin, Joan, 1989, *Women and Marriage in Nineteenth-Century England*, London: Taylor and Francis.

Probert, Rebecca, 2008, 'Examining Law through the Lens of Literature: The Formation of Marriage in Eighteenth-century England', *Law and Humanities* 2.1, pp. 29–48.

Probert, Rebecca, 2009, *Marriage Law and Practice in the Long Eighteenth Century: A Reassessment*, Cambridge: Cambridge University Press.

Taylor, Diane, 2013, 'Sperm Donors who Know Parents can Apply to see Children, Court Rules', *The Guardian*, 31 January 2013, www.guardian.co.uk/lifeandstyle/2013/jan/31/sperm-donors-parents-apply-contact-children.

Wiesner, Merry E., 2008, *Women and Gender in Early Modern Europe*, Cambridge: Cambridge University Press.

Wiesner-Hanks, Merry E., 2000, *Christianity and Sexuality in the Early Modern World*. London: Routledge.

Woodhead, Linda, 2013, 'Do Christians really oppose gay marriage?', www.religionandsociety.org.uk/events/programme_events/show/press_release_do_christians_really_oppose_gay_marriage.

Woodhead, Linda, 2014, 'What People Really think about Same-Sex Marriage', *Modern Believing* 55.1, pp. 27–38.

4

Thinking About Marriage with Scripture

BEN FULFORD

Introduction

Discussions of biblical texts loom large in Christian debates about same-sex marriage. The provocation for this chapter is the observation that far too often writers do not stand back from the detailed engagement with texts to ask deeper questions about how we should use the Bible to think theologically about forms of vocation in respect of human beings as sexual creatures. In this chapter I want to propose one way of addressing that issue and, in so doing, to put it more firmly on the agenda.

For those who have grown used to reading books and blogs that go straight to the disputed biblical passages in order to derive from them conclusions about human sexuality, this chapter is going to be frustrating. That frustration is a necessary one, however, if we are to unlearn those bad habits of short-circuiting a scripturally resourced discernment on these questions and find ways of pursuing that task more adequately. We desperately need to, on both sides of the debate. I hope to model, in a brief and sketchy way, one approach. It takes its basic cue from the link between who Jesus is in the New Testament story about him, and the claims upon addressees of the gospel story that concerns him.

My tentative proposal, then, is that Christians in their theological reflections on belief and practice should take themselves to be bound primarily to the story that culminates in the story of Jesus, and to be addressed by God and by Christ in and through it, in being called to the reorientation and common life it demands. Part of that reorientation is the call to understand every facet of being human, including human sexuality and institutions like marriage, in light of how we are to identify ourselves and others (including other creatures) as related to God in creation, salvation and in eschatological consummation. In this task we should take the biblical literature as not only the indispensable form in which the story is mediated, but – taking a lead from some early Christian ways of thinking about the Bible – also as offering a sort of training or education in learning to embody that story in the way we think, feel and relate to one another.

The Need to Think About How We Use the Bible on this Question

Turn to most books (or blogs) dealing with same-sex marriage and Scripture and after a while we know what to expect: a trawl through the much-debated passages like Genesis 19, Leviticus 18 and 20, and Romans 1.18–32 and the historical backgrounds most likely to illumine their patterns of reasoning; and a minute dissection of passages relating to marriage, such as Jesus' sayings about divorce in Mark 10, the depiction of sexual differentiation and marriage in Genesis 1—2, and Pauline and Deutero-Pauline teaching on marriage in 1 Corinthians 7 and Ephesians 5.22–33 (for example, see Brownson 2013; Countryman 2001; Gagnon 2001; see also more popular treatments such as John 2012; Schmidt 1995; Vines 2014). Writers emerge, after lengthy wrestling with a mountain of scholarship, grasping a conclusion about whether or not biblical teaching on homosexuality excludes faithful, permanent same-sex couples from marriage. While many of them seek to uncover underlying rationales and ask about their applicability for today, very few seem to reflect on deeper questions about how one should use Scripture to draw theological conclusions about these issues, and what sort of assumptions underlie their focus on this short list of contested texts as a way of reaching theological conclusions about human sexuality and marriage.[1]

Nor is it enough to urge the return to a traditional pre-critical approach to the plain, canonical meaning of the Bible, as though traditional ways of approaching the canon (which canon?) were beyond serious theological challenge or demonstrably capable of yielding theologies of sexuality rich enough to address the questions before us (see, for example, Seitz 2000 and Roberts 2007). The examples of anti-Semitism, slavery and women in the history of biblical interpretation suggest otherwise, and wishful appeals to the 'trajectories' of Scripture

---

1 There are some exceptions, such as Song 2014 or Hays 1997, though Hays' treatment of homosexuality does not do justice to the promise of his methodology and he only briefly alludes to his underlying theology of Scripture. Analogies with the inclusion of the Gentiles are another exception. For one of the most significant treatments, see Rogers 1999.

on these questions fail to reckon with the question of what qualifies as a meaningful and decisive trajectory in the canon or why it took so very long for these trajectories to be noticed by wise and thoughtful Christian readers. An appeal to some form of basic tradition of Christian reading practice is necessary, however, since in themselves the texts of the various Christian biblical canons may be read and used in all manner of ways and the form of the canon itself imposes relatively little guidance about how to use biblical texts in theology. In other words, we need to begin a long way back from where the debate is happening.

Scripture in Christian Communities and the Theology of Scripture

This last point suggests that the proper setting for thinking theologically about uses of Scripture in relation to questions of human sexuality and marriage is in Christian communities and the uses to which they and their members put biblical texts. All this is the proper setting for a theology of Scripture; that is, the attempt to understand the ways God is present and active in all these uses of Scripture. It is also the place to make proposals about what ways of using biblical texts might more fully accord with that understanding.

The alternative to this approach would be to find a theory that will tell us how any text has meaning and should be interpreted, and make sure our scriptural interpretation conforms to it. The price for such a general theory, however, may be that in its generality it fails to account for Christian ways of reading and the particularly Christian ways they make sense – and ends up excluding them.

There are properly Christian reasons, of course, for wanting to respect scriptural texts just as texts. They are the products of other creatures' communicative intentions and so out of respect for those intentions we should in our interpretations respect the ways they have been put together. Even so, such respect allows for a wide variety of ways of using texts, including plain disagreement with their authors! We need another way to think in more specifically Christian terms about the status of these texts, the authority we should accord them and what might be appropriate ways of using them in Christian communities. One way forward, suggested by the theologian Hans Frei, would be to take a cue from a (so far) stable, practical consensus about reading Scripture in Christian tradition that offers an approach to these questions.

The Priority of the Story of Jesus

Frei argued that, amid all their disagreements about biblical interpretations, Christians have in practice prioritized the stories about
Jesus in the New Testament over other texts in the Bible. They have
read them as stories primarily about the character Jesus Christ. They
have taken them to represent him adequately to us. And they have
understood his story to be the culmination of the story of God's concern for Israel and the world in Israel's Scriptures (Frei 1990, pp. 8–18;
Frei 1993).[2] Insofar as those stories have a similar basic way of identi-
fying who Jesus was – in terms of his life, death and resurrection – we
may talk of a single story rendered in various ways. It is to that story,
then, in its connectedness to Israel's Scriptures, that Christian theology
is most basically accountable.

In *The Identity of Jesus Christ* (Frei 1975), Frei offered a reading
of the synoptic Gospels (and especially Luke–Acts) that is in keeping
with this consensus. He argued that the Synoptics answer the question, 'Who is Jesus?', above all in the way they tell the story about
him, and that in that story his identity (who he is) emerges through the
sequence of the story. As the story comes to its climax in the passion–
resurrection sequence, Jesus' identity is most clearly set forth. There
we see Jesus carrying out his most characteristic intentions in going to
the cross out of love for human beings and obedience to God. There,
in the continuity of what he does and undergoes as a human body,
he is seen in his unrepeatable uniqueness. Just in that sequence, however, it becomes clear also that his identity is forever and inescapably
entangled with who God is.[3] In the story, God is mysteriously active
in and through contingent historical events and agencies. That divine
presence and action culminates in the resurrection of Jesus, where God
is present directly. The form that God's active presence takes is the
risen Jesus. The resurrection has revelatory force for Frei: it discloses
the profound unity of Jesus of Nazareth and Israel's God and the centrality of this human being to all God's activity in history, and to the
way God relates to every human. This claim offers us a basis for thinking about Scripture, once we clarify the relation between Scripture and
the identity of Christ.

---

2 This consensus therefore excludes certain groups claiming a Christian identity
but rejecting Israel's Scriptures, a position traditionally labelled 'Marcionism' after the
second-century teacher Marcion.

3 See also Kavin Rowe's exegetical development of this argument with respect to
the term *kyrios* ('Lord') in Luke's Gospel, in Rowe 2009b.

A Theology of the Gospel as Story

In Frei's account, the logic of the way the story identifies Jesus Christ is such that, for the believer who accepts it, Jesus Christ cannot be thought not to live. In this way the story implicitly claims a very strong form of authority: if we accept its identification of Jesus Christ, we must understand him to be the living one.

We can fill out a theology of the story and the nature of its authority a little more if we trace the connection between it and the one it identifies. Following Frei's focus on Luke's Gospel, we might turn to its companion volume, the Acts of the Apostles, where this connection between Jesus Christ and the spreading of his story is set forth. I take the narrative episodes of Acts to portray the activity of apostles as they disseminate the gospel about Jesus of Nazareth in such a way as to offer a Christian way of re-imagining the world.[4]

In Acts, the apostles and others retell Jesus' story repeatedly before different audiences, Jewish and Gentile, in Judea, Samaria and various destinations on the way to the ends of the earth.[5] In the text this story has the status of human testimony, the witness of those who had been with Jesus from his baptism to his ascension, to his resurrection from the dead, reporting 'God's deeds of power' in and through Jesus of Nazareth. In the episode of Pentecost and the sermon of Peter, Acts relates that testimony to its subject, Jesus Christ.

According to Peter's sermon in Acts 2, the apostles' testimony is to be understood as the fulfilment of prophecy in light of the identity of Jesus. The apostles are witnesses of God's resurrection of the one whom God had attested to Israel through deeds of power, who had been handed over to the Gentiles to be put to death according to God's plan. The apostles' witness at Pentecost is the manifestation of the promised Spirit, which Jesus has poured out, having received it from the Father. By this Israelites are to know 'with certainty that God has made him both Lord and Messiah, this Jesus whom you crucified' (Acts 2.36).

In this crucial moment of his sermon, Peter not only identifies the risen Lord and the earthly Jesus as the subject of the apostles' wit-

---

4 Here I am following the way of conceiving Acts taken by Rowe 2009a, though without attempting to match the sophistication or erudition of his treatment.

5 The story varies in the telling, but the resurrection and exaltation of Jesus is always the decisive moment, usually preceded by his attestation by God through the deeds of power he performed followed by his (unwitting) rejection by the people of Israel and their leaders. Sometimes that story is made the conclusion to a rehearsal of the story of Israel; sometimes it is the conclusion to a story about God the gift-giving creator.

ness; he also picks up on two key terms by which Luke depicts Jesus' identity in Luke–Acts. As Kavin Rowe has shown, Luke in his Gospel uses the term *kyrios* ('Lord') of God but also of Jesus, and uses the ambiguity about which of the two the term denotes to express both the unity and the distinction between Jesus and God (Rowe 2009b). As Rowe also argues, Luke's use of the term *christos* ('anointed one') helps clarify that pattern of unity and identity between God and Jesus. Jesus of Nazareth is the Anointed One in virtue of the way the Spirit shapes his life from his conception, through his baptism, temptation and in his ministry. The Spirit of the Lord is the Power of God. The construction of these terms, we may infer with Rowe, serves to express the freedom and intimate engagement of the God who is present and active in this world (Rowe 2009b, p. 47). It is the effect of the activity of the Spirit of the Lord in the human life of Jesus, uniting him inseparably to God, which justifies Luke's extending the divine title *kyrios* to Jesus (Rowe 2009b, pp. 47–9). But Jesus is Lord in a distinct way: as Christ, as the one who receives the Spirit, who is entirely dependent on God in this unique way.

The force of Peter's sermon is that the extraordinary apostolic testimony of Pentecost as the outpouring of that same Spirit marks the further gift of God's Power to other human creatures, in and through Jesus. We can thus identify two factors that make possible the apostles' witness – their story about Jesus Christ as Lord. Both inhere in Jesus' identity as given in the story itself and his relationship to God in the Spirit of God. First, the identity of Jesus as something that can be told is made possible by the extraordinary role of the Spirit in shaping who Jesus is from the very beginning of his life: a human being living from a unique relation to God whose life therefore has a pattern that a human story can relate. Second, in his unity with God, marked by the shared title 'Lord', and as disposing of the same Power that shaped his existence as 'Christ', Jesus impels and empowers the telling of the story by bestowing that Power of God as a gift on his witnesses.[6] As a result this story that humans tell is a means whereby God speaks. It conveys a divine call to repentance and promise of forgiveness and the gift of the Spirit (2.40). Hence at times in Acts the apostolic testimony about Jesus Christ is called 'the word of God' (e.g. Acts 6.2, 7). At the same time, the apostles speak in the name of Jesus Christ (4.18), and their message is described as 'the word of the Lord' elsewhere (13.44, 48). If we bear in mind the way Luke uses 'Lord' to express the unity of God and

---

6 See also Paul's description of the origins of his apostolic ministry and his gospel in Galatians 1.1, 11ff.

Jesus, we can see that Jesus is included in this divine speaking through the apostles' story (see Rowe 2009a, pp. 111–12 for the same argument with respect to the use of 'Lord' in Acts 2). For the same reason we may take Jesus to be, with God, the Lord who makes this message efficacious (Acts 2.47; 11.21) (Rowe 2009a, pp. 128–9).

Jesus' identity is crucial to the efficacy of this divine communication: it is to those who repent and are baptized in the name of Jesus Christ that the Spirit and forgiveness are to be given. As a vehicle of divine communication, the story that the divinely empowered apostles tell demands and evokes a response that orientates the responder wholly to the subject of the story: the risen Lord himself.[7] In the fullness and continuity of his identity, he himself is the truth of the story and the source and end of its authority, of the demand it makes of its hearers. The story of Acts illustrates further the nature of that authority and the scope of that demand.

According to Peter's sermon at Pentecost, the apostolic witness calls its hearers to a fundamental reorientation away from sin and towards this same Jesus, by means of the rite of baptism involving the invocation of Jesus' name (cf. Acts 22.26). By being orientated to Jesus in this way through baptism, hearers of the story become those who also receive the end-time gifts Jesus gives: forgiveness of sins and the Holy Spirit.

It also entails their joining a community of those who share this fundamental shift in self-identification, gathering in the temple and in homes. Their common life is marked by practices in which they learn to live out that shift in the way they think, in their emotions, and in the manner in which they act toward one another. They 'devote themselves to the apostles' teaching and fellowship, to the breaking of bread and the prayers'; they sell their property and goods to meet one another's needs; they eat food together 'with glad and generous hearts' (2.42–47). Here we have a picture of the mode of authority of the story of Jesus Christ reflected in the ideal response set forth in the narrative of Acts. It demands the reorientation of lives in identification with Jesus Christ, the story's subject, embodied through appropriate practices, emotions and dispositions in a common life.

---

7 Similar claims could be made of the story as told in the other Gospels in the New Testament, and also in Paul, where it is God's immanent activity – God's Power or Spirit – that makes the gospel effective (1 Cor. 2.4–5; Rom. 1.17). Here too the story and its apostolic tellers are vehicles of an address that is at once from God and from Christ (2 Cor. 5.18–21), and can be called in this sense God's word (2 Cor. 2.17).

The extension of the apostolic mission to the Gentiles discloses further elements to our understanding of the authority of the story of Jesus. It is a message of reconciliation extended to all people on earth, to whom also the eschatological blessing is also extended. But the story demands a more basic reorientation within the turn to Jesus as Lord. It demands a turning to Israel's God as creator, radically different from everything else as the source of all life and blessing (Acts 14.14–17; 17.22–28). Of Gentiles, then, the story requires a learning to see the world as creation, oneself as creature. It is to relate the goods we enjoy and our enjoyment of them to God as their source. It demands this recognition and along with it a redirection of worship, trust and hope from creatures to their creator whose goodwill is disclosed in the particular human being, Jesus of Nazareth.

The Authority of Scripture in a Historical World

If we follow the logic that relates Jesus Christ to the story about him, we find that, just as he is seen to be central to God's relation to the world, so he and his story form the centre of gravity for Christian Scripture. It does so in two ways.

First, it does so with respect to Israel's Scriptures. The story of Jesus calls us to recognize that the God of Israel has come to Israel and to the world in and through Jesus Christ (Acts 2.20). In this way it presents itself as the culmination of a story about God and Israel told in those Scriptures (Acts 2.16–36; 3.12–26; 7.1–53; 8.30–35; 13.16–41 etc.). Just so, the story of Jesus asks believers to receive and understand those Scriptures in those terms. On the one hand, Israel's Scriptures provide the context in which Jesus' story is to be understood. On the other, Jesus' story claims to be the lens through which those Scriptures are to be read in Christian community. It asks us to see anticipations of the end of the story in earlier episodes and especially in the promises made to Israel and the visions of its prophets. What authority Israel's Scriptures have for Christian communities is mediated through this relationship to the story of Jesus. Second, Jesus' story forms a centre of gravity in relation also to the texts of the New Testament. In effect, the book of Acts contextualizes itself (and the gospel of Luke) by narrating the story of the apostles and their message into the world. It thus implies a distinction between the story of Jesus and the text of Luke–Acts in which that story is related. We may be used to thinking that the reliability and authority of a text is our guarantee as to the truth of its message. Thus if we can show that the story is divinely authored, or historically reliable, or true to a more general sense of what it is to be human, then we can have confidence in what it tells us. The story Acts tells about the apostles, however, upsets our expectations about this relationship between the reliability of the text and our confidence in the story it tells. By contextualizing itself in the story of the apostles' mission, Luke–Acts signals that as a text its reliability depends on the apostolic testimony it relates. And as we have seen, according to that testimony, Jesus of Nazareth as Lord is One who makes his story true and authoritative, and shapes the nature of that authority. Jesus Christ as the Living One is the ultimate ground of assurance of the truth of the teachings for the text's addressee, Theophilus, and for all the readers he stands for (see Luke 1.1–4).

In this respect Luke–Acts offers a pattern for thinking about all New Testament literature. Luke mentions other orderly accounts besides his own, and the New Testament includes three of these. This mention also relativizes these accounts to the common basic story that all tell in their different ways. Those different ways of telling serve the purpose of assisting readers and hearers to the truth of what they have been taught. They offer different ways into Christ's identity and presence and into following him. We might extend the point to other New Testament literature. For example, Paul offers ad hoc theological argument and instruction in response to the issues raised by his correspondents in their particular circumstances, drawing on the implications of the story of Jesus Christ in the context of Israel's Scriptures and the story they tell. In other words, Acts helps us contextualize New Testament literature *theologically*, rather than primarily as a historical source – though it may be useful in this way also.

Our circumstances too are, like those of the writers, contextualized by the ending of the story of Israel in Jesus' story. They are nevertheless quite particular and distinct from the historical worlds reflected in scriptural texts. Those texts, moreover, confront us with a Lord who is not constrained by the limits of historical location. Therefore we cannot always simply repeat the ways these writers and their contemporaries set forth faithful living in conformity with Christ. Difference of historical context can mean, on the one hand, that we are faced with circumstances not addressed by biblical teachings, or that biblical teachings involve appeal to common sense or scientific knowledge that is not valid for other readers in other contexts (think of Paul's natural law argument about hair coverings, or hair length, in 1 Corinthians 11.2–16: see the account of Paul's reasoning in Schoedel 2000, pp. 59–64). Yet in responding to this Lord, we are afforded in these texts, under the

Spirit's guidance, a sort of education. It is a training in the 'transform-ation of the mind' (Rom. 12.2) and life in accordance with the way God and Christ are identified in the story and with the way all people are identified in relation to them. Acknowledging the authority of this literature, then, means learning to think with it in dependence upon the Spirit of God. Such a model of scriptural authority also allows us, where appropriate, to bring our own knowledge to bear, where the texts make room for an appeal to such knowledge, and to relate it to what Scripture discloses about the identities of God, Jesus Christ and creatures.

I would suggest that we might extend this way of thinking about Scripture to Israel's Scriptures also, read in the light of the story of Jesus (see above). Here too we have a highly varied set of texts that serves to offer provocations, principles or paradigms to think with theologically. Wisdom literature is obviously suited to this sort of appropriation but so too is narrative, and many legal texts can be taken in this way also.[8] To indicate more fully what this proposal might look like would take more space than I have here, but it does seem to be one way of follow-ing the pattern of Paul in 1 Corinthians 10.1ff. ('These things happened to them to serve as an example, and they were written down to instruct us, on whom the ends of the ages has come') and the guidance offered by the author of 2 Timothy 3.16 ('All Scripture is inspired by God and is useful for teaching, for reproof, for correction, and for training in righteousness').

This discernment must also be critical in at least two ways. First, we must be attentive to ways of following the teaching of Scripture that have led to promoting the suffering and denigration of other creatures. Such suffering and denigration are contrary to their dignity as God's creatures and as addressees of the gospel. We must be prepared to scrutinize and revise our performances of the text accordingly.[9] Second, for the same reason we must be alert to the potential in scriptural litera-ture for being appropriated in such ways. We can also guard against harmful readings by reading Scripture in conversation with other mem-bers of Christian communities past and present, far and near. And for all these reasons, this sort of thinking with Scripture demands that we are being formed already.

---

8 On narrative and law, see also Barton 2014, pp. 137–48, 170–4.

9 I'm borrowing this shorthand from Stephen Barton (among others) (Barton 1999).

Thinking about Human Sexuality and Marriage in the Context of Creation

In the gospel the Lord asks of believers to recognize who they are in relation to God. The most basic recognition here is to learn that we are creatures. I want to take this learning as my focus in offering a worked example of thinking with Scripture about human sexuality and marriage. I do so largely in conversation with David Kelsey's *Eccentric Existence* (2009).

A key decision that needs to be made at this point is where to begin to focus our thinking within the biblical canon. Theologians at this point traditionally turn first to Genesis, as the first book in the canon and which begins with stories about creation. In doing so they follow the direction of at least two strands of New Testament teaching, one of which is directly concerned with marriage: Paul's depiction of Christ as a Second Adam in 1 Corinthians 15 and Romans 5, and Jesus' teaching about divorce in Mark 10 and parallel passages.[10] And in doing so they find two passages concerned with human sexuality and with the origins of marriage. It is hard to dispute the need to follow this direction in thinking theologically about these subjects, but these are not the only texts to which the New Testament directs us. Paul's identification of God as creator in Acts 14.16–17 and 17.26 describes divine creative activity in terms that echo not only Genesis ('From one ancestor he made all nations …') but also the portrayal of God in biblical Wisdom literature who allots times of human lives (Eccles. 3.1–15), who gives life and breath to creatures (Ps. 104.29–30) and provides them with good things (Ps. 104.10–28), and whose providential ordering of human lives is the background belief asserted and tested in that literature. Furthermore, in the Johannine Prologue and in Colossians 1.15ff., the writers connect creation and salvation in Jesus Christ using the figure of divine Wisdom that we find in Proverbs and other texts (cf. Prov. 8.22–31).

Kelsey has argued that there is a particular value in turning to Wisdom literature first in order to shape our thinking about God's creative relation to creatures. For here we find this topic treated on its own terms. In Genesis, Isaiah and the New Testament it is used to illuminate stories of how God reconciles creatures to Godself, and its distinctive logic is subordinated to the logic of those stories of salvation (Kelsey 2009, pp. 161–2). A further advantage of this way of proceeding within the biblical canon, Kelsey argues, is that it helps block the tendencies

---

10 One might add Romans 1.18ff.

of traditional readings of the tales of origins in Genesis 1—11 (the 'primeval history') to understand Genesis 1—2 as descriptive of an ideal world before the 'Fall' of Genesis 3 (Kelsey 2009, pp. 297ff.). For the consequence of this way of reading Genesis 1—3 (which also interrupts the structure of Genesis 1—11) has been to equate the created existence of Adam and Eve with human perfection.[11] In this way these readings seem to imply that human beings are, in their created existence, imperfect because of the Fall and hence imperfectly human, so casting suspicion on their full humanity.

Kelsey uses Job's protesting description of being created by God in Job 10.8–19 to guide his reflections on human beings as created by God. He finds two mini-stories here. Job 10.8–10 describes Job as being created by God in and through his birth from his human mother. God is freely and directly engaged in this process, so that Job's creation is both utterly gratuitous and natural, and on a par with the way other animals are created. Kelsey proposes, in effect, that we follow the model the text offers for thinking about humans as creatures. The text speaks of God's creative action by way of Job's birth in terms of the knowledge of its time (the coagulation of semen in the womb – Job 10.10). We think with the text by speaking of God's creative action through human birth, using the scientific knowledge of *our* time. And so we say that God creates human beings through their complex development before and after birth, as they interact with their biological and social environments. Thinking with the text in this way allows Kelsey to acknowledge the frailty and finitude of humans as living bodies and affirm their goodness as such.

The second mini-story, Job 10.11–12, depicts Job as the recipient of his human body, the recipient of a gift from God. Job takes this gift to be a mark of God's commitment to him in something like a social institution between two parties. This commitment from God forms the basis for Job's complaint. Job 10.11–12 also depicts Job as capable of being held to account by God for his actions (cf. Job 10.13–17) and just so worthy of respect. Finally, Kelsey also notes that in Job, and in Genesis 2.4b—3.24, God actually makes human beings accountable and responsible (and capable of response) by addressing them through the medium of ordinary human language, so establishing between God and humans something like a public space with commitments and obligations for the parties involved (Kelsey 2009, pp. 291ff.). What lines of

---

11 On this point about the abstraction of Genesis 1—3 from Genesis 1—11, see Westermann 1994, pp. 2–4.

thought about human sexuality and marriage might we develop from the orientation these scriptural texts afford us?

First, they indicate that we should see human reproduction, and hence the form of sexual differentiation it involves, as a good through which God creates human beings, just as Job was created. In this light we can understand the significance of the creation of humans as male and female and God's blessing of them (Gen 1.27–28) and subsequent generations in the Genesis primeval history and beyond. Yet once we learn from Wisdom texts not to see Genesis 1—2 as a depiction of perfect humanity, and not to absolutize the ancient social forms in which scriptural teaching is given, we need not see reproduction as normative for every human being or every act of sexual intimacy, or as determinative for human gender roles. Nor need we conclude that sexual differentiation is significant only in reproductive encounter (as Robert Song seems to imply – Song 2014, p. 25). The malign effects of assuming the normativity of reproductive sex for full humanity in respect of many who are single, or who do not desire someone with whom they could reproduce in this way, or who find themselves unable, or no longer able, to do so, urge the importance of such considerations.[12] We would also have space to see the nurture offered by non-biological parents, guardians and other carers as modes of divine creation.

Second, Job's story also encourages us to take seriously the possibility that attention to the development of human sexuality might trouble readings of Genesis 1—2 that derive from those texts a two-sex model of human sexual differentiation.[13] I am thinking here especially of certain intersex conditions and the way they problematize thinking of biological sex as male and female (Cornwall 2010; Cornwall 2012; Fausto-Sterling 2012, pp. 43ff.; see also Susannah Cornwall's essay in this volume). If we take seriously the priority of thinking with creation with Wisdom texts, it may be difficult to block this challenge by asserting the fallen imperfection of intersex bodies. At the same time, we should take seriously Kelsey's insight from Job and from the second Genesis creation narrative that God personalizes us by addressing us through ordinary human language. For this insight directs us to attend to the ways our linguistic contexts form us as persons responsible to

---

12 Here one might have sympathy with Elkanah's argument in 1 Samuel 1.8. A passing comment by Rachel Muers alerted me to the significance of this passage for this topic, and her reflections on Elkanah are developed in more depth in her Afterword to this volume.

13 Note the complexity of this development and the scope for discontinuity between various levels of sex/gender identity in Fausto-Sterling 2012.

God and one another. Such reflection must consider the ways categories of human sexual differentiation and its lived expression (sometimes called 'gender') vary historically and across cultures (Laqueur 1990; Fausto-Sterling 2012, pp. 70ff.; see also Raphael Cadenhead's essay in this volume). It must consider the possibility that the categories of sexual differentiation and gender roles found in scriptural texts may not be natural or normative, even as they are part of the fabric of texts through which we are addressed by God.

Third, Wisdom literature indicates to us that part of our proper response to God's creating us and our everyday world is a delight in God's creatures. This delight is patterned for us in the delight Wisdom takes in her fellow creatures. For humans this delighting includes taking delight in one's sexual partner through sexual intimacy. In the texts, reproduction is logically separable from such sexual delighting. The two are found together in Proverbs 5.15–20, but while a concern to restrict the addressee's production of offspring to the relations with his wife is urged as a major reason for sexual fidelity, the aim of sexual activity here is not strictly subordinated to reproduction.[14]

The Song of Songs offers an extended account of sexual intimacy in which passionate mutual delight between the lovers, framed in terms of the delightfulness of other creatures, is to the fore. Here there is scant reference to the possible reproductive results of their love-making.[15] In this light we need not subordinate the delight expressed by the earth-man in Genesis 2, or the one-fleshed union for which the first pair are the etiological explanation, to the focus on blessing and reproduction in Genesis 1.27–28 (and might also note the apparent equality between the man and woman). Such lines of reflection give further cause for not seeing reproduction as a normative expectation of every human couple in their sexual intimacy, even if it is enjoined upon humanity as a species. By understanding God to create us as fragile, dependent beings set in our everyday contexts, we may also see that the desire for another to take delight in one in this way is a proper creaturely need.[16]

Nevertheless, this kind of affirmation of taking sexual delight in another is qualified in Wisdom literature. For the desire it involves is

---

14 Ecclesiastes 9.7–10 seems to suggest partners take mutual delight in sexual encounter, but makes no reference to reproduction.

15 The closest the text comes is when the woman connects their intimacy of their love-making to the birth and rearing of their mothers in Song of Songs 3.3; 8.1–2 and 8.5, which is of a piece with the way the man addresses her as his sister in places (e.g. 4.9–12; 5.1–2).

16 See also Kelsey on need and desire in general as features of human finitude, not marks of imperfection, in 2009, p. 268.

relativized by being compared to a desire for something far more desirable: wisdom.

Wisdom is here a way of navigating the world in its orderliness so as to flourish. Such wisdom, says Woman Wisdom in Proverbs 8.11, 'is better than jewels, and all that you may desire cannot compare with her'. We are thus directed to respect the priority accorded here to the desire for wisdom over other forms of desire that we experience as creatures. Hence the life conducted in search of wisdom will seek a wise way of conducting oneself with regard to sex that should guide Christians in seeking to shape and to inhabit (and perhaps in part subvert) the marital institutions of their contexts.

One line of reflection here might, like Rowan Williams in 'The Body's Grace', consider the form of partnership that best makes for mutual delight in another to be respectful and dignifying (Williams 2002; see also Brett Gray's chapter in this volume). Such a line of reflection might attend to the way language is a vehicle for the mutual delight of the lovers in the Song of Songs. Sex here is so much more than 'genital acts'. It is just as much a conversation in which the language of words (expressing desire, praising, inviting and beseeching, narrating episodes of intimacy) and the language of physical intimacy (seeking, looking, touching, welcoming, entering) are interwoven in what is a thoroughly mutual taking of intimate erotic delight. These are highly vulnerable communicative acts because they are highly self-involving. They involve a singling out of the other for particular regard that involves the whole of oneself; that entails a mutual possession: 'I am my beloved's and my beloved is mine' (Song 6.3). The woman seeks a permanency to their love: she would be a seal upon his heart and arm because love is as strong as death (8.6). The text does not tell us whether this desire was met, and it is clear this Solomon had many queens and concubines (Song 6.8–10), suggesting the mutuality of their love might be questionable on the part of the man.

To this ambiguity we can bring the concern of Proverbs for truthful language and faithfulness to one's conversation partners. As Kelsey relates, Proverbs represents this concern by contrasting the behaviours of Woman Wisdom and the foolish or adulterous woman (Kelsey 2009, pp. 229ff.). Woman Wisdom makes a truthful, public offer. The foolish woman subverts such ordinary public speech by her deceitful offer and by her breach of the marital covenant with her husband. It is a problematic image, taken from a male perspective, but its depiction of the way our ordinary speech commits us to those we speak with can be applied to the conversation of the lovers in the Song of Songs without such gender bias. The lovers' conversation is a deeply self-committing one. In light of Proverbs' concern for truthful, faithful speech, the lovers' verbal and physical conversation can be seen to tend towards a life-long and exclusive commitment on the part of both. Such commitment would also demand an appropriate public formalization and recognition by wider society. In putting these things together we may find here a condition for wise loving that envisages forms of marriage that would echo *on both sides* the other-respecting, hospitable self-commitment of God to creatures symbolized in God's relation to Wisdom in Proverbs 8.22–31.

Conclusion

So much depends on *how* we think with Scripture. The worked example I have just offered illustrates the difference it makes to approach the task in light of the model of scriptural authority I have sketched above, and to consider carefully the way we deploy the resources of the scriptural canon. By thinking with the texts in terms primarily of how they identify God and creatures, and by thinking first with texts from the Wisdom tradition, and then reading texts from Genesis and elsewhere alongside them, we may find new ways of thinking theologically about human sexuality and about marriage. Thinking with Scripture in these ways might allow us to recognize ourselves as created by God through human reproduction, biological development and socialization, without taking reproductive sex as a norm for all human sexual relationships. It would let us consider the phenomena of human sexual difference within a scripturally shaped framework and allow them to disturb our assumptions about sex and gender. It would move us to seek wise forms of relationship in which the deep self-commitment to the other enacted in truly mutual sexual delight is expressed in a wider pattern of life, and publicly recognized.

But when, some might be wondering, do we get to the difficult passages that everybody argues about most? The short answer is: not yet. To get there I would need to develop this worked example into a much fuller theological account of human sexuality and of ways of thinking about human relationships involving sexual intimacy. Such an account would need to expand on the work done here in respect of humans as creatures. It would have to add to it similar exercises in thinking with Scripture in respect of humans as creatures reconciled to God and on the way to final fulfilment with God. It is only in the context of a theological use of Scripture of that order that we can adequately assess the most appropriate *use* of the teaching of passages like Leviticus 18.22 and 20.13 or Romans 1.18–32 and their appeals to what is appropriate to male status or to the natural order.[17]

For, as I have shown throughout this chapter, to help Christians address the character of marriage in any given context we need a God-centred way of thinking about it that allows us to draw upon, sift, order and deploy the varied testimony of the Scriptures, taking seriously both their normative function and their human, historical character. It will be one that allows us to pay attention to the complex lived reality and variety of marriage practices in our own context, and teaches us to see how they might better reflect the good purposes of God. I have sought to show how we can take the Scriptures primarily as testimonies to the identities of God and creatures, and as patterns proposed to the people of God for discerning their lived response to God. I have argued that recognizing these patterns does not bring our thinking to an end, but sets us on a pathway of theological thinking, taking into account our experience and other data and discoveries about human sexuality. We think 'biblically' about marriage when our reasoning about particular forms of marital institutions and practices takes its shape from those patterns, as critically governed by the way Scripture identifies God and human beings in relation to Jesus Christ.

References

Barton, John, 1999, 'New Testament as Performance', *Scottish Journal of Theology*, 52.2, pp. 179–208.

Barton, John, 2014, *Ethics in Ancient Israel*, Oxford: Oxford University Press.

Brownson, James, 2013, *Bible, Gender, Sexuality: Reframing the Church's Debate on Same-Sex Relationships*, Grand Rapids, MI: Eerdmans.

Cornwall, Susannah, 2010, *Sex and Uncertainty in the Body of Christ: Intersex Conditions and Christian Theology*, London: Routledge.

Cornwall, Susannah, 2012, 'Intersex and Ontology: A Response to *The Church, Women Bishops and Provision*', University of Manchester: Lincoln Theological Institute.

Countryman, L. William, 2001, *Dirt, Greed and Sex: Sexual Ethics in the New Testament and their Implications for Today*, London: SCM Press.

Fausto-Sterling, Anne, 2012, *Sex/Gender: Biology in a Social World*, London: Routledge.

Frei, Hans, 1975, *The Identity of Jesus Christ*, Philadelphia, PA: Fortress Press.

---

17 Robert Song offers a good example of this sort of assessment in 2014, pp. 62ff. For one of the best treatments of the rationale behind these texts, see Nissinen 1998.

Frei, Hans, 1990, *Types of Christian Theology*, New Haven, CT: Yale University Press.

Frei, Hans, 1993, 'The Literal Reading of Biblical Narrative: Will it Stretch or Will it Break?', in George Hunsinger and William C. Placher (eds), *Theology and Narrative: Selected Essays*, New York, NY: Oxford University Press, pp. 117–52.

Gagnon, Robert, 2001, *The Bible and Homosexual Practice: Texts and Hermeneutics*, Nashville, TN: Abingdon Press.

Hays, Richard B., 1997, *The Moral Vision of the New Testament: A Contemporary Introduction to New Testament Ethics*, Edinburgh: T&T Clark.

John, Jeffrey, 2012, *Permanent, Faithful, Stable: Christian Same-Sex Marriage*, London: Darton, Longman & Todd.

Kelsey, David, 2009, *Eccentric Existence: A Theological Anthropology*, Louisville, KY: Westminster John Knox Press.

Laqueur, Thomas, 1990, *Making Sex: Body and Gender from the Greeks to Freud*, Cambridge, MA: Harvard University Press.

Nissinen, Martti, 1998, *Homoeroticism in the Biblical World: A Historical Perspective*, Minneapolis, MN: Fortress Press.

Roberts, Christopher Chenault, 2007, *Creation and Covenant: The Significance of Sexual Difference in the Moral Theology of Marriage*, London: T&T Clark.

Rogers, Eugene, 1999, *Sexuality and the Christian Body: Their Way into the Triune God*, Oxford: Blackwell.

Rowe, Kavin, 2009a, *World Upside Down: Reading Acts in the Graeco-Roman Age*, New York, NY: Oxford University Press.

Rowe, Kavin, 2009b, *Early Narrative Christology: The Lord in the Gospel of Luke*, Grand Rapids, MI: Baker Academic.

Schmidt, Thomas E., 1995, *Straight and Narrow? Compassion and Clarity in the Homosexuality Debate*, Leicester: IVP.

Schoedel, William R., 2000, 'Same-Sex Eros: Paul and the Greco-Roman Tradition', in David L. Balch (ed.), *Homosexuality, Science, and the 'Plain Sense' of Scripture*, pp. 43–72, Grand Rapids, MI: Eerdmans.

Seitz, Christopher, 2000, 'Sexuality and Scripture's Plain Sense: The Christian Community and the Law of God', in David L. Balch (ed.), *Homosexuality, Science, and the 'Plain Sense' of Scripture*, Grand Rapids, MI: Eerdmans, pp. 177–96.

Song, Robert, 2014, *Covenant and Calling: Towards a Theology of Same-Sex Relationships*, London: SCM Press.

Vines, Matthew, 2014, *God and the Gay Christian: The Biblical Case in Support of Same-Sex Relationships*, New York, NY: Convergent Books.

Westermann, Claus, 1994, *Genesis 1–11*, Minneapolis, MN: Fortress Press.

Williams, Rowan, 2002, 'The Body's Grace', in Eugene Rogers (ed.), *Theology and Sexuality*, Oxford: Blackwell, pp. 309–21.

5

Taking Time Over Marriage:
Tradition, History and Time in
Recent Debates

FRANCES CLEMSON

Introduction

In his book on the blessing of same-sex unions, Mark Jordan underlines
the importance of time in thinking about relationships, particularly
marriages. The passing of time transforms two people into a couple:
an initial connection becomes a relationship that endures. The 'dur-
ation' of such a relationship 'marks time for the partners in it, but also
for their families, friends, and communities'. A long-term relationship
'holds memories' (Jordan 2005, p. 21). Jordan also draws attention to
the way Christian thinking about marriage has developed over time,
as a response to life in the 'meantime' of history, before the eschaton
(2005, p. 108). He suggests, however, that anxiety around what it
means to live within this 'meantime' often prompts Christians to seek
to contain time-taking practices like marriage within stable, timeless
definitions (2005, pp. 109–10). Such definitions require that the history
of Christian thought about marriage be stabilized also. So it is, Jordan
states, that the language of 'tradition' is caught up in the Church's 'confusions of time around marriage' (2005, p. 110).

   In this chapter, I examine the interconnections between time, history
and tradition in our thinking theologically about marriage, opening up
Jordan's claim that anxieties about time affect the way tradition is used
in current debates. I begin with some reflections on tradition as the
Church's activity of handing on, before turning to the connections made
between tradition and history, and between marriage, complementarity
and time, in two recent Church of England documents. Following my
critique of these documents I offer a constructive theological account
of how married lives and the handing on of the life of the Church can

inform one another, as time-taking practices, caught up in the activity of the Spirit.

Handing On, Handing Over and the Joining of Hands

Mention of 'tradition' when speaking about marriage evokes a number of associations, from the idea of a 'traditional' wedding to 'traditionalist' as a synonym for 'conservative' (in contrast to 'progressive' or 'liberal') in debates about same-sex marriage (see, for example, Sachs 2009). 'Tradition' can signify either what is customary – from the colour of the bride's dress to the sorts of jokes the best man tells – or what has been believed and thought for a long time, the status quo. These meanings are important in thinking theologically about tradition but they only partially capture what tradition means for the Church. In this section, through reflection on a poem, a painting and a moment in the Church of England's marriage liturgy, I start to sketch an account of tradition in terms of the handing on of the Church's life, a life centred on encounter with Jesus.

I begin with some lines by the French poet Charles Péguy, as quoted by the Roman Catholic theologian Yves Congar in his book *The Meaning of Tradition*. These lines trace the movement of the hands of worshippers as they touch holy water, pass bread and make the sign of the cross. The poem continues:

> In the same way, from hand to hand, from fingers to fingers,
> From finger-tip to finger-tip, the everlasting generations
> Who go to Mass age after age,
> One generation succeeding another,
> Pass on the word of God, in the same hope,
> In the same breasts, in the same hearts, until the world itself is
>   buried.
> (Congar 2004, p. 11)[1]

For Congar this poem evokes the remarkable continuity of the Church's tradition. Such continuity is possible, Congar says, only because the transmission of the Church's tradition follows on from God's revelation of Godself to us in Christ and Christ's handing over of the gospel to the apostles. Since the handing on of the Church's tradition is an activity that follows from and participates in God's action in handing over

---

1 For the full poem in translation, see Péguy 2005.

'saving truth' to us, the 'spiritual riches' of tradition can be enjoyed by and passed on to every generation, without loss or decay. In and by the power of God, tradition becomes 'the sharing of a treasure ... [which] represents a victory over time and its transience' (Congar 2004, p. 12).

Péguy's poem instantiates the continuity Congar describes not only in its content but also in its form. The section of the poem given above is a single sentence, through which the reader is led in a continuous flow from one line to the next. Yet it is also the case that the poem enacts one of the central problems in thinking theologically about tradition. The repetition of 'same' across the lines quoted above simultaneously suggests continuity *and difference*. Each time we come to this repeated word we are at a different point in the poem; the word 'same' is set in a different context, creating phrases – 'same way', 'same hope', 'same breasts', 'same hearts' – which carry different resonances. Likewise, the fingers and hands that appear throughout the poem both signify the connection existing between the faithful *across* time and suggest the physical uniqueness of each person. The poem thereby raises the question of how it is that God may be looked for and found in and among specific, embodied communities *within* time.

Following on from Péguy's imagery of hands and finger-tips, we turn now to a painting by Caravaggio, *The Incredulity of Saint Thomas* (*c*.1601), which depicts the moment in John 20.27 when the disciple Thomas is invited by the risen Jesus to 'Put your finger here and see my hands. Reach out your hand and put it in my side.' The viewer's attention is drawn in this painting to Thomas' hand as he probes Jesus' wounds, and Jesus' hand which, holding Thomas by the wrist, draws him close.[2] The painting presses upon the viewer the embodied particularity of the encounter, from the discomfortingly detailed depiction of Jesus' gaping wound to his pierced hands and Thomas' dirty fingernails.

This image of the handling of Jesus' body is important for our purposes for two reasons. First, I want to suggest that whatever else the Church seeks to 'hand on', the movement of tradition that Péguy's poem traces is fundamentally connected with this moment when Thomas' hand is taken in Jesus' hand and led into his wounded side. This may appear to be a curious claim given that emphasis is often placed on the difference between Thomas' encounter and the experience of the faithful who 'have not seen and yet have come to believe' (John 20.29). If we carry this emphasis through into our viewing of Caravaggio's painting, we could see this image either as a tantalizing glimpse of a faith con-

---

2 For further discussion of this point, see Ward 2005, pp. 125–6.

firmed by sight and touch (an assurance that only Thomas enjoys) or as an exposure of Thomas' simplistic reliance on the material. In either case, there would be a division between the event depicted in the painting and the faith of the viewer.

Though Thomas' error in demanding to see the risen Jesus is frequently identified with an overly crude focus on the materiality of the resurrection, Rowan Williams has suggested that Thomas' mistake might better be understood as rooted in his unwillingness to accept the testimony of the community to which he belongs, requiring instead his own individual confirmation. That he is granted this encounter with Jesus, Williams suggests, is for the purpose of reincorporating Thomas into this community. So it is that Williams stresses the central importance of the fact that *both we and Thomas* are being invited into the same faith in the risen Jesus and into the community constituted by that faith (Williams 2002, p. 94). Caravaggio's image of Thomas' hand, grasped by Christ's hand, touching Christ's wound, directs our attention both to a particular moment of encounter and to the identity of the Church as the community that hands on this moment when Jesus is known to be 'My Lord and my God!' (John 20.28).

The second reason Caravaggio's image is important for our thinking about tradition is that the contact of Thomas' hand with Jesus' wound recalls for us a significant duality of meaning in the New Testament verb *paradidomi*, which can be translated 'to hand on'. This verb can also mean 'to hand over', in the sense of 'betray'. As Graham Ward highlights, in 1 Corinthians 11.23 Paul plays on the dual meaning of this term (Ward 2006, p. 249). Paul's use of both connotations of the word is evident in the NRSV translation of this verse: 'For I received from the Lord what I also *handed on* [*paredoka*] to you, that the Lord Jesus on the night when he was *betrayed* [*paradideto*] took a loaf of bread.' Thomas' hand in Jesus' hand, drawn to touch his wounded side, reminds us that what the Church is handing on is news of the one who was handed over to death. At the heart of the Church's tradition is a broken body, a betrayal, a failure to keep faith.

The activity of handing on that the Church performs entails continual wrestling with sameness and difference. It requires both thinking about connections across time and giving our attention to embodied particular persons and communities within time. Handing on the good news is an activity of a community formed around encounter with Jesus Christ, as the one who is handed over for us. The handing over of Jesus requires that in thinking about the Church's activity of handing on we remain always alert to our capacity to betray and to falsify, even as we rejoice, as Congar suggests, in the power of God to heal and preserve us against loss.

How might marriage matter to this process of handing on? In the marriage liturgy of the Church of England there is a point at which the couple's marriage is proclaimed to all who have come to witness it. At this moment the priest joins together the couple's right hands, sometimes binding them with a stole, and may then present their joined hands to the congregation. This moment can be understood as an affirmation of the intimate and exclusive nature of the couple's union, particularly given that at this point the priest says 'Those whom God has joined together let no one put asunder.'[3]

Understood in this light, the joining of hands fits with a claim made in the Faith and Order Commission of the Church of England's 2013 study document, *Men and Women in Marriage*. Marriage, the authors state, 'plays a central role in the transmission ... [of] the life of the church' (Archbishops' Council 2013, p. 11). Marriage does this, the document suggests, through procreation and the raising of children. Viewed in conjunction with this claim, the joining of hands in marriage – understood as an act that defines the couple in terms of their exclusivity – can be seen as a sign also of a clearly defined role for marriage in the Church's activity of handing on. The married couple join together to become 'one flesh' (Gen. 2.24) and their union allows for, as *Men and Women in Marriage* states, both 'the transmission of the human race' through 'biological reproduction' and 'care, education and equipment' of children 'for the moral and spiritual tasks of life' (Archbishops' Council 2013, p. 11). What I want to begin to do here is affirm this role for marriage but suggest also that there is more to say about marriage's part in the Church's activity of handing on.

Marriage often does bring into being (through procreation but also in many other ways) new families. The familial (and other) bonds that marriages can create allow for the handing on of memories, stories, behaviours, ethics, beliefs and practices across generations. Yet thinking about these bonds intensifies our appreciation of the fact that any handing on across time occurs only in and through relationships *in* time, in a process that is often far from clearly or straightforwardly delimited.

Rachel Muers, in her book on intergenerational theological ethics, emphasizes the extent to which the process of handing over to the next generation is in important ways 'uncontrollable' (Muers 2008, p.

---

3 The *Common Worship* marriage service can be found at www.churchofengland. org/prayer-worship/worship/texts/pastoral/marriage/marriage.aspx.

135). This handing on occurs through multiple complex relationships of dependence and nurturing, in and over time. We find that we cannot fully control what we inherit, just as we do not have full control over what the next generation receives from us. This is not to say that the process of handing on is a failure but rather to recognize that it is not a tightly bounded process whose lines we can always trace with ease (Muers 2008, pp. 127–35). Handing on from one generation to the next is ultimately the work of whole communities, and communities in time are by nature, Muers suggests, 'open at the seams' (Muers 2008, p. 133). Certainly, communities have a 'form and structure' (2008, p. 133); they work with and within certain givens and time-tested understandings;[4] yet we cannot give an adequate account of a community without reference to its ongoing life, influenced by the past and looking towards the future (2008, p. 133).

There is an echo here of a comparison made by the novelist, playwright and theological thinker Dorothy L. Sayers between artistic creativity and human procreation: in both cases, Sayers writes, 'creation settles nothing' (Sayers 1994, p. 152). The last thing we should be able to say of procreation is that it generates anything that is 'final, predictable, or complete' (1994, p. 151). Analogous to the vast diversity of responses that a work of art may elicit – in many cases leading to further creative acts in different modes (1994, pp. 93–7) – so the arrival of the next generation adds to the ever-burgeoning diversity of our responses to one another and to our past.

To return to the joining of hands in the marriage ceremony, my brief discussion of procreation and handing on suggests that we should take note of the multiple layers of meaning present in this moment. We should affirm (as Julie Gittoes does in this volume) that the joining of hands involves both a binding together and a reaching out, not merely as each partner reaches out to the other but in the ways the couple become involved in processes of handing on and receiving from their wider family and their society. This reaching out recalls too Jesus' invitation to Thomas to 'reach out' his hand towards him: an invitation to draw close to our God and a reminder that hands can betray as well as bind and bless. Marriage does contribute to the handing on of the life of the Church, but even the process of handing on from parents to children, let alone through the other familial and communal connections that marriage fosters, is a process that at its fullest does not allow us to describe or demarcate it neatly or conclusively. It is an embodied

---

4 See below for further discussion of how the Church as a community in time works with 'givens'.

process that takes time; it is necessarily marked by continuity and difference, by the continual formation and re-formation of relations of dependence and by a flourishing diversity of response.

I want to return later in this chapter to this discussion of what marriage can say to the Church about the activity of handing on. The account I have offered thus far treats the handing on of the Church's life, in which marriage is involved, as an ongoing time-taking practice. Before developing this account further, I want to turn to some of what Jordan calls the 'confusions of time' evident in some recent Church of England documents about marriage.

Tradition, History and Marriage

In the Church of England's response to the UK government's consultation on same-sex marriage (2012), the authors define the 'traditional understanding' (Church of England 2012, §8)[5] or 'traditional institution' (2012, Annex, §20) of marriage as 'a lifelong union of one man with one woman' (2012, §1). The authors' insistence on the value of this 'traditional institution' rests in part on the claim that marriage has been, and continues to be, essentially an unvarying human practice and, as such, that it is an institution that has the weight of history behind it. The document emphasizes that though 'marriage has evolved … in many other ways', the 'traditional' definition of marriage as between one man and one woman has been a 'constant' across time. Marriage has 'always' been understood in this way (2012, §7). Traditional marriage is 'ages-old' (2012, §8); 'deeply rooted in our social culture' (2012, §7). It has, the authors claim, *from the beginning of history* been the way in which societies have worked out and handled issues of sexual difference' (2012, §11; my emphasis).

The Faith and Order Commission of the Church of England's *Men and Women in Marriage* is less firmly insistent on the consistency of past understanding and practice in relation to marriage. However, the authors do suggest that marriage has some 'basic structural features', as an exclusive lifelong partnership outside an existing family group between one man and one woman, and that these have persisted across time (Archbishops' Council 2013, p. 6). The document acknowledges that historically there have been 'compromises' in areas such as monogamy but states that 'these compromises have tended to be of

---

5 This understanding, the document states, is 'derived from the Scriptures and enshrined within … authorised liturgy' (2012, §2).

limited scope': 'Many differences there have been, but they hardly amount to a significant challenge to these structural foundations' (2013, p. 6). *Men and Women in Marriage* also briefly makes reference to the 'common traditional understanding of marriage' as a 'human, not only a religious act' that the Church shares with wider society, indicated in the Church of England's recognition of all marriages, whether entered into through a religious ceremony or not (2013, p. 14).

In these documents, particularly in the former, the vocabulary of 'tradition' is associated with a conception of marriage that, it is suggested, the Church shares with society and that accords with the historical reality of how marriage 'has always been'. The 'traditional understanding of marriage' consists here in the tracing of a pattern of sameness across time. The most obvious criticism to which this view is open is that this pattern of sameness is not an accurate representation of the history of marriage.

A number of scholars have pursued this line, drawing attention to the variety in evidence in thinking about marriage, and in the practice of marriage, within and beyond the Church over time. Charlotte Methuen, in her chapter in this volume and elsewhere, has underlined that understandings of marriage have been far from static (Methuen 2014). Linda Woodhead has sought to demonstrate that in recent debates the Church of England has been 'forgetful of its own past' (Woodhead 2014, p. 291). In claiming that the Marriage (Same Sex Couples) Act 2013 represents the first time that the 'general understanding and definition of marriage ... in law' will diverge from the Church's definition of marriage, the Church 'forgot', as Woodhead demonstrates, historic divergences between Church and state over remarriage after divorce and over the legality of a man's marriage to his deceased wife's sister (2014).[6] Eugene Rogers suggests that the idea of marriage as 'a lifelong public union of one man and one woman for the procreation of children' represents a nineteenth-century construal of marriage (Rogers 2006, p. 152). He stresses too that, in practice, Christians' recognition of what counts as marriage already functions more along the lines of discerning a family resemblance than in finding a strict consistency between the many different ways marriage has been and is now entered into and understood (2006, pp. 154–5).

In taking note of such critiques, however, we should not imagine that their aim is *merely* to disturb and disrupt a pattern of sameness

---

6 For the original claim, see the House of Bishops' Pastoral Guidance on Same-Sex Marriage, 15 February 2014, Appendix, §9, www.churchofengland.org/media-centre/news/2014/02/house-of-bishops-pastoral-guidance-on-same-sex-marriage.aspx.

by pointing to instances of difference. The point I want to raise here is similar to that which Mark Jordan sets out in his discussion of arguments for and against Christian same-sex marriage that are constituted by the tracing of 'liturgical genealogies' (Jordan 2006). As Jordan explores, arguments by reference to such genealogies often presume either that the constancy of a line of sameness across time – excluding irrelevant distant branches or illegitimate divergences – can be taken as an authoritative pattern for today, or that the identification of a significant lost ancestor, in some way at variance with the main line, legitimates and provides a model for further variation in the present. Jordan suggests that it is worth asking whether such genealogies do in fact function as authoritative for current liturgical practice in either of these ways. This is not to say that the past does not matter – far from it. Rather it is to say that the past *matters more* and matters *more complexly* than is allowed for by some of those who summon 'the ghosts of weddings past' for or against reform (2006, pp. 102–3, 112–15). The risk inherent in an argument from a liturgical genealogy is that a practice of public prayer and blessing, a practice that in each instance is possessed of its own density, its own singular texture, woven out of the interrelation of text, time, context, community and so on, may be reduced to a single function: signifying 'sameness' or 'difference', fitting the pattern or breaking it.[7]

Methuen, Woodhead and Rogers are all sensitive to this danger. Methuen's attention to the history of marriage not only highlights the variety found across this history but also demonstrates that stripping back the detail from any account of marriage – a necessary step if one is to make a claim for the basic consistency of this institution over time – inevitably avoids grappling with the reality that marriage has 'often been an institution which has not fostered women's flourishing' (Methuen 2014, p. 160). Attention to history thus not only provides precedents for change but also forces us to take account of the way particular marriages have been informed by and have concretized oppressive accounts of gender difference. Woodhead insists that attempts to reduce marriage to a 'timeless legal definition' fail even to begin to capture the theological and social richness of past thinking and practice (Woodhead 2014, pp. 288–9).

Rogers gives an explicitly theological grounding to the argument that we should remain closely attentive to the density and complexity of the history of marriage. To recognize and engage with the diversity

---

7 I am here building on Jordan's emphasis on liturgy as *performed* (Jordan 2006, pp. 115–17).

and particularity of past history and present practice is, for Rogers, to recognize and engage with the work of the Spirit as 'she gathers the diverse and diversifies the corporate' (Rogers 2006, p. 159). The Spirit's work is not simply to deliver (or indeed disrupt) a pattern. The Spirit rests, Rogers says, on particular bodies at particular times and places, rejoicing in, as well as drawing together, the diversity of creation (2006, pp. 159–60; see also Rogers 2005, pp. 61–72). What Rogers begins to point us to here is a theological understanding of history as the place where God is present and active. Rogers' description of the way the Spirit works suggests that discerning God's presence in history requires that we do more than gain an overview or trace a pattern; it calls for attention to particulars. To respond to the handling of the history of marriage in the two documents discussed above, we need *both* to underscore how the telling of this history smooth over aspects of the past, *and* resist the temptation to respond only by citing disrupting instances of difference. To be more than disruptive and to give due attention to the particularity of marriage(s) as a practice, we must offer, as Rogers indicates, a theological account of history.

Before we go deeper into the theology that we have begun to examine here, I want to look at another 'confusion of time' in the Church of England Faith and Order Commission's document; for here, as we shall see, the significance of time in thinking about marriage risks being lost altogether.

Time and Complementarity

On occasion *Men and Women in Marriage* points towards the time-taking nature of marriage. Yet it does so in a way fundamentally shaped by the authors' commitment to the logic of complementarity. In their chapters in this volume, Susannah Cornwall and Raphael Cadenhead treat the problematic role of gender and biological complementarity in thinking about marriage. Here I am concerned more narrowly with the understanding of time that a commitment to complementarity entails.

Echoing some of the points Jordan makes, discussed at the beginning of this chapter, *Men and Women in Marriage* describes marriage as a form of sociality that structures the course of many people's lives (Archbishops' Council 2013, pp. 2–3, 5). Over time, different 'strands' of the marriage bond are evident, from sexual enjoyment, to cooperation in raising children, to the sharing of memories (2013, pp. 5–6). The multi-faceted nature of marriage becomes apparent over the long term, across the 'full length of a couple's life' (2013, p. 6). Going further, the document states that Christians understand marriage as supporting the 'spiritual growth' of a couple, offering a 'bridge' between our 'physical needs' and our 'spiritual vocation' (2013, pp. 10–11).

What kind of growth over time is this? For *Men and Women in Marriage* all these forms of development over time have as their basis our nature as male or female: this nature constitutes our 'foundation for growth', the 'natural endowment' that provides the scope for our 'spiritual creativity' (2013, p. 10). Here the document draws on an earlier Church of England Report, *Marriage, Divorce and the Church*, which describes marriage as offering couples 'healing and growth on the basis of progressive mutual completion' (Archbishop's Commission 1971, §40; Archbishops' Council 2013, p. 10). The original context of this earlier statement is a broad discussion of psychological theories about how human maturity develops through different familial attachments. In *Men and Women in Marriage* the statement acquires, however, more specific reference to the way a man and a woman, acting from the basis of their maleness and femaleness, are able to complete one other. It is the 'complementary gifts of men and women', the nature of marriage as 'partnership of male and female', that allow 'each to make good what the other lacks, over time and throughout life' (Archbishops' Council 2013, pp. 11, 12). Curiously, it seems therefore that the process of 'mutual completion' is in fact largely predetermined. The experience in and over time of particular couples does not carry weight here, for the capacity of each to 'make good' any lack in the other resides in their pre-existent and unchanging sexed identity, an identity that is effectively timeless. The document seems clear that an individual does not become a man or a woman; an individual is male or female and it is this basic 'fact' of identity that decides – outside of the couple's life together over time – the growth that their marriage will bring.

As in the case of our discussion of the Church's handling of the history of marriage in the previous section, one possible response to the approach that the Church of England Faith and Order Commission takes is to question how far this picture of timelessly established complementarity involves 'forgetfulness' of the history of sex and gender. For example, one might draw attention the work of the historian Thomas Laqueur, which suggests that the idea that there are two sexes that fit or match each other is a relatively recent development in Western thought (Laqueur 1990).[8] Acknowledging that this is the case does not mean we are falling into the trap that the Church of England Faith and Order

8 Cf. William Stacy Johnson's response on these lines to Karl Barth's assumptions about complementarity in Johnson 2012, p. 303 n.16.

Commission's document names when it states that it is wrong to 'turn our back upon the natural, and especially biological, terms of human existence' (Archbishops' Council 2013, p. 4). To situate our discussion of human bodies more firmly and more transparently within the history of different understandings of sex and gender enables us, as Susannah Cornwall suggests, to be more aware, not less, of the temptation to gloss over the (often discomforting) physical reality of sexed bodies.

Yet I also want to respond directly to the tension in the document between descriptions of marriage that emphasize its time-taking nature and the overshadowing of these descriptions by the timelessness of complementarity. To understand more clearly the problem here, we can draw on an examination by the theologians Todd Salzman and Michael Lawler of a similar tension in Roman Catholic thinking. Salzman and Lawler point to a contradiction in Catholic thought between what they term 'ontological' and 'existential' complementarity (Salzman and Lawler 2008, p. 208). Ontological claims about complementarity posit that male and female are the two essential or natural modes of human being and that – independently of any particular cases – they make one whole when brought together. Existential complementarity refers to claims about the ways, in actuality, particular men and women enter into relationships that develop over time and, in and through these relationships, in a phrase from John Paul II, *'become* a gift for each other' (Salzman and Lawler 2008, p. 208, citing John Paul II 1997, p. 58) in ways that are *'continually developing'* (2008, p. 208; Salzman and Lawler's emphasis in both cases). Ontological complementarity both feeds and is fed by tendencies to collapse the whole of marriage into two once-and-for-all acts that legitimate a marriage within Catholicism: consent and consummation (2008, p. 209). As soon as a marriage is deemed to have taken place through these acts, the 'fact' of complementarity has been achieved. For Salzman and Lawler this fails to do justice to experiences of the 'unfolding of human relationship' within actual marriages in time, marriages that are as unique and richly complex as each of the individual partners (2008, p. 210).

Salzman and Lawler seek to address the tension between onto-logical and existential complementarity through a more 'historically conscious' account of human being and incorporate this into a much broader understanding of complementarity that is not simply dependent on binary sexual difference (2008, p. 211). They re-envision comple-mentarity as 'a multi-faceted quality, orientational, physical, affective, personal, spiritual, possessed by every person, which draws him or her into relationship with another human being ... so that both may grow, individually and as a couple ... into human well-being and human flourishing' (2008, pp. 156, 211).

This expansive form of complementarity is experienced by couples as an 'evolving reality', a process that takes place over time (2008, p. 211). This re-description of complementarity appears to do better justice to those parts of *Men and Women in Marriage* that indicate that marriage is a time-taking discipline or vocation. It does not, I suggest, entail 'turn[ing] our back' on our bodies as sexed and gendered (Archbishops' Council 2013, p. 4). Rather, by attending more closely to the historical nature of human life, Salzman and Lawler's approach presses us to recognize that we are situated fully in the material world,[9] calling us to attend to actual bodies in time. It is an approach that insists, with *Men and Women in Marriage*, that 'Persons in relation are not interchangeable units ... They are individuals who bring to the relationship unique experiences of being human in community, unique qualities, attributes and histories' (2013, pp. 8–9).[10]

In addition to highlighting both the historicity of the Church of England Faith and Order Commission's claims about the sexes and the tension between its depiction of marriage as time-taking and the timelessness of the complementarian logic, there are also questions to be asked about the document's envisioning of the couple's growth in terms of 'making up a lack' or completing one another. There is a further tension here between the suggestion that marriage can be 'a way of

---

9 Again, this is something that *Men and Women in Marriage* urges us to recognize (Archbishops' Council 2013, p. 4).

10 The Church of England Faith and Order Commission's complementarian logic is further underpinned by assumptions about natural law that correspond, I suggest, to Gerard Loughlin's description of what he calls 'crude natural law theory'. This construes natural law as delivering a 'universal, non-contextual ethics', supposing that it is simply 'possible to read off from nature a series of precepts for human behaviour' (Loughlin 2004, p. 93). Crude natural law theory fails to recognize the interpretative lens that is brought to the task of deciding what will be found to be 'natural' and what 'unnatural'. So in this case the idea that men and women form two complementary halves (which is not, as Laqueur shows us, an ahistorical, universal understanding) is represented as a timeless natural law, knowable by any person through neutral observation. As Loughlin says, crude natural law theory requires that we are 'wearing the right spectacles before we start looking at nature' (2004, p. 93). This does not mean that there is no place in Christian thinking for natural law. Loughlin suggests rather that we need to go back to richer and more nuanced thinking about natural law in the Christian tradition; for example, in Aquinas, for whom natural law 'is the name for the movement of nature toward ... [its] end [in God]' (2004, p. 97). Natural law here is not a set of universal, de-contextualized principles but a firmly theological account of how all creation is 'caught up into the movement of God's desire for God' (2004, p. 97). This latter account of natural law resonates with my argument below.

sanctification' and the implication that what this way leads towards is an end point of 'completion' (2013, pp. 10, 12). The document is in danger of skipping ahead to this end, as though we can know, before it has happened, what sanctification looks like for married couples. Equating holiness with a certain kind of wholeness, a state of being 'finished', places what we are growing towards within our grasp. In the final section of this chapter, I want to insist that the end of marriage is not graspable in this way because the growth that marriage can allow for is growth towards God, whose superabundance always exceeds our knowing and desiring.

Inhabiting Time

At the beginning of this chapter, I drew attention to Jordan's argument that 'confusions of time' in thinking about marriage are fed by anxieties about our life in the 'meantime' of history. Ben Quash offers us a different perspective on this 'meantime' by reference to Jesus' words to his disciples in John 16.16: 'A little while, and you will no longer see me, and again a little while, and you will see me.' Like Jordan's use of the 'meantime', this 'while' can be anxiety-inducing because it does not allow us to step back and survey our position. As Quash states: '"While" is a concept that resists any overview, because of its indeterminacy ... A "while" is something one is in the middle of' (Quash 2002, p. 99; see also Quash 2005, p. 220). Yet this 'while' is the time Christ gives to the Church to inhabit. In this final section, I want to follow a line of thought developed by Quash, and by Eugene Rogers, which treats time as given by God, to see how such an understanding of time can help us address some of the problems in recent Church of England debates, as outlined above.

In *Found Theology*, Quash explores how we might understand 'ongoing history' as a 'gift of the Holy Spirit', a 'God-given medium of encounter with God' (Quash 2013, pp. 1, 10). In this understanding, history and our historical existence is not a 'given' in the sense that it may be *taken for granted*, that its story can be taken 'as read' (2013, p. 6; emphasis in original). Rather, understanding history as the medium in and through which God makes Godself known means that we are called to practise, repeatedly, close attention to human life in time, past and present, to see what is there to be found. This activity of attending, searching and finding within history is an activity that responds to the movement of the Spirit in and through history. The Spirit guides us into 'all the truth' (John 16.13), 'is able to accomplish abundantly far more than all we can ask or imagine' (Eph. 3.20), and opens up for us, in Quash's words, 'the "moreness" of meaning in the unfolding of history' (2013, pp. 76, 275).

This seeking and finding approach, which endeavours to remain open to the action of the Spirit, will take particularity seriously, for particulars are history's fabric, its texture (2013, p. 19). At the same time, understanding history as the medium in which God makes God-self known and which is given for us to inhabit as we seek God, means that we can trust in the 'connectedness and coherence' of that history (2013, p. 133). The past is not alien to us; inhabiting time we are able – in, by and through the action of the Spirit – to find (continually) in the past, the 'more', the abundance, of God's presence. This is not to say that history is not marked by sin and error, by our forgetfulness and by tragic events that do not appear to be occasions for finding (2013, pp. 73, 76, 140, 288). It is to say, however, that in all these cases we are called to attend to the possibility that God may turn moments of loss or failure into moments of discovery or rediscovery and that to discern this we must treat 'each new encounter ... with utter seriousness in its own unique particularity' (2013, p. 18).

There are some significant resonances here with my description of the handing on of the Church's life in the first part of this chapter. The understanding of history that Quash proposes guards against a view of human historical existence in which the diversity of particulars that make up history are understood purely in terms of division and dissim-ilarity, such that the past becomes a 'foreign country' to us. It is this divisiveness, this loss of connection, that Congar is concerned about when he writes of tradition overcoming the 'transience' of time. At the same time, Quash suggests that the activity of seeking and finding in response to the work of the Spirit requires us to allow ourselves to be drawn deeper into particular moments, relationships and encounters to see what God discloses to us in the time given to us.

What of the Church's tradition in the sense of specific teachings and practices through which the Church seeks to 'hand on' the encoun-ter with the broken and risen Christ? Tradition in this sense is woven through this approach to human historical existence. The activity of finding described by Quash is undertaken when we are always already 'in the middle of' time, and this includes the extent to which we are situated within and have been shaped by the Church's tradition of thinking and practice. Quash's proposal is not made in opposition to the 'givens' of this thought and practice. Rather, his approach under-lines the importance of avoiding allowing these 'givens' to lose their character as gifts of God, becoming instead ideas and practices that we take for granted as our possessions (2013, pp. 5–6). Taking account of the divine source of these 'givens', and of the movement of the Spirit who made history and who works within history, encourages us instead to expect that we may find more in and among our 'givens' as the living God discloses Godself to us, in an ongoing 'mutual and dynamic relationship' between the given and the found (2013, p. 17).

When thinking about marriage this theological account of human historical existence presses further a number of the points made in the preceding sections of this chapter. It suggests the importance of attentiveness to the particulars of marriage – particular relationships, particular bodies – rather than merely to generalized patterns. It suggests that it is possible for the Church to find out new things about marriage but also that we should not expect this finding to take place in isolation from the 'givens' of the Church's life: principally Scripture, but also the Church's history and tradition. It is an account of history that gives assurance that we are connected to past generations and their practices, while also showing us that we should both expect surprises and be alert to forgetting and failure in our activity of seeking God in marriages, past and present.

Yet it is not only that this account of history opens up new possibilities for our thinking about marriage. I also want to suggest that marriage itself, as a time-taking practice, is one of the ways we may be schooled in inhabiting time as given by God. In my treatment above of the 'confusions of time' that a complementarian logic can lead to, I highlighted a disjunction between a vision of the progress towards completion that marriage allows that is so predictable that it is effectively timeless, and an understanding of growth in marriage that makes space for the unfolding of particular relationships over time. To the extent to which marriage can foster the latter kind of growth, making for a diversity of forms of time-taking flourishing for couples and communities, marriage can be seen as revealing to us our creaturely nature as beings made for growth over time towards God. As Rogers states:

Creatures are made to grow; their createdness is a movement from God to God. God might have made creatures static, but that is a different story ... from the biblical one. The Spirit therefore wants to foster the virtues, or powers, particular to each of us, so that we may not be left out of our own destiny. For creatures, time-dwellers, it is strictly appropriate to *come* to God over time. That is the flowering that the Spirit presents to the Father and the Son ... (Rogers 2005, p. 65, emphasis in original)

Progress in the sense of an ordered progression towards becoming 'finished' is replaced here with what theologians call the *exitus–reditus* (going out and returning) movement – whereby all things, including all people, have their origin and their end in God.[11] Growth starts with our creatureliness; it starts with us where we are, in time, in our bodies, in our relationships, and draws us towards the fulfilment of creation in intimacy with the one who made us. To say that growth starts with our creatureliness is emphatically *not* to say that we can map out this growth, knowing straightforwardly our predetermined path and end. The *exitus–reditus* movement is neither predictable nor containable, for it is a movement from and to God whom we can never fully comprehend, the one of whom there is always superabundantly more than we can grasp. And it is this God who is continually showing us 'far more than all we can ask or imagine' in the while of history, as the time given to us for our growth.

Elsewhere, Rogers suggests that marriage encourages growth towards God by offering a form of life comparable to monasticism, 'in which God uses the perceptions of others one cannot easily escape to transform challenge into growth, into faith, hope, and charity' (Rogers 2006, p. 151). Marriage takes time and over time can school us in the discipline of inhabiting time, as we remain with, respond to and continually give ourselves over to another.[12] Desire for a certain kind of completion or satisfaction, for a form of fulfilment that has a clear end-point, can be transformed in marriage by the time-taking practice

11 For Quash's discussion of the Spirit's role in this 'towardness', see Quash 2013, pp. 250–65.

12 Rogers' mention of monasticism should signal to us that marriage is not the only time-taking practice that does this. There are different forms of committed relationship to others that, as Quash says, 'seek to be sustainable through time, taking time as their medium' (Quash 2012, p. 117). In each case the 'timeful' nature of these forms of relationship should draw us to pay more attention to their specificity, to the particular differentiated ways marriages, life in community and other forms of commitment allow people to grow towards God and to draw others into this movement. Note that the value given to commitment over time here should not be confused with blindness to the possibility that committed forms of relationship do fracture and breakdown. Quash also describes how the breakdown of a marriage can 'without negating the pain and cost ... be an occasion of grace'. It 'can lead to a life in which there is greater acknowledgement of one's need, vulnerability, and dependence on God and other human beings' (2012, p. 119). It may be that the breakdown of a marriage can, by grace, turn us back to, rather than away from, practices of relating to others that make for our spiritual growth.

of living with and being vulnerable to another. In and by the Spirit's work in time, each partner's desire for the other may be opened out so as to lead the couple into the unending movement of desire for God. Being transformed in this way, human desire begins to be caught up into God's desire for creation. The couple's desire for one another is reconfigured through orientation to God as the one who desires us, not out of lack but out of a 'plenitude of longing love' (Coakley 2013, p. 10). Marriage, by asking of couples that they take time together to attend to each other, can be one way to learn the time-taking attentiveness to particulars needed in our seeking and finding of God in history. Marriage, when it fosters the growth of partners towards one another, as well as the growth and flourishing of families and communities, can open on to and make known to us our movement as creatures 'from God to God'.

Conclusion

In the final part of this chapter, I have suggested, first, that a theological account of history as the time given to us by God calls us to practise, continually, attentiveness to the past and present, alert to the interplay, in Quash's terms, of what is given with what may be found. This means that in telling the history of marriage it is not sufficient to trace a general pattern and assume that we need look no further. It also means that we are called to do more than simply brush prior thought and practice to one side, concentrating only on the new. For the Church this means that thinking about marriage is rightly situated within and shaped by the Church's tradition. Yet this account of history is also a call to the Church to be open to being drawn repeatedly into the depths of that tradition, as a place where there is ever more to be found, conscious of our capacities for forgetfulness and betrayal.

I have suggested too that this theological account of life in time is not merely an external framework that we can apply to thinking about marriage, but that marriage itself, as an ongoing time-taking practice, can teach couples and those around them about the nature of time as given to us by God. Marriage can foster our learning to live in time as creatures and to attend to the particulars of life in time, seeking in and among them, in and by the power of the Spirit, the presence of the self-giving God. Marriage has the capacity to reveal to each partner, and often also to their communities, both that we are called as creatures to return to God, and how, in time, through the time-taking transformation of our desires, we may be caught up in motion towards 'the love that moves the sun and the other stars' (Dante, Canto XXXIII, l.145; Sayers and Reynolds 2004, p. 347).

Returning to the specific question of marriage's role in the handing on of the Church's life, there is one final connection to be made here. As Peter Candler has argued, the Church's continuous tradition, the ongoing activity of handing on, 'implies the motion of the pilgrim city of God towards its own source and end' (Candler 2006, p. 125). The Church's handing on – which has at its heart encounter with the one who was broken for our redemption – is for the sake of this motion of return towards our Lord and our God, our maker and redeemer. The time-taking learning, faithfulness and growth of married couples can disclose to the Church something of the character of this movement of return. I suggest, then, that it is not simply the case that the Church's activity of handing on shapes our thinking about marriage. More than this, the joining of hands in marriages and the unfolding of married lives may reveal to the Church ways of inhabiting time as a people being drawn to God.

References

Archbishop's Commission, 1971, *Marriage, Divorce and the Church: The Report of a Commission Appointed by the Archbishop of Canterbury to Prepare a Statement on the Christian Doctrine of Marriage*, London: SPCK.

Archbishops' Council of the Church of England, 2013, *Men and Women in Marriage: A Document from the Faith and Order Commission Published with the Agreement of the House of Bishops of the Church of England and Approved for Study*, GS Misc 1046, London: Church House Publishing.

Candler, Peter M., 2006, *Theology, Rhetoric, Manuduction, or Reading Scripture Together on the Path to God*, Grand Rapids, MI: Eerdmans.

Church of England, 2012, 'A Response to the Government Equalities Office Consultation – "Equal Civil Marriage" – from the Church of England', www.churchofengland.org/media/1475149/s-s%20marriage.pdf.

Coakley, Sarah, 2013, *God, Sexuality, and the Self: An Essay 'On the Trinity'*, Cambridge: Cambridge University Press.

Congar, Yves OP, 2004 [1964], *The Meaning of Tradition*, trans. A. N. Woodrow, San Francisco, CA: Ignatius Press.

House of Bishops, 2014, 'Pastoral Guidance on Same-Sex Marriage', 15 February 2014, www.churchofengland.org/media-centre/news/2014/02/house-of-bishops-pastoral-guidance-on-same-sex-marriage.aspx.

John Paul II (Pope), 1997, *The Theology of the Body: Human Love in the Divine Plan*, Boston, MA: Pauline Books.

Johnson, William Stacy, 2012, *A Time to Embrace: Same-Sex Relationships in Religion, Law and Politics*, 2nd edn, Grand Rapids, MI: Eerdmans.

Jordan, Mark D., 2005, *Blessing Same-Sex Unions: The Perils of Queer Romance and the Confusions of Christian Marriage*, Chicago, IL: University of Chicago Press.

Jordan, Mark D., 2006, 'Arguing Liturgical Genealogies, or, the Ghosts of Weddings Past', in Mark D. Jordan with Meghan T. Sweeney and David M. Mellott (eds), *Authorizing Marriage? Canon, Tradition, and Critique in the Blessing of Same-Sex Unions*, Princeton, NJ: Princeton University Press, pp. 102–20.

Laqueur, Thomas, 1990, *Making Sex: Body and Gender from the Greeks to Freud*, Cambridge, MA: Harvard University Press.

Loughlin, Gerard, 2004, 'Sex after Natural Law', in Marcella Althaus-Reid and Lisa Isherwood (eds), *The Sexual Theologian: Essays on Sex, God and Politics*, London: T&T Clark, pp. 86–98.

Methuen, Charlotte, 2014, 'Thinking About Marriage: An Excursion Through Christian History', *Modern Believing* 55.2, pp. 149–62.

Muers, Rachel, 2008, *Living for the Future: Theological Ethics for Coming Generations*, London: T&T Clark.

Péguy, Charles, 2005, *The Portal of the Mystery of Hope*, trans. David Louis Schindler Jr, London: Continuum.

Quash, Ben, 2002, 'Making the Most of the Time: Liturgy, Ethics and Time', *Studies in Christian Ethics* 15.1, pp. 97–114.

Quash, Ben, 2005, *Theology and the Drama of History*, Cambridge: Cambridge University Press.

Quash, Ben, 2012, *Abiding*, London: Bloomsbury.

Quash, Ben, 2013, *Found Theology: History, Imagination and the Holy Spirit*, London: Bloomsbury.

Rogers, Eugene F., 2005, *After the Spirit: A Constructive Pneumatology from Resources Outside the Modern West*, Grand Rapids, MI: Eerdmans.

Rogers, Eugene F., 2006, 'Trinity, Marriage and Homosexuality', in Mark D. Jordan with Meghan T. Sweeney and David M. Mellott (eds), *Authorizing Marriage? Canon, Tradition, and Critique in the Blessing of Same-Sex Unions*, Princeton, NJ: Princeton University Press, pp. 151–64.

Sachs, William L., 2009, *Homosexuality and the Crisis of Anglicanism*, Cambridge: Cambridge University Press.

Salzman, Todd A. and Michael G. Lawler, 2008, *The Sexual Person: Toward a Renewed Catholic Anthropology*, Washington, DC: Georgetown University Press.

Sayers, Dorothy L., 1994 [1941], *The Mind of the Maker*, London: Mowbray.

Sayers, Dorothy L. and Barbara Reynolds (trans.), 2004, *Dante Alighieri, The Divine Comedy 3: Paradise*, rev. edn, London: Penguin.

Ward, Graham, 2005, *Christ and Culture*, Malden, MA: Blackwell.

Ward, Graham, 2006, 'Tradition and Traditions: Scripture, Christian Praxes and Politics', in Justin S. Holcomb (ed.), *Christian Theologies of Scripture: A Comparative Introduction*, New York, NY: New York University Press, pp. 243–60.

Williams, Rowan, 2002, *Resurrection: Interpreting the Easter Gospel*, 2nd edn, London: Darton, Longman & Todd.

Woodhead, Linda, 2014, 'Questioning the Guidance', *Modern Believing* 55.3, pp. 286–91.

6

A Perfect Crown:
Towards a Liturgical Theology of Marriage

JULIE GITTOES

Introduction

In her Prologue to the *Report of the House of Bishops Working Group on Human Sexuality*, Jessica Martin acknowledges that we 'cannot talk about same sex relationships in isolation'; nor can we say anything about human sexuality without 'speaking first of our sense of the body and bodily relationships as holy' (Martin 2013, p. xiv). Christianity is incarnational. In Christ, body and God come together; the life of the Church is characterized by the language of being a body with many members. Therefore anything we think about same-sex relationships, especially when we disagree, has 'no value except as part of this larger vision of all our human relationships' (Martin 2013, p. xiv).

Marriage is part of that larger vision. The language we use, the expectations and aspirations we have, are shaped liturgically. The liturgical character of marriage expresses a public commitment that is both exclusive and inclusive. Exclusivity in terms of 'forsaking all others' (*CW*, p. 106) is held alongside the expectation that marriage 'enriches society and strengthens community' (*CW*, p. 105).[1] It expresses a generous and outward-looking aspect to this vocation – the gift of marriage is a source of 'refreshment and joy' (*CW*, p. 112) as well as 'strength, companionship and comfort' (*CW*, p. 105). This 'perfect crown' (Oliver 2012, p. 12) is an inclusive relationship that is connected to other forms of social life (to the wider community, including those who are single and networks of non-biological kinship). It is *a way* of expressing the call to holiness and discipleship rather than the *only* expression of maturity. Although marriage is a public celebration of intimacy, there

---

1 Quotations taken from the Church of England's *Common Worship: Pastoral Services* (Archbishops' Council 2000) will be cited *CW* followed by the page number.

is something provisional about it. Marriage is a way of life lived in the hope of the kingdom of God and in the face of death.

This chapter begins with a consideration of Rembrandt's capacity to reflect on human relationships – and the way his painting *The Jewish Bride* conveys inclusivity and exclusivity. This expression of marriage is then set alongside the research and analysis of the Church of England's Weddings Project. This serves to highlight the importance of drawing on a deep vein of resources to think about marriage, rather than colluding with the pressures of a wedding day. The liturgy draws us into God's purposes and the promise of love. It does so recognizing the penultimate reality of our human frailty and the ultimate hope of God's kingdom.

'Let their love for each other be a seal on their hearts and a crown upon their heads'

The art critic Laura Cumming described the exhibition *Rembrandt: The Late Works* at the National Gallery in 2014–15 as presenting both 'ethereal vision and earthly worlds' (Cumming 2014). Rembrandt takes us on a journey through life, captivating us with moments of intensity. In these episodes something of the beyond breaks in. We are drawn into the company of the saints irradiated by light, and radiating that light into our lives as we encounter them.[2] Rembrandt takes us to the heart of human life. He powerfully and compassionately enables us to gaze on faces that have loved and lost, hoped and endured. He lends dignity to our frailty, infusing every gesture and glance with grace. He holds us between life and death; without losing passion for the former he makes us confront the latter. No wonder that in her review, Cumming describes the exhibition as 'dark, impassioned, magnificently defiant' (2014).

Rembrandt looks on human beings with absolute attention; his portraits scrutinize us: the tenderness and sensuality of a sleeping woman; the injustice and brutality of a hanged teenager. We are caught up in Bathsheba's moment of decision as she holds David's letter – loyalty to king or husband weighs on her heart. We are captivated by the moment of distraction in the face of the young Titus, Rembrandt's son, as he daydreams at his desk. We ponder what meaning, consolation or inspiration the old woman is finding in the book she is reading with

---

2 The reflections on Rembrandt are based on a sermon preached at Guildford Cathedral on 2 November 2014, Evensong for All Saints' Sunday.

undivided attention. Rembrandt captures things that are statements of public intent or position; he also draws back the veil on the inner thoughts of men and women. In one painting in particular, he reveals a love that is both a crown and a seal.

In *The Jewish Bride* the love of a nameless couple endures.[3] The richness of the fabric catches the light yet pales in comparison to the luminescence of their faces. There is something compelling about these two individuals. Rembrandt has observed them with a depth of attention, with the result that the portrait has a profound impact: he reveals something recognizable and affecting; something that touches human longing. Cumming describes it as 'a secular altarpiece, an inspiration to patience, humility and kindness' (Cumming 2014). If it serves as an altarpiece, it is one that conveys the sacred. In paint and brush-stroke, Rembrandt expresses what Christian liturgy declares in word and gesture.

Their posture captures the exclusive intimacy of love. It is a seal upon their hearts as their hands touch; hers resting on his, across her breast. Tenderly, yet without possession, his arm reaches across her shoulder. We do not know if they are newly married or celebrating the longevity of their commitment. They are not surrounded by an entourage or children; they are not gazing at each other. Regardless of their age, there is a maturity beyond romantic captivation. They look out at us with the assurance of companionship that is generative. They inspire and embody virtues – patience, humility and kindness. We see beyond the luxurious dress to a generous love that responds to others; a love that is a crown upon their heads.

In this painting Rembrandt presents a compelling and poignant vision of marriage. It reflects both the public and private aspects of that commitment. In doing so he echoes the words of the Song of Songs: 'Set me as a seal upon your heart, as a seal upon your arm; for love is strong as death, passion fierce as the grave' (Song of Songs 8.6). This conception of marriage is picked up within the *Common Worship* marriage service as the priest says: 'Let their love for each other be a seal on their hearts and a crown upon their heads' (CW, p. 111).

Such love is expressed in an intimate and exclusive relationship. It is not a solely private commitment because the married couple are connected to, and live within, a wider network of social life. Their exclusivity expresses an equally radical inclusivity. The liturgy gives voice to marriage as a way of life that reflects the call to holiness, the

3 I am grateful to David Tregunna of IAP Fine Art for helping to shape my reflections on *The Jewish Bride*.

call to discipleship. It is not the only expression of such maturity, hope and living well. The language of covenant – inclusivity and exclusivity – is rooted in God's faithfulness to us; it draws us into the inner life of the Trinity. Whatever our marital status, we share in this generative, loving fellowship. Robert Song writes that 'in our finite covenant relationships, we bear witness to the eternal covenant relationships within the very being of God' (Song 2014, p. 10). The language used of such transformed relationships is 'holiness' – with the cross of Christ as the crucible burning away the 'fragmentation between human beings and God'; with worship as formative of a holy people, open to moral density and intimacy of relationships (Hardy 2002, pp. 490, 498).

All that marriage celebrates and affirms – intimacy, hospitality, exclusivity and inclusivity – is an expression of living well within the Church and world. Such life is costly and demanding; its abundance is rooted in vulnerability and fragility. The love it embodies is rooted in the mystery of incarnation and as such is an expression of life lived in hope of the kingdom of God. This is not least because it is life lived in the face of death, in the light of the resurrection. For some, marriage is primarily an expression of permanence, faithfulness and procreation; for others there is recognition of a series of shifts in the understanding of Christian marriage.[4] I will argue that our liturgical expression of marriage deepens our understanding of participation in the kingdom of God. In addition it enables us to acknowledge the provisionality of such covenantal commitment in the face of the penultimate contingencies of life and death, and the ultimate consummation of the heavenly wedding banquet.

'May their marriage be life-giving and life-long'

Before exploring the theological horizons of the liturgy it is worth pausing to consider the expectations of those seeking to get married in church. The Church of England Weddings Project, which began in 2007, set out to explore why couples choose to be married; it reflects their experience of the Church from the point of making initial contact to the wedding day and beyond. The project resulted in *The Church Weddings Handbook* (Oliver 2012), which is described in the Preface by Archbishop John Sentamu as a 'wake-up call' to clergy and parishes seeking to respond with warmth and imagination to those wanting to marry in church. He writes: 'People want to be married in church ...

---

4 Song 2014 and Wilson 2014 reflect these approaches.

there is a recognition that there is something important in a wedding that only begins to make sense when there is space for the sacred' (in Oliver 2012, pp. v–vi).

By drawing on conversations with couples and visits to hundreds of churches, the book seeks to dispel myths and complacency in order to give this pastoral office more impetus and to remove unnecessary barriers. John Barton reflects on the competition among secular wedding venues, which show no interests beyond the reception. He says, 'Surely we, the servants of Christ who lavished his generosity on an unsuspecting couple at Cana, are not motivated by profit and can add value to all that' (in Oliver 2012, p. xi). To take the wedding at Cana seriously means doing more than 'adding value' to the wedding as an event; the liturgy shapes a vision of marriage that faces the hopes and challenges of human commitment, while also pointing beyond an institution to God's kingdom.

The Weddings Project focuses on three tasks: to attract more weddings in church; to build public awareness of the Church's enthusiasm for marriage; to care for couples and guests well, so that more of them want to 'stick with the church after the day' (Oliver 2012, p. 6). It does not aim to set out a theology of marriage; rather, it seeks to inform pastoral ministry with secular research. Yet it is precisely the question of how we think theologically as well as pastorally about marriage that has become urgent following the headlines in the wake of the government's decision to legislate for same-sex marriage.[5] In the light of that decision, the research and analysis of the Weddings Project uses language that merits further consideration.

Marriage is seen by heterosexual couples surveyed by the Weddings Project as an expression of life-long commitment; and church is seen by the majority of those as the 'proper' context for the wedding itself. The *Handbook* acknowledges a sense of spiritual seriousness – seeking God's blessing, making vows before God, affirming the sacred, affirming personal or family faith (Oliver 2012, pp. 14–15).[6] Yet it also sees spending and lavish celebration as a corollary to this culmination of

---

5 The government's Marriage (Same Sex Couples) Bill received Royal Assent on 17 July 2013, having been passed by both Houses of Parliament. The Church of England made a formal response to the 2012 consultation and issued briefing papers: www.churchofengland.org/our-views/marriage,-family-and-sexuality-issues/same-sex-marriage.aspx. The Faith and Order Commission published *Men and Women in Marriage* in April 2013, as discussed in detail in Mike Higton's chapter in this volume: www.churchofengland.org/media/1715479/faoc%20marriage%20doc.pdf.

6 More than 80 per cent of respondents gave reasons other than the appearance of the church building, and above all these reasons related to God.

commitment: 'A perfect crown is what they are yearning for, when they yearn for marriage' (Oliver 2012, p. 12).

The *Handbook* reminds us that an approach to marriage that is liturgically rooted is concerned with connections: between the assumptions and hopes of the couple; between the nature of God's love and human commitment; between those who are married and the wider community. It commends the use of visual symbols that reflect the story of the couple, which is held within the context of the overarching story of God's love from creation, in redemption and in eschatological hope.[7]

By engaging with the liturgical expression of private and public commitment, we uncover something of God's purposes for human flourishing. The phrase 'the perfect crown' is used as an expression of lifelong commitment: how might a liturgical expression of this imagery deepen our ecclesial understanding of marriage, educating our desires and enlarging our minds?[8] As responses to Rembrandt's *The Jewish Bride* suggest, the capaciousness of marriage opens the couple to the cultivation of virtues. How might liturgy express a vision of the sanctification of human lives now, in the hope of the ultimate fulfilment of God's purposes?

Alongside legal and historical developments, the richness and challenges of the biblical tradition and the deepening understanding of human gender and sexuality, our liturgical framework opens up ways of engaging theologically and pastorally with the question of marriage.[9] Might same-sex marriage might be a continuation of a liberating trajectory in understanding marriage? Might our liturgy itself shape our understanding of marriage in a way that transcends inequalities between men and women; indeed, might extending this perfect crown to same-sex couples via the possibility of Church of England marriage be a redemptive step (Methuen 2013a)?[10] This liberating trajectory in our understanding of marriage is rooted in the light of tradition and in the hope of the fulfilment of the kingdom of God.[11]

---

7 For example, the lighting of candles representing the couple and their marriage is one such additional liturgical ritual, which lies beyond the scope of this essay.

8 Such an imaginative vision is inspired by David Ford's first Bampton Lecture, 'Theology at Full Stretch', which invites us to be daring in our theological thinking by being open to a horizon of truth and love in the power of the Spirit (Ford 2015).

9 I will be focusing on the rites and ceremonies of the Church of England as set out in *Common Worship*. Space precludes a comparison with the liturgical texts of other traditions; however, the imaginative, theological and relational questions are intended to open up a generous and enriching dialogue.

10 See also Charlotte Methuen's chapter in this volume.

11 Frances Clemson's chapter in this volume addresses our understanding of tradition as more complex than simply sameness and difference.

'God is love'

The first text to be cited in the Church of England marriage service is 1
John 4.16 (Archbishops' Council 2001, p. 104). It declares that 'God is
love'. It is statement not just about the nature of God, but also of our
capacity to reflect divine love in our lives: 'Those who live in love live in
God and God lives in them.' This is a call to life lived within the love of
God in the midst of community, rather than a description of romantic
love embodied by the couple. At the very outset of the liturgy, marriage
is set within a wider vision of all our human relationships. The opening
prayer calls us to acknowledge God as not only the source of life, but of
love, wonder, joy and grace. With echoes of 1 Corinthians 13 and the
Church of England's Collect for the nineteenth Sunday after Trinity,
the prayer continues, 'Without you we cannot please you; without your
love our deeds are worth nothing.' The Holy Spirit is invoked, not just
upon the couple but upon the whole congregation gathered together.
The Spirit pours into human hearts the 'most excellent gift' of love
whose purpose is both worship and service. This in part echoes the constitution of the Church – as a community formed by facing the holiness
of God in worship and enacting that holiness in the world.[12]

The Collect that follows the declarations focuses on the generosity
of God in creation – from the beginning, blessing it with abundant life.
This vision for creation – and its redemption – rooted in the nature of
God is also reflected in the prayer of blessing for the couple. The hope
is that they may be joined in 'mutual love and companionship, in holiness and commitment to each other'. The emphasis is striking in that
it recognizes that abundance is a gift of God to all creation, and that
this is not specifically related in terms of procreation to those about
to be married. Rather, the prayer is for a flourishing of their relationship. This is focused on mutual love and holiness, which are to be the
marks of all God's people, and also on companionship and commitment within their life together. In Christ, stable relationships are built
up in mutual trust. They are undergirded by grace and love, which are
transformative because we are seen as precious; we are wanted.

Rowan Williams explores how 'the whole story of creation, incarnation and our incorporation into the fellowship of Christ's body tells
us that God desires us, as *if we were* God, as if we were that uncon-
ditional response to God's giving that God's self makes in the life of

---

12 I am indebted to Daniel W. Hardy for the pneumatological vision of ecclesiology expressed in his books *Finding the Church* and *Wording a Radiance*, which
shaped my own book *Generous Ecclesiology* (Gittoes, Green and Heard 2013).

the trinity. We are created so that we may be caught up in this; so that we may grow into the wholehearted love of God by learning that God loves us as God loves God' (Williams 2003, p. 3; emphasis in original). It is this incorporation in the community of God's holy people that makes sense of the body's grace; that gives space and time to come to the knowledge of our bodily selves and desire. Williams talks about sex as risky – and not invariably graced. Locating 'sexual union in a context that gives it both time and space, that allows it not to be everything' enlarges our vision of physical intimacy and nourishes our sexuality (2003, p. 10). The liturgy gives a framework within which to explore joy, desire, stability and faithfulness, which are rooted in God's love for us. Its imagery and language is relational and generative; it speaks of enriched communities and heavenly fulfilment. The coming together of two human lives in love, two bodies crowned and two hearts sealed, speaks of fruitfulness beyond procreation. This liturgical space revalues sexuality and embodiment with a generosity and challenge.

'Marriage is a gift of God'

It might be said that the words of the Preface most clearly set out what the Church of England believes about the nature of marriage – in relation to God's purposes, the world and the intimacy of life together as a couple. While the point is made that the couple marry each other (something picked up in *The Church Weddings Handbook*), the liturgy acknowledges that they do so in the presence of God and before a whole company of witnesses (invited guests and members of the Church community). The purpose of the gathering together with them is to pray for God's blessing on them, as we have seen, but it is also to share in their joy and celebrate their love. This is a public marking of a prior commitment – of love that has grown and flourished. The relationship is to be a source of joy and celebration not just for the couple (a private matter) but for the wider community (a 'perfect crown').

Marriage is described in the Preface as a 'gift of God in creation' through which husband and wife 'may know the grace of God' (*CW*, p. 107). To speak of gift and grace, creation and divinity, broadens and deepens our understanding of marriage beyond the terms of a legal or civil contract (the earthy framework within which all legally recognized marriages are governed). It is an invitation to explore the nature of marriage as a way of life open to the cultivation of virtues – a way of holiness, a dynamic outworking of Rembrandt's relational 'altarpiece'.

Robert Song emphasizes three themes in relation to Genesis: that marriage is a *created* good; that it is a created *good*; and that it has a structure: faithfulness, permanence and openness to procreation (Song 2014, pp. 3–4). Yet to attend to deeper meanings of gift and grace, within a biblical as well as liturgical framework, is an invitation to model our patterns of life on Christ – whether in the home, work-place or church. As Alan Wilson puts it, the 'spiritual and relational aspects of marriage are developed beyond considerations of sex, gender or children' (Wilson 2014, p. 99). That does not undercut the funda-mental goodness of marriage, nor the way it reflects the generative nature of creation. However, it roots faithfulness and permanence in God's purposes.

A liturgy that shapes a theological vision of partnership and the 'crowning summit' of a committed loving relationship resonates with human longings (Wilson 2014, p. 120). Alan Billings expresses the power of the liturgy in giving a 'voice' to the couple as they seek to deepen an established relationship, and also articulating a vision that marriage is something good and God-given – enabling couples to flourish and live faithfully, and to raise children together (Billings 2004, pp. 75–9). However, given the trends he outlines in the rise of cohabi-tation and contractual relationships, the liturgy expresses a deeper and embracing vision of covenant that reflects a longing for stability and intimacy. It expresses a desire for fruitfulness and holiness directed out-wards towards the world. It articulates an understanding of covenant as crown and seal. As Jessica Martin puts it, 'No relationship in Christ can be transactional or contractual'; rather, there is a depth of attention as we seek to recognize and be recognized, as bodies become 'the site of the sacred or holy' (Martin 2013, p. xv).

Entering into marriage is the continuation of growth in love and trust. As deepening and flourishing of relationship takes place, 'they shall be united with one another in heart and body and mind' (CW, p. 105) as Christ is united with his bride the Church. By being rooted in Christ's relationship with the body of Christ, categories of gender, sexuality and procreation are set in a radical vision of self-giving, mutuality and generosity. The gift of marriage brings husband and wife together in private and public ways: in the 'delight and tenderness of sexual union, and in joyful commitment to the end of their lives' (CW, p. 105). The grace of growth in physical intimacy, with the corresponding deepen-ing of emotional, spiritual and intellectual bonds, is to be a delight in itself. This is not selfish or self-enclosed, but perhaps a subversion of the self-contained nuclear family. To live a life of joyful commitment in marriage, here and now, is a form of living well that may enable us to articulate a vision for dying well (regardless of marital status). Joyful commitment is an invitation to live intensely, yet lightly; to think about how we exercise our gifts and determine our priorities; to allow ourselves to love and be loved, to forgive and be forgiven. Marriage is a vocation that has the capacity to enable the couple of flourish but also causes us to reflect on a wider network of commitments.

None of this is to deny that part of the givenness of marriage is that it is the foundation of family life. This is expressed in a way that is not limited to parenthood. It is the context within which children are born 'and nurtured' (CW, p. 105) – a phrase that itself recognizes or alludes to the diversity of family life. The pastoral reality of this might include the couple's own children as well as step-children; there might be the financial and emotional pressure to conceive through IVF or the decision to foster or adopt; some might be caught up in the lives of godchildren and grandchildren. As Martin states, biological kinship is not 'the last word in permanent relationships' (Martin 2013, p. xv). The liturgy includes the expectation that each member of the family (in good times and in bad) may find strength, companionship and comfort. There is more than a suggestion that this stretches our care and concern beyond the nuclear family; marriage, according to such an interpretation, is to be a gift to strengthen others. Again, growth in both maturity and love is to be a mark of married life – not just for the couple but for all those whose lives are bound up with theirs.

That marriage is a way of life made holy by God, which also enriches community, is a theme to which we will return. Dan Hardy's work deepens our understanding of the call to holiness as part of the vocation of the people of God, which situates marriage within a wider network of ecclesial and social relationships. It is unsurprising that the liturgy makes reference to the wedding at Cana, because it is the only reference to Jesus' attendance at a marriage feast. However, it also expands our vision of marriage. The blessing is not just upon the couple, who in John's Gospel do not feature in the narrative; the wedding itself is blessed by the presence of Christ 'with those celebrating' (CW, p. 105). Again, this is an expansive vision of community life as the context for marriage; and, in interpretation of the Gospel text, something of the foretaste of the kingdom of God and that reveals the identity of Christ.

'Marriage is a way of life made holy by God'

This multi-layered revelation reveals our calling: that our humanity has to be transformed by divine love. Jean Vanier reflects both on the particularity of marriage and on the cosmic vision. For Jesus, says Vanier, marriage is 'the sign of a sacred union, enfolded in love that enables people to grow in forgiveness, tenderness, kindness and compassion' (Vanier 2004, p. 52). This event is also offering the transformation of the ordinary; just at the point at which our human resources run out, 'the drudgery of duty' becomes a 'new passion of love' (2004, p. 53). The cries of humanity for the fulfilment of the promise of love echo throughout the Scriptures in language of wine and feasting, bridegrooms and brides, in abundance and generous invitation. That yearning is sated at the wedding feast of the Lamb: 'The Spirit and the Bride say "Come." Come, Lord Jesus!' (Rev. 22.17, 20). All drawn to this feast find community and love. The vision is eschatological; but the reality is glimpsed in human promises and celebration.

How does the liturgy point to the kingdom of God's breaking into our midst? Marriage can be expressed at a basic level as a legal contract. The advent of civil partnerships, and the subsequent legislation regarding equal marriage, highlight a human longing to express something more. Marriage is a sign of unity and loyalty that all should uphold and honour. This is not just because unity and commitment are worthy of celebration at a human level or because the risk of self-giving is a beginning and end in itself; rather, it is because this promise of fidelity – worked out with patience, humility and kindness in the face of death – is what Vanier calls 'a taste and sign of eternity, a sign of the covenant that bonds God to his people' (Vanier 2004, p. 58).

Again there is a mirroring of expectation between the life of the Church and the commitment in marriage; and there is a reciprocal call for support too. We live out this promise against the backdrop of hurt, disagreement and betrayal. It is because Jesus came to renew all things that our broken and fragile humanity is called into a new unity. The Church is called to be one, which is Jesus' prayer; but as a microcosm of such relating, marriage is to be a sign of unity. Loyalty (or elsewhere faithfulness) is an expression of commitment that echoes the nature of God's faithfulness to humanity. The honouring and upholding of this sign of marriage is not confined to the inner dynamics of the couple's relationship. Rather, it is a responsibility that rests with all members of society.

Vanier describes the importance and beauty of the 'bonding of man and woman in the oneness of human sexuality'; for such bonding to be affirmed at Cana reveals a deep desire and need to love and be loved (Vanier 2004, p. 59). Regardless of sexuality, such a biblical and liturgical vision of a love that is crown and seal is a prophetic vision for human life. Marriage, according to the Church of England liturgy, 'enriches society and strengthens community' (CW, p. 105): there is reciprocity and logic about such a statement. The couple needs the support of others to hold their shared life; their life together becomes a blessing in return. When human life is ordered along the patterns of mutual love and commitment, common life flourishes. It is a demanding pattern – as any reflection on the life of the Church or wider community reveals. Therefore it is to be entered into reverently and responsibly in the sight of God; as with the baptismal promises, this is not a place of selfishness. The commitment being made is not to be undertaken lightly. It is also a journey of hope: we cooperate in faith, trust and hard work.

Dan Hardy uses the term 'sociopoiesis' to capture the way relationships are formed and transformed in relation to God. As it embraces all spheres of personal and social activity including politics, economics, love and ethics, it seems appropriate to see marriage within this lens too. It holds together both the shaping of our individual personhood and the societal expressions of such transformation as our desires are redirected towards God, as well as seeking the well-being of friend and stranger. It is also a language that enables us to speak about the complexity and subtlety of the relationship between Church and world, which is pertinent when thinking about marriage within society and within God's economy.

Hardy describes the way 'care for the other' draws on sacramental energy, for example (Hardy 2010, pp. 51–2). This finds expression as a crown and seal of love in marriage but it also reflects the challenge to pastoral care raised by the Weddings Project. The prophetic and priestly calling of the Church also imagines, speaks and enacts a calling to something better as society moves towards the fulfilment of God's kingdom. A liturgical vision of marriage expresses something of the dynamism of this movement of attraction to God and calling to holiness.

The liturgy sets the commitment of the couple in the context of worship; it brings the light and love of God into their journey of deepening intimacy. It is a process of transformation as love is sealed and as it becomes a crown. Holiness and God are mutually defining. Divine holiness attracts, calls, refines; it is relational and performative as we improvise upon its 'beauteousness'.[13] Like Cumming's description of *The Jewish Bride*, this is a trajectory of humility, patience and kindness. Hardy also argues that social institutions have a key role to play in the performance of holiness, and marriage is unequivocally part of the legal and civil fabric of society. In Hardy's terms, these are 'provisional approximations to the good'; for 'every attempt to guide, to enact justice, to embody mercy, and to punish and forgive, must pass through the refining fire of God's justice in order to partake of the unnamed qualities of holiness and to be energized by it' (Hardy 2001, p. 19).

To set marriage in the context of worship means facing the holiness of God, as well as performing it within the realm of human social life. It is an anticipation of the kingdom of God. It is a moment of being drawn into the light and love of God, as two people who have journeyed together in mutual affection take the risk of entrusting all that they are and all that they have to each other. They do this in the face of our human propensity to make mistakes and the fragmentation caused by our misdirected desires.

'United with one another in heart, body and mind'

It is God's self-giving holiness that forms us, lifts us up and calls us into a pattern of life that moves us towards the good. Within the marriage service, entering this way of life is marked in three ways: mutual consent, solemn vows and the giving and/or receiving of rings as a token. There is freedom, promise and a sign. All these are reliant on the invocation of the Holy Spirit for guidance and strength – that they may fulfil God's purpose for their earthly life together.

The wording of the Declarations that follow express the freedom to lawfully marry, but also express the qualities of marriage – love, comfort, honour and protection. The declarations are mutual and exclusive. Each party commits to forsake all others and to remain faithful as long as they live. Such exclusivity is followed by an expression of commitment on the part of the congregation who agree to support and uphold the couple. A marriage is not self-sustaining – they cannot forsake each other, nor is the community to forsake them.

The vows are made in the presence of God and according to God's holy law: that from this day onwards, until death, each party will have and hold regardless of circumstance, loving and cherishing the other for

---

13 This is a word coined by my colleague Canon Dr Andrew Bishop as a conflation of the phrase 'the beauty of holiness'.

better or worse, richer or poorer, in sickness and in health. The words are so easy to recite we forget just how all-encompassing and demanding they are. They are rooted in the covenantal promises of faithfulness. The fruitfulness of such a reciprocal bond is open ended. The bonding of sexuality and embodiment of which Vanier speaks is something that is beyond our human capacity to love; we will fall short of love's promises. And yet, in God, we know the forgiveness and renewal that become the grounds of our human offering of love. All our human loves are rooted in God:

> God is the end and fulfilment of human desire, and our generously conceived desires point beyond their objects towards God. Desire's balancing point between past and future means that is can only exist as a gift nourished by a promise. Desire joins what has been to what will be, and when it is hallowed by an exclusive choice it can grow into a shared common life, faithfully given all the way to its last breath. (Martin 2013, p. xvi)

The rings are to be a token: a 'symbol of unending love and faithfulness' (CW, p. 109) and a reminder of the vow and covenant made in marriage. They are given and/or received within the love of God. All our human acts of trust and commitment are held within the unending love of one who is faithful; this act undergirds and sustains the frailty, vulnerability and imperfections of our human expressions of love. The words said express a physical honouring of the other and a sharing of resources or possessions. They are also an expression of the giving of oneself to the other; such mutual self-giving is something to which the people of God are called. It is in the giving of self that the other enables them to become more fully who they are. It is not a romantic sense of being 'completed' by the other but the opening up of something new and a deepening of capacity. It is a pattern rooted in God's gift of God's self in the incarnation.

It is following the consent, vows and the exchange of rings that the couple have declared their marriage; that marriage is proclaimed and acclaimed (often with applause as a precursor to the solemnity of the binding of hands and the affirmation that God has joined them together). The prayers of blessing over the couple ground this particular human expression of love in God's generosity and creativity. God creates joy, gladness, pleasure, delight, love, peace and fellowship. Divine and human come together in this expression. God pours out abundance at the start of this new chapter of life together; it affirms and bears witness to a relationship that has already begun; and their love is to be both a seal on their hearts and a crown upon their heads. Just as the vows express commitment in all the complexity and conditions of life we experience, so God's blessing is asked upon the spouses in work and companionship, wakefulness and sleep, joy and sorrow, life and death. All this is held within the perspective of God's eternal kingdom.

Blessing, help and the riches of God's grace are invoked that in marriage the spouses may please God in body and soul; and that 'living together in faith and love' they may 'receive the blessing of eternal life' (CW, p. 111). The provisionality of marriage in the face of death and in anticipation of the kingdom draws our attention to God: the source of blessing and the one whom we are called to delight. It is a modelling of a way of holiness; holiness in the sphere of companionship, marked by a seal and crown.

'In joyful anticipation of heaven'

The prayers of intercession are for the couple and for their deepening engagement with the lives of others. To begin with, prayers of thanksgiving for the couple on their wedding day are couched in the nature of God, in God's faithfulness and holiness, in echoing the opening prayer naming God as the source of life and spring of love. The prayer for a life-giving and lifelong marriage is also set in the context of God's love and grace: that the relationship may be enriched and strengthened by God's presence – in order that the spouses may bring comfort and confidence to each other in faithfulness and trust. Again, the nature of our human relating, in its most intimate sense, should mirror the divine and be sustained by it. This should be the pattern of all human relationships – as we grow in mutual affection and learn to become ambassadors of reconciliation.

The prayers are also about the public aspect of marriage and its impact on deepening the quality of our social networks. The home should be a place of hospitality – bringing 'refreshment and joy to all around them' (CW, p. 112). Love is not to be contained within the couple or directed solely to their immediate family. Rather, their love should 'overflow to neighbours in need' and 'embrace those in distress' (CW, p. 112). The perfect crown of a public commitment of love in marriage is expansive and generous. It is a way of holiness that is undergirded by the love and support of those who have shared in blessing, witnessing and celebrating the wedding. Marriage is not a private arrangement. It is one of the 'goods of community' that is worked out over a lifetime, within a rich tapestry of relationships; it is a 'highly demanding' kind of 'lived out commitment' of self-giving, which is a seal on the heart and a crown upon the head (Martin 2013, p. xiv).

Order and purpose for the spouses' lives is to be discerned in God's word; with the Holy Spirit to 'lead them in truth and defend them in adversity' (*CW*, p. 112). There is something generous and expansive about this, which sits alongside the vision of abundance amid paucity, blessing in the ordinary, as expressed at the wedding at Cana. Nurturing a family demands devotion; and seeing children 'grow in body, mind and spirit' (*CW*, p. 113) is part of the fruitfulness of married life. This is not a restrictive statement: it might include godchildren, adoptive children and the assumption that marriage enables a trust in the future and the nurturing of relationships.

All this is set within the context of death: that, at the end of their lives, the spouses' hearts might be content, and that they might live in joyful anticipation of heaven. This extends the understanding of marriage beyond an earthly covenant or legal contract to a vision of God's kingdom: life now that mirrors the ultimate kingdom. Finally, words are addressed not just to the couple but to the whole congregation: that the Holy Trinity may make them strong in faith and love; that they may be defended on every side and be guided in truth and peace. Lives lived corporately in the power of the Spirit: this is a pneumatological vision that undergirds human commitment.

'You have blessed creation with abundant life'

If Rembrandt presents us with an altarpiece of virtues associated with marriage – as a crown and seal, inclusive and exclusive – it is perhaps Mike Leigh's film *Another Year* that presents us with a secular challenge to how we understand marriage in relation to the complex network of relationships within which we live. Leigh captures our human frailty with great honesty, both in tenderness and challenge, but also with a surprising hopefulness. Tom and Gerri are a mature, professional married couple: they exude comfort and contentment. Over the course of a year – marked by shifts in seasonal tones – they are surrounded by family and friends, who experience varying degrees of unhappiness and tribulation.

Their son Joe longs to be in a relationship and find fulfilment; his parents certainly wish that for him. He meets Katie, and their delight in each other and intense commitment serve to magnify his parents' contentment. Yet Tom and Gerri's friends, Mary and Ken, by contrast, find their loneliness and longing exaggerated. They are depressed, dependent, disillusioned; fragile, yet taking risks in their longing for love, intimacy and commitment. Then there is Tom's brother Ronnie – recently bereaved, with an aggressive and unpredictable son.

Tom and Gerri fret, judge, cajole and support from their vantage point of stability. Around them is the maelstrom of hurt, grief, brokenness and longing. They are generous up to a point; they are tolerant within certain bounds. Their faithful commitment in marriage ought to enable hospitality, support of those in distress, the nurturing of relationships. In reflection on liturgy we have focused on faithfulness and intimacy as a crown on the head and seal on the heart; on exclusivity for the purpose of including others.

What we say about marriage relates directly to what we might want to say about the life of the Church (and indeed God's world and God's kingdom). Each one of us, alone and together, is called up to offer hospitality, comfort, encouragement, challenge. In Leigh's film it is in the all but silent ritual of making tea and sitting at a table that we see compassion breaking in. A grief-stricken widower and distressed singleton show an intense level of mutual recognition and compassion.

Love and marriage can be a cause of deep hurt and frustration as well as a life-enriching blessing. Lives unravel through a lack of intimacy, through unfaithfulness or the inability to adjust to change within a marriage. Being human means finding ourselves caught up in a cycle of pain, brokenness, guilt and betrayal. The frailty of our mortality means that we find ourselves 'alone' because of divorce, death or never finding a partner; others might fear commitment or seek fulfilment in sexual 'encounters' rather than stable relationships. The question of loneliness, however, affects those who live alone and those who share their homes with others.[14] Any liturgical theology has to address those realities. It does so from the perspective of an ultimate reality.

It speaks of love as crown and seal; not as perfect in itself but a breaking in and affirmation of what God has already done in Christ. What Vanier describes as a deep bonding of our sexuality is about fostering intimacy: emotional, spiritual, intellectual as well as physical. Marriage has the potential to be a crucible where lives are refined in holiness. It is a deep bonding that cultivates virtues – the gifts of

---

14 The BBC set aside a day of programming called A Life Less Lonely on Friday 12 December 2014 to explore the effects of loneliness in the UK. A BBC poll commissioned in 2013 as part of the Faith in the World Week revealed that 48 per cent of adults feel varying degrees of loneliness: www.bbc.co.uk/news/uk-england-24522691.

patience, kindness and humility. Thus it is also to be a crown as well as a seal – there is a radically inclusive public engagement born out of the trust of exclusivity. In that sense liturgy educates and directs our desires and it enlarges our minds. It moves beyond quirky responses to the Weddings Project to a hopeful and challenging vision of marriage that is rooted in community and in God.

As John Bradbury hints in this volume, within the life of the Church perhaps we need to recover a sense of marriage as being *a* way of holiness – supporting those who enter into it after serious thought but also upholding those for whom it is a longing or a disappointment. As a holy people we are also to 'think single', as John Pritchard expresses it (Pritchard 2013, p. 122). Part of being able to think that way is to think more holistically about what it is to be members of a body – called to that same level of intimate commitment in Christ yet also sent out in the power of the Spirit to witness in the world. Liturgy expresses the depth of God's love and holds open the long view of God's future, which is our ultimate hope. That perspective transforms and upholds the complexity of our lived reality. The provisionality of our human relationships, our propensity to fail, is redeemed. As Martin writes with honesty and compassion, 'We will fail. Because we are flawed ... we need to forgive each other even as we hope to be forgiven. Relationships too will fail; but no bond of love can ever be forgotten or belittled' (Martin 2013, p. xvi). A liturgical vision of marriage is a challenge to both Church and society as it expresses a theological account of a union that is both intimate/exclusive and generous/inclusive. It presents a vision of God's Kingdom that seals the deepest levels of trust and affection; but that also crowns relationships with a love that seeks the transformation of the world. To think liturgically about marriage is to think imaginatively at full stretch – to continue a trajectory that is rooted in the nature of God and that does justice to human lives. Perhaps we should be wary of making things too tidy this side of the eschaton. As Rowan Williams expresses it in his haiku on John 2:

Poured from this stone, the water
stings, the mind lurches, suspects
joy, chaos. (Williams 2014, p. 33)

References

Archbishops' Council of the Church of England, 2000, *Common Worship: Pastoral Services*, London: Church House Publishing.

Billings, Alan, 2004, *Secular Lives, Sacred Hearts*, London: SPCK.

Cumming, Laura, 2014, 'Rembrandt: The Late Works Review: Dark, Impassioned, Magnificently Defiant', *The Observer*, 19 October, www.theguardian.com/artanddesign/2014/oct/19/rembrandt-late-works-review-national-gallery-magnificently-defiant.

Ford, David F., 2015, 'Theology at Full Stretch', Bampton Lectures, University Church of St Mary the Virgin, Oxford, 20 January 2015.

Gittoes, Julie, Brutus Green and James Heard (eds), 2013, *Generous Ecclesiology: Church, World, and the Kingdom of God*, London: SCM Press.

Hardy, Daniel W., 2001, *Finding the Church: The Dynamic Truth of Anglicanism*, London: SCM Press.

Hardy, Daniel W., 2002, 'Worship and the Formation of a Holy People', in Stephen Barton (ed.), *Holiness Past and Present*, London: T&T Clark, pp. 477–98.

Hardy, Daniel W., 2010, *Wording a Radiance: Parting Conversations on God and the Church*, London: SCM Press.

Martin, Jessica, 2013, 'Living with Holiness and Desire', in *Report of the House of Bishops Working Group on Human Sexuality*, Archbishops' Council, pp. ix–xvi, London: Church House Publishing.

Methuen, Charlotte, 2013, 'Marriage: One Man and One Woman?', www.opendemocracy.net/ourkingdom/charlotte-methuen/marriage-one-man-and-one-woman.

Oliver, Gillian, 2012, *The Church Weddings Handbook: The Seven Pastoral Moments that Matter*, London: Church House Publishing.

Pritchard, John, 2013, *Living Faithfully: Following Christ in Everyday Life*, London: SPCK.

Song, Robert, 2014, *Covenant and Calling: Towards a Theology of Same-Sex Relationships*, London: SCM Press.

Vanier, Jean, 2004, *Drawn into the Mystery of Jesus through the Gospel of John*, London: Darton, Longman & Todd.

Williams, Rowan, 2003 [1989], *The Body's Grace*, London: Lesbian and Gay Christian Movement.

Williams, Rowan, 2014, *The Other Mountain*, Manchester: Carcanet.

Wilson, Alan, 2014, *More Perfect Union? Understanding Same-Sex Marriage*, London: Darton, Longman & Todd.

7

Faithfulness to Our Sexuate Bodies:
The Vocations of Generativity and Sex

SUSANNAH CORNWALL

Introduction

For many Christians marriage can, by definition, only take place between a man and a woman. This belief strongly underlay the Church of England's submission to the UK government's consultation on same-sex marriage in 2012. The document claimed that something about males' and females' complementary nature would be lost if same-sex couples were allowed to marry (Church of England 2012, pp. 3–4), as Mike Higton discusses further in this volume. But in this chapter, I suggest that the binary nature of biological sex is not quite as obvious and self-evident as it seems. I show that biological maleness and femaleness may not be a firm ground for the distinctness and complementarity the Church of England submission and many other mainstream theologies of marriage claim. I suggest that human sexedness in relation to God is more primary than human sexedness in relation to other people, and that while *being* sexed is an irreducible facet of personhood, *how* we are sexed is less significant. Finally I argue that being a sexed person is a vocation and that theologies of sex in marriage would do well to take fuller account of the diverse complexities of the ways sex and sexuality permeate human interactions with the world.

Christian theological accounts of marriage often ascribe special significance to the spouses' respective maleness and femaleness, asserting that sexed differences are not insignificant or coincidental but carry both earthly and cosmic significance. The partners' sexed differences matter, in this account, first because the spouses' roles as wife and husband are intimately tied to their potential (and subsequently actual) roles as mother and father to children. To remove the necessity of sexed difference from marriage (as some critics believe occurs in the legalization of same-sex marriages) would break the intimate association between marriage and parenthood (Catholic Bishops Conference 2013). Second, by this logic, being of different sexes also means being of different genders, reflecting different aspects of God and bringing different skills and aptitudes to marriage. Third, for these theologians, maintaining sexed difference as a prerequisite for marriage means engaging with specificity, taking different kinds of bodies seriously and celebrating diversity rather than privileging only males or only females. I will respond to these positions in turn, before sketching out an alternative account of sex as vocation.

1 Sex and Generativity

First, as critics inside and outside the Church have pointed out, the connection between spousehood and parenthood is not universal or necessary even in partners of different sexes. Some couples are unable to have their own biological children; others choose not to and, even if this decision has often been maligned as selfish or immature, it may be made for compelling reasons such as the desire to minimize straining the resources of an already overpopulated world or to parent existing children via adoption. Indeed, many couples (including same-sex couples) become parents through adoption, and to argue that relationships between adoptive parents and children are inherently 'lesser' than those between biological relations is deeply problematic, especially given the Christian tradition's long emphasis on the importance of non-kinship relationships and communities.

Furthermore, biological procreation is not the only kind of 'reproduction' possible. Couples who adopt their children may still pass on to them their beliefs, values, family histories and cultures. A strong stream within Christianity advocates caring for and including non-relations: Jesus said that his mother and sisters and brothers were whoever did the will of God, and the Church's involvement with monasteries, children's homes and other contexts of community and care for non-biologically related people over the years testifies strongly to the idea that the Christian idea of family transcends biology. Gerard Loughlin says,

> Children [are] born to the Church, and not merely to their parents ... This is why ... not everyone in the Church has to look for the gift of children, why not every particular relationship or sexual act has to be open to the gift of children, in short, why there can be infertile straight couples and gay couples; why there can be celibates,

consecrated virgins and single people. For in the imagination of the Church, children are first and foremost gifts that arrive through the nuptial union of the Church with her beloved, Jesus Christ. (Loughlin 2004, p. 97)

It therefore seems strange that most theologies of marriage appeal to biological reproduction as necessarily protected and promoted by opposite-sex marriage. Furthermore, denominations that allow contraception for married couples already acknowledge a distinction between spousehood and parenthood: a husband is not always or necessarily a father, or a wife always or necessarily a mother. Rowan Williams compellingly makes this point in his essay 'The Body's Grace' (Williams 2002), discussed in more detail by Brett Gray in this volume.

Even so, sex differences in the genital anatomy are particularly prominent, and a particular focus for accounts of male and female difference. The Church of England submission to the same-sex marriage consultation says, 'Distinctiveness and complementarity are seen most explicitly in the biological union of man and woman which potentially brings to the relationship the fruitfulness of procreation' (Church of England 2012, p. 3). Reproduction is a source of joy and delight for many couples, but to make it the crowning mark of difference is potentially problematic. First, not everyone's body fits neatly into the either–or, male–female system. Intersex people – as many as 1 in every 2,000 people in total, about the same as the number of people with cystic fibrosis or coeliac disease – cannot usually reproduce with their partner. Indeed, some intersex people may not be able to have penetrative vaginal sex – which most easily and frequently leads to conception – at all, because of the specificities of their anatomy. Some intersex people have a shallow or closed vagina, no uterus or no functioning gonads. While some intersex people consider themselves a 'third' gender in between masculine and feminine, many identify strongly as ordinary men or women despite their difference of physical sex. The Church of England does not seem to acknowledge that not everyone's body fits clearly into the male–female, ideally procreative account of sex. It is unsurprising that this has been the case, for until recently intersex was much more shadowy and 'hidden' than it has become since the rise of the intersex advocacy movement in the 1990s. (For a fuller account of this movement, and some of the theological implications of intersex, see Cornwall 2010.) But now that we are more aware of the science of foetal development and the non-binary nature of human sex, it seems important to engage with it in our theological anthropologies.

However, as Mark Jordan comments, theologians and church authorities are frequently happy to invoke evidence from science only when
it helps their case. This points to an inconsistency significant in the sex
and marriage debate:

> If God's intentions for human nature are to be inferred only from
> what we hypothesize about Adam and Eve in Eden, we will not be
> able to reason about those intentions very convincingly. Nor can we
> invoke scientific evidence on one page of theological argument and
> then reject it out of hand for the next. If our medicine and biology
> reveal nothing theologically significant about sex, then we shouldn't
> trust them in other cases either – say, in constructing arguments about
> abortion or alcoholism or insanity. (Jordan 2002, p. 150)

The Church of England's close link between complementarity and
reproduction may also take too little account of people who are infertile and cannot reproduce biologically. Many people who cannot have
children experience sadness and hurt as a result, and may feel even more
wounded by being told, implicitly or explicitly, that it is in reproduction that humans are most fully sexed. Men who feel they are not really
accepted as men until they are fathers, and women who find themselves
infantilized because they are not mothers, are nonetheless sexed just as
irreducibly as anyone else. Theologies that overemphasize the good of
reproduction as the sole or highest facet of being sexed also negate the
full personhood of single and celibate people who never engage in the
kind of 'biological union' the submission endorses. Julie Gittoes notes
in this volume that marriage is only *one* expression of mature discipleship (so that overemphasizing biological reproduction undermines the
specific value and contribution of single people), and that marriage as
an institution is not to be understood as final or perfect.

2 Sex and Gender

Pope John Paul II asserts that human males' and females' orientation to
each other is built into them by God (John Paul II 2006). This mutual
sexed orientation is, he believes, inherently 'nuptial': that is, designed
to tend toward marriage. Male–female relationships also symbolize
a deeper truth about the relationship between God and humans. To
hold that marriage is about the relationship of *any* two persons, rather
than a male and a female, is, believes John Paul II, to detract from
the specificities of their embodiment. Males are not males *regardless* of

their bodies, but *in and through* their bodies; and it is in and through this maleness that they relate to females and to God. Sex difference as male and female is universal, and communicates something onto-logical about human persons. Human sexed bodies are manifestations of human sexed spirits.[15]

For John Paul II this is significant because God's love for the Church is a larger, maximized version of the love between human spouses. Indeed, God's love for the Church is, in itself, 'spousal'. To deny or frustrate the way human marriage imaged this divine love would be to block marriage's capacity to be sacramental: that is, to mediate God's grace both to the spouses and to other members of the community, including their own children.

The Pope's intentions are to ensure that embodiment and materiality are not disparaged, and no one tries to 'rise above' their embodiment. In this way his position chimes with Christian theologians from Augustine of Hippo onwards who have insisted that bodies are not inconvenient vessels to be transcended but integral to our being and the way we meet God and one another.

But it is for exactly this reason that there is a flaw in John Paul II's argument. If body identities are specific, good and not to be disparaged, and if it is in and through sexed bodies that all human–human and human–divine relationships occur, then it matters that we are faithful to *these* sexed bodies, not to mythical or theoretical ones. Faithful-ness to real, actual sexed bodies means not using them to communicate falsely with, either to ourselves or to others. For some individuals, communicating falsely will mean engaging in sexual relationships with those to whom they are not attracted (e.g. a homosexual man who marries and has a sexual relationship with a woman); for others it will mean denying the truth of their gender identity. Faithfulness to sexed and gendered bodies must include theological acknowledgement that their sex and gender are not quite like other people's (though no less real), and that to squeeze all humans into one of two categories does not tell the whole story of sexed and gendered personhood.

Furthermore the Pope conflates being sexed in relation to other humans with being sexed in relation to God – which, as I will argue in more detail in a moment, is problematic. In fact although both encoun-ters take place in and through sexed bodies, our relationships with other sexed persons and our relationships with God, who is not sexed, are of different orders.

---

15 See, for example, the claims in John Paul II's *Theology of the Body* at sections 9.4, 14.1, 20.5 and 45.2.

John Paul II wants to argue that sexual intercourse is most pro-foundly about self-giving (which is why he wants it to be open to the procreation of children). Indeed, both in the *Theology of the Body* and elsewhere (e.g. the 1988 letter *Mulieris Dignitatem*), he strongly links the sex act to the inherent parental relationship communicated in it: women are 'naturally' hospitable mothers who welcome children into their bodies, and this is demonstrated by the female 'welcoming' of the male penis into her body during sex or the 'gift of interior readiness to accept the child ... [which] is linked to the marriage union' (John Paul II 1988, section 18). Like many other Roman Catholic theologians, he holds that sexual intercourse may only have justice done to it in the con-text of the permanent, committed, exclusive relationship of marriage: this is key to the time-taking that the development of the relationship to its fullest extent needs. He believes that same-sex marriages are not possible, because only in male–female sexual relationships are males and females fully themselves and fully reflective of divine–human rela-tionships. Importantly, he does also acknowledge that one can also be fully female or fully male as a celibate whose sexuality is not expressed genitally with other people at all – but one's sex is still a decisive factor for one's interactions with the world, as demonstrated by the tradition of single-sex/single-gender monastic communities.

In John Paul II's account, bodies are an irreducible ground on which sexuality and gender identity supervene. Ontology comes first, fol-lowed by the embodiment that speaks to its irreducible truth, followed by subsidiary matters of orientation and identity. To be embodied is the key thing, and from this that orientation and gender identity flow (so that it is possible to have a more or less 'correct' orientation and a more or less 'legitimate' gender identity, depending on one's sex). It is here where I think the Pope's good impulse to value embodiment and specificity, and to refuse the Gnostic disavowal of materiality, leads him to take too little account of the complexity of how sex, gender and sexuality interrelate, and to overemphasize the cosmic significance of sexual orientation towards people of the opposite sex.

The social theorist Judith Butler suggested in the early 1990s that gender was not something that unproblematically stemmed from bio-logical sex and could therefore only happen along certain lines. Rather, she suggested, gender was *performed*; gender identity is something constructed, not something that somehow naturally stems from our biological sex. Cultural beliefs about sex and gender mean that some characteristics are more associated with males and some with females, but these things are contingent, not timeless or self-evident truths. As individuals, she suggested, we all do things that reinforce the gender identity we inhabit and project (Butler 1990). Butler has often been slightly misunderstood and misrepresented. Importantly, for Butler, saying that gender is 'performed' does *not* mean that it is always totally freely chosen or that we are always conscious about reinforcing our genders. Certain choices and behaviours are associated with certain genders. It is harder, for example, to be an eight-year-old boy who likes wearing flouncy dresses and sparkly nail polish than an eight-year-old girl who likes these things, because in most Western societies dresses and nail polish are usually considered exclusively feminine. A boy who wears them is likely to encounter – from peers and adults – the message that 'Boys don't do that' or that 'Nail polish is only for girls'. The point, Butler might argue, is that *both* boys and girls who wear frills and glitter are performing their gender, but that because feminine girls perform gender in a 'typically' female way, it is considered legitimate and unremarkable. On the other hand, Western females who make 'unfeminine' choices such as allowing their facial and body hair to grow unchecked in adulthood are likely to encounter people who believe that they are somehow failing to be 'real women', because body-hairlessness has come to be associated with femininity. So according to Butler, every one of us performs our gender but we may not realize it because many of us have been socialized into gender performances that nobody considers remarkable.

Transgender people experience a strong disjunction between their biological sex and their gender identity. Some choose to have surgery to alter their bodies and make them 'match' their genders. Transgender people are performing their gender no more or less than anyone else, but attract more attention because they are making a strong statement that gender identity does not always 'match' biological sex. Theologians writing about marriage almost always assume that 'normal', 'healthy' people are non-transgender people, and that God intended sex and gender to match only in certain ways. Or, more often, theologians do not distinguish between sex and gender at all, or acknowledge that being a male is not always the same as being a man. One reason why some Christians oppose sex reassignment surgery for transgender people is that it seems to 'interrupt' the capacity of these individuals to take part in penetrative sexual intercourse in the way that someone who had not had such surgery would be able to do. Sex reassignment surgery is saying 'no' to the body as God has given it. Theologies of marriage have often taken little or no account of the experiences of transgender and gender-non-conforming people, assuming that these betray psychological disturbance or a failure to accept the God-givenness of one's body. However, in this way such theologies risk negating the important evidence of transgender people's own relationships with God and their bodies, which make clear that otherness and difference in embodied life are complex and multiple.

This is theologically significant and, moreover, may point to something the mainstream Christian tradition has sometimes forgotten, namely that binary gender is not, if it ever was, a primary demarcation. In Christ gender no longer means what it once meant (Gal. 3.28); rather, gender is disrupted and relativized – which does not mean that it is erased but does render it interrupted, transgressed and rendered 'subject to the labile [i.e. frequently changing] transformations of divine desire' (Coakley 2013, p. 57).

3 Sex, Difference and the Cosmic Order

Another reason for insisting that marital partners must be of different sexes is, for many Christians, the belief that male–female marriage reflects something important about the order and hierarchy built into the cosmos. For the Swiss Reformed theologian Karl Barth, writing in the middle of the twentieth century, it was crucial that marriage occurred between people of different genders because marriage testified to a greater theological truth about the relationship between God and humanity. Barth believed that the whole story of salvation history was about God initiating and humans responding. He saw, in marriage, a mirror image of this pattern: men led and women followed (Barth 1961, pp. 169–71). The relationship of husband and wife in marriage was a version of the relationship between Christ and his Bride, the Church.

Barth believed that part of the good of marriage was its repetition and endorsement of sexual difference. A key question, then, is whether Barth (and those who have followed him) was right to hold, first, that sexed difference is a God-ordained good, and second, that the difference brought to marriage by the spouses necessarily happens along sexed or gendered lines. Is it really the case that there are particular patterns of emotional, mental and spiritual life into which men and women respectively fall?

Barth was a strong critic of natural theology, the idea that we can discern theological truths from what we see around us in the world. Rather, for Barth, everything focused on God's self-revelation in Jesus. We could not know anything about God if God had not first chosen to reveal it to us. Barth revisits this idea throughout his writing and, in particular, the huge *Church Dogmatics*, which was still unfinished when he died in 1968. However, some theologians believe that Barth fell into the very trap he believed should be avoided and that his theology of initiation and response was based on what he observed in human beings, projected back on to God – that it was, itself, a kind of natural theology (see, for example, discussions in Kärkkäinen 2014, pp. 114–18 and Ward 1994, p. 17). Barth, critics suggest, looked at social norms about how men and women should behave in marriage and society and projected from these social norms theological truths about the nature of the cosmos.

Importantly, some theologians suggest, Barth's valuable point about the significance of difference in human relationships – a reminder of the difference between God and humanity – loses something when he assumes that the most irreducible kind of difference between spouses is that they are of different sexes. Barth held that what makes humans different from other animals – uniquely reflecting the image of God – is that humans are distinguished only by sex, not by breed or kind as other species are. Writing in a Europe recently ravaged by National Socialist ideology in Germany, it was important for Barth to insist that divisions of ethnicity, race and class were not of ultimate significance and that eliminating a people-group on the grounds of race or religion was utterly reprehensible.

Barth understood sex as ontologically different from these other divisions. But he seemed to mistake the cultural gender norms he observed around him for timeless, self-evident truths. Critics of this kind of account might note that relationships between men and women, inside and outside marriage, vary greatly across times and cultures. They might also note that an indicative is not an imperative: in other words, just because things *are* a certain way (or tend to be a certain way), that is not necessarily the best or only possible way for them to be.

Barth himself recognized that sexed difference was relatively minor when compared with all the things that human males and females shared, and that the partners in marriages brought both similarity and difference to the relationship. We might agree that there are good reasons for exhorting difference as good: it means that each partner may be a check on the other's inadequacies and excesses; it makes for richer mutual understanding between the partners and, more broadly, of others; it echoes the multiplicity and creativity of God's world. But the most serious flaw in Barth's position is assuming that this difference could most reliably and irreducibly be brought to a marriage by virtue of the partners' being of different sexes.

For it is not the case that all men have things in common that they share with one another but with no women. There may be particular *tendencies* within each gender but there is also huge variation. Moreover there is crossover: two men may or may not be more alike in a given way than one of those men is like a woman. While many of us follow certain gender conventions that may mean we have similarities or affinities with others who follow the same conventions, these are at least as much social as they are 'natural'. Gender is a complex combination of a variety of factors such as upbringing, social convention, the effect of hormones on the prenatal brain and so on. Gender expressions vary across time and culture; what looks unmistakeably feminine in one context (such as wearing ornate lacy and ruffled clothing in contemporary Britain) has been deemed faultlessly masculine in others (such as the sixteenth-century European royal courts). Many people today believe pink is obviously meant for girls and blue for boys, and would be shocked by someone dressing a baby in the 'wrong' colour, but this convention was fluid (and even reversed) prior to the 1930s (Paoletti 2012).

Furthermore, as we have already begun to see in the case of intersex, even biology may be less irreducible and self-evident than it seems. Although there are many things shared by most females that are not true of males (such as the ability to menstruate, become pregnant and breastfeed), there are enough exceptions to this rule to make it a shaky ground on which to build an entire theological anthropology. Menstruation is shared by most females but not absolutely all. Many women do become pregnant, give birth and breastfeed but many do not. Transgender man Thomas Beatie has borne three children, and there are intersex people whose bodily specificities do not fit into the male–female pattern at all. Of course, this does not mean that specifically male or specifically female embodied experiences are unimportant. Rather, it means that these are not the *only* important experiences, and that the most significant thing about a given male's or female's bodily experience consists of something other than the fact that it is shared with other males or females.

Barth did not make claims about men initiating and women responding in sex but, using the initiation–response logic, the Church of England's bishops did do so several decades later:

In terms of our relationship to God we are essentially 'female-like' and feminine and he is 'male-like' and masculine. God always has the initiative and our duty is to respond. Because, psychologically and symbolically and, to an important extent, biologically, taking the initiative is male, it was therefore appropriate that the Word was incarnate as a male human being and not as a female human being. The particularity of maleness assumed in the incarnation and taken into the Godhead signifies divine initiative. (Central Board of Finance 1988, p. 27)

But the ways initiation and response play out within sexual relationships are various: in a heterosexual relationship the initiator might as easily be female as male. Initiation–response play might form part of sexual activity for same-sex couples too. To claim that males 'naturally' initiate biologically, and that this has cosmic significance, is to read too much both into and out of an observation of a particular kind of sexual behaviour that is not universal.

Questioning the link between males and females in sex and marriage, and God and humanity in salvation history, does not mean rejecting the idea of sexed difference in creation and marriage as good. However, as Sarah Coakley notes, sex and gender in light of God must always be appraised in the context of the divine desire that is the ground for all human relationality: 'The certainties of this world ... can be remade in the incarnate likeness of Christ ... Embodied difference ... is here not to be eradicated ... but to be transformed; it still "matters", but only because God desires it to matter and can remake it in the image of his Son' (Coakley 2013, p. 55). What we cannot do so straightforwardly, therefore, is to make a leap to saying that 'difference' always happens along unambiguously male and female lines, or that same-sex relationships cannot have the same mixture of similarity and otherness as heterosexual ones. Furthermore, we can note that biological sex is only *part* of the mix of similarity and difference that spouses bring to a marriage relationship. Those who hold 'traditional' views of marriage as legitimate only between partners of different sexes (which, as Augur Pearce and Charlotte Methuen show in this volume, may not be so traditional as they are purported to be) often maintain that this is all part and parcel of the Christian tradition's positive focus on embodiment and incarnation. It matters, they hold, that spouses are of different sexes; it matters that not all bodies are the same and that God's image may be reflected in them variously. But by their insistence on only opposite-sex marriages as theologically licit, those who hold this kind of position precisely risk *not* taking bodies seriously. Bodies are, indeed, various and multiple – but they do not come in only two kinds. By painting all humans as either male or female and building attendant assumptions about gender identity, parenthood and marital role on supposed biological sex, 'traditionalists' exclude whole swathes of people. This might include intersex people; it might also include infertile people, who cannot have biological children, and transgender people, whose sense of gender and self does not 'match' their biological sex.

Sex and Vocation

How can we take seriously the specificity and diversity of bodies and sexes and ensure that they continue to receive due attention in the Christian theological context, without either essentializing or dismissing them? One strategy is to insist that if embodiment is an irreducible and undeniable aspect of what it is to be a person, then theologies of embodiment that diminish or write out some kinds of bodies will be inadequate ones. More specifically, we might say that theologies that try to make sense of what it is to be a sexed person must engage with the multiple realities of human sex, not just the apparently straightforward maleness and femaleness of the majority.

Focusing too much on only certain kinds of sexual activity, and only certain body parts, as carrying all the cosmic significance about what it means to be a sexed and gendered person in relationship is problematic for several reasons. First, focusing only on penetrative vaginal intercourse means that people physically unable to have sex of this kind may find their own modes of sexual relationship erased, ignored or figured – arbitrarily – as less than ideal. Second, an opportunity is missed for exploring how same-sex sexual relationships might be specific sites of God's revelation and grace, which might (as Rowan Williams, Eugene Rogers and others have begun to show) have important lessons to teach heterosexual people precisely because they are *not* procreative ones with obvious biologically generative 'ends' (Williams 2002, p. 318). Third, reducing legitimate or cosmically significant sex only to penetrative vaginal sex, and insisting that what is *really* significant about this kind of sex is that it is potentially procreative (whether or not a given couple is capable or desirous of this), detracts from all the other ways sexual intercourse has of imparting meaning and relationality. If the procreative imperative is removed from the equation it is difficult to see why penetrative vaginal sex should *necessarily* be considered more potent or more resonant than the other forms of sexual activity in which partners may engage. Physical touch, skin-to-skin contact, the exchange of bodily fluids with all its potential risk and vulnerability, the sharing of heightened sensation and orgasm and feelings of emotional closeness and intimacy are possible via multiple kinds of sexual activity. Indeed, focusing too much on the potentially procreative aspect of sex might actually undermine sex's other good aspects, such as bonding, building intimacy and being something physically pleasurable and mutually rewarding in which couples engage together.

This is important, particularly if (as we are arguing throughout this volume) one of the most theologically important and distinctive things about marriage is that it is a relationship in which the partners have publicly committed to marking out time and commitment for letting the relationship grow, for the benefit of the spouses themselves and others of their community. Julie Gittoes and Frances Clemson show effectively in their chapters that marriage might be understood as living tradition, which both reflects and feeds into the Church's own commitment to tradition and taking care of its relationships in shared time – and which is characteristically outward looking, committed to the well-being and nurture of those who are not married (including children, young people, willingly and unwillingly single people, widowed people, separated and divorced people, celibate lay and religious people) as well as those who are. Commitment does not guarantee fidelity or the success of a relationship, but it testifies to the intention to make it so and communicate it as so. As Margaret Farley says, 'Commitment is love's way of being whole while it still grows into wholeness' (Farley 2013, p. 44). The act of promising and committing, she believes, is part of what converts the heart, turns us outwards from ourselves to the other, and 'helps to effect what it assures' (2013, p. 44): that is, safeguarding us 'against our own inconsistencies' (2013, p. 43) and making us into the kind of people who could have made such an awesome promise. Other theologians, including Eugene Rogers (2006) and David Matzko McCarthy (2004), have already shown that commitment to taking time and *making* time for the grace that marriage brings about needs to exist and be recognized in same-sex relationships as well as heterosexual ones.

Furthermore, as I hinted earlier and as bears fuller reflection, the human experience of being sexed in marriage is secondary to the prior experience of being sexed in relation only to God. What is true about human sex must fundamentally still be so even in the context of solely the self and the divine – even if there were no other humans present to define one, or to whom one could relate. God must be the final point of reference for any discussion of desire, and it is in light of desire that human sex is created (Coakley 2013, p. 10). For this reason human sexedness as male or female (or some other kind of sex), which only makes sense in the context of another *sexed* person, must be less primary than one's existence as a human before God (who has no sex at all). There are many ways humans differ from God, so it is not that it is insignificant to God that any given human is sexed – but it cannot be fundamental to God's relationship with an individual *how* they are sexed, be it female, male or other. Being sexed is, irreducibly, part of being human; fitting a particular category of maleness or femaleness is not. We are who we are in relation to God more primarily and more absolutely than we are who we are in relation to other human beings (though human relationship is the mechanism by which we are nurtured and sustained – and how we come to know God at all – right from infancy).

If marriage understood in its fullest light is a calling, something into which the spouses enter for others as well as for themselves, and which will require time, commitment and work to sustain, then the way sex and gender come to be experienced and expressed in marriage might also be figured as a calling. Justin Tanis (2003) has suggested that for transgender people, gender is a vocation that shares characteristics in common with other vocations. For example, it may be permanent or something to which one is called for a time; it may become obvious all at once in a moment of revelation, be a sense of having 'always just known' or it might unfold gradually. The experience of shifting gender may seem unique to transgender people but actually many non-transgender people also understand their self-identity as a sexed and gendered person changing over time. Expressions of gender at six or 16 are unlikely to be quite the same as at 30, 60 or 90. Our processes of working out what it means to be a sexed person in relation to God and other people may develop over time and in the context of our own specific sexual relationships. Theologies of marriage will be lacking if they do not acknowledge that sex – even the sexuate nature of a single given individual across their own lifespan – is as much shifting, transient and uncertain as it is stable, permanent and irreducible.

What does it mean to be faithful to our vocations as sexed persons, and what might this mean for theologies of marriage?

1 Sexed persons are **embodied**. Being faithful to our sex is being faithful to our own body in its specificity and to the multiplicities of embodiment in others. Faithfulness to sex means endorsing the

goodness of materiality and physicality, as well as acknowledging the pain and discomfort embodied people experience. Embodiment is not something to be escaped, explained away, apologized for or dismissed. Our sexuate nature is a reminder that we encounter God in and through our physical senses, and that embodiment is good.

2 Sexed persons are **generative**. Sexuality is energy, a capacity for making and celebrating. This kind of generativity, sometimes called *poiesis*, from a Greek term meaning to make or do, has been variously understood as poetic creativity bringing about transformation or as the production of something that transcends and may outlive the individual. We often focus on the biologically generative aspect of sex – that is, procreation – without recognizing that single, celibate, infertile and voluntarily childless people also create and that many people experience their creative interactions with the world as a sense of unity and wholeness that echoes the sense of unity generated in sexual relationship even if they are never genitally active with others.

3 Sexed persons are **relational**. Our sexed bodies are places of meeting with God and others. Sex therefore cannot be written out or divided from either our relationship with God, which is prior, or those with others, which are secondary. In the context of our relationship with God, it matters *that* we are sexed (as something irreducible to being human) but not *how* we are sexed. In our relationships with others the specificities of our sex are more relevant but still not the primary or most irreducible locus of our selfhood. Physical sexual intimacy is one kind of relationality but sexedness travels with us in all our relationships, even those with the vast majority of people with whom we will never have any genital or romantic relationship. Our status as sexed reminds us of our predisposition for relationship and our irreducible interconnection with the world. Desire is not alien to true humanity but something that drives us to seek out relationship.

4 Sexed persons are **unities of body, soul and spirit**. Sexuality permeates our physical sensations and desires but also our emotions, proclivities and spiritualities. Bodies require adequate nutrition, sleep, rest and care in order to function well; sexuality benefits directly from such care but may also benefit from its own specific 'maintenance', such as attention to how well we are integrating our sexed selves with our publicly projected identities. Faithfulness to our sex means faithfulness to our inner selves, acknowledgement that we are spiritual and ensouled creatures who do not exist as

bodies alone, and whose bodily actions affect our emotional and spiritual lives.

5 Sexed persons are **concrete**, situated in time and space, with relationships to human societies, economies, networks and structures, and extra-human ecosystems. Being faithful to our sex also means being responsible for what we do with it and the ways it impacts on other people and the non-human world. Using our sex exploitatively, destructively, humiliatingly and hurtfully is an abuse of its power.

6 Sexed persons are often **worshipping** persons, whose interactions with their communities of faith take place in the same bodies that feel, yearn, masturbate, make love and give birth. Each member of a community of faith brings to worship a unique and individual sexed body, meeting God and others in it. Being faithful to our sex means continuing to be open to the revelation of what bodily specificity means here, now, for this community.

7 Sexed persons are **damaged** persons, whose sexualities and desires are affected by the results of living among the debris of personal and structural sin. Sexuality is powerful and life-giving but also vulnerable. Persons who have been damaged invariably damage others; being faithful to our sex therefore means being aware of the ways our own hurts and wounds in this area may dispose us to inflict hurt on others. It also means putting appropriate measures in place to protect ourselves from further damage, which will mean nurturing healthy self-esteem, the confidence to refuse undesired intimate relationships and committing to work through events from our pasts in order to minimize the harm they may bring to our present and future relationships.

8 Sexed persons are **animals**, mammals whose sexes involve tissues, organs, hormones and sensate flesh. As animals we are capable of sustaining physical harm; being faithful to the animality of our sex means acknowledging the fragility of our bodily boundaries. Our sexes are affected by our chemical environments and our sexual activities may have implications for other aspects of our animal materiality (e.g. exposure to infection, genital rupture or other damage, the possibility of pregnancy). As animals, sex permeates multiple aspects of our embodiment and is not located in genitals alone. As animals, our bodies also decay and die. Faithfulness to our sex means due attention to how sex, sexuality and self-identity may change as we age and perish, and what this means for how we relate to God and others.

9 Sexed persons are often, and frequently, **non-sexual**. Being sexed only somewhat rarely entails being biologically reproductive or engaging in genital sexual activity. Sexuality may be understood as energy and creativity but there is also a sense in which many of our relationships are, in a narrower sense, appropriately non-sexual ones. Faithfulness to sex sometimes means allowing sex to exist in the background of our everyday lives, present and integrated but not shouting for attention, with an acknowledgement that it is often less relevant than most other aspects of our physicality, which are shared with all humans regardless of sex.

10 Sexed persons are **enchanting**, worthy of joy and celebration and capable of appreciating the value and wonder of others. Sexual relationship is one way we can communicate to others that they are joyous and delightful and come to understand that we too are prized, astonishing, marvellous persons. Rowan Williams calls this 'the body's grace', since desiring and being desired by another person in sexual relationship can help us to appreciate a little of what it is to desire and be desired by God (Williams 2002). But God's delight in humans exists 'just because', regardless of whether we discover this grace through sexuality for ourselves.

Conclusion

If theologies of sex in marriage focus mainly or solely on sexual intercourse as potentially reproductive, and the male or female sex of the individual as the primary locus of personhood and seat of gendered identity, then a wealth of other aspects of our sexuate status is erased. As I have shown in this chapter, there are a variety of reasons why the sex or gender of the partners in a marriage is not necessarily the best way to determine whether this marriage is licit, optimal or a means of mediating grace. Sex and gender are callings just as marriages are, and the spouses' distinctiveness and difference from each other is not most reliably, consistently or profoundly marked by their having different sexes or genders.

For this reason, I have suggested, the fruitfulness and fecundity that any marriage has must be understood more broadly than in a strictly biological or procreative way. And if reproduction is relativized, then so is sex. Crucially, this does not make sex unimportant: indeed, as I have shown, it is in and through sexed bodies that we live and work out our relationships to God and the world. But it does mean that some of the *meanings* ascribed to sex in theological contexts might bear further questioning. If sex does not inevitably need to 'mean' reproduction, male initiation and female response or particular gender roles, then sex might be freed up to 'mean' other things or to 'mean' more broadly. By allowing sex not to be shorthand for a whole range of other things, sex might be understood more broadly as the creative, generative embodiment we all share, regardless of whether we have genital sexual relationships, who we have them with or whether children result. In this way the significance of human sex for marriage will be understood as a broader significance for human relationality in general, but with an acknowledgement that aspects of a specific marital relationship and commitment may allow for the further blossoming of sex in its fullness.

Mark D. Jordan, one of the most sophisticated contemporary writers in the area of sex, sexuality and theological ethics, has observed that Christian teachings on sex are always also to do with the exercise of power. Biblical texts on sex are occasions for divine instruction (Jordan 2002, p. 44): they do not so much impart it, as though the texts themselves had agency, as shine a torch on how moral truths are assembled and disseminated. Certain texts have become authoritative in Christian talk about sex not because of what they say but because of what they allow particular communities of Christians to say (2002, p. 46): 'Texts only have fleshly voices when we let them speak through ours – when we give them our attention in the present' (2002, p. 175). The Church has largely carried on as before in its pronouncements on sex, without recognizing the shift that has taken place, namely that both believers and non-believers now look elsewhere (including to the state) for their authority on sexual matters (2002, pp. 134–5). Christian theologians and ethicists now have to examine their own power and ask by what authority they speak (and why anyone should listen), after Christendom (2002, p. 146).

The Church's power may be waning but it still has authority in many areas: over its own clergy in how they may and may not conduct their sexual lives and, in some denominations, to what extent they are at liberty to celebrate and consecrate the relationships of others; over millions of ordinary people in contexts where the Church controls access to contraception, sex education, adequate health insurance and safe legal abortion; and ideologically, where the Church colludes with homophobia and misogyny and gives them a veneer of theological legitimacy rather than uprooting them and throwing their poisonous husks on to the fire. We have more work to do on what it means to be sexed human beings in relation to God and one another, and what this means for our institutions and social structures. What is clear is that being sexed is both a more irreducible and a more hazy aspect of being human than Christian theologies and pronouncements on sex have thus far been able to acknowledge.

References

Barth, Karl, 1961, *Church Dogmatics III/4: The Doctrine of Creation*, trans. A. T. Mackay et al., Edinburgh: T&T Clark.

Butler, Judith, 1990, *Gender Trouble: Feminism and the Subversion of Identity*, New York, NY: Routledge.

Catholic Bishops Conference of England and Wales, 2013, 'Statement on the Passing of the Marriage (Same Sex Couples) Act', www.catholic-ew.org.uk/Home/News/Marriage-Same-Sex-Couples-Act.

Central Board of Finance, 1988, *The Ordination of Women to the Priesthood: A Second Report by the House of Bishops of the General Synod of the Church of England*, London: General Synod of the Church of England.

Church of England, 2012, 'A Response to the Government Equalities Office Consultation – "Equal Civil Marriage" – from the Church of England', www.churchofengland.org/media/1475149/s-s%20marriage.pdf.

Coakley, Sarah, 2013, *God, Sexuality, and the Self: An Essay 'On the Trinity'*, Cambridge: Cambridge University Press.

Cornwall, Susannah, 2010, *Sex and Uncertainty in the Body of Christ: Intersex Conditions and Christian Theology*, London: Equinox.

Farley, Margaret, 2013, new edn, *Personal Commitments: Beginning, Keeping, Changing*, Maryknoll, NY: Orbis Books.

John Paul II (Pope), 1988, 'Mulieris Dignitatem (On the Dignity and Vocation of Women)', www.vatican.va/holy_father/john_paul_ii/apost_letters/documents/hf_jp-ii_apl_15081988_mulieris-dignitatem_en.html.

John Paul II (Pope), 2006, *Man and Woman He Created Them: A Theology of the Body*, Boston, MA: Pauline Books and Media.

Jordan, Mark D., 2002, *The Ethics of Sex*, Oxford: Blackwell.

Kärkkäinen, Veli-Matti, 2014, *Trinity and Revelation*, Grand Rapids, MI: Eerdmans.

Loughlin, Gerard, 2004, 'Sex After Natural Law', in Marcella Althaus-Reid and Lisa Isherwood (eds), *The Sexual Theologian: Essays on Sex, God and Politics*, London: T&T Clark, pp. 86–98.

Matzko McCarthy, David, 2004, *Sex and Love in the Home: A Theology of the Household*, London: SCM Press.

Paoletti, Jo, 2012, *Pink and Blue: Telling the Boys from the Girls in America*, Bloomington, IN: Indiana University Press.

Rogers, Eugene F., 2006, 'Trinity, Marriage, and Homosexuality', in Mark D. Jordan (ed.), *Authorizing Marriage? Canon, Tradition, and Critique in the Blessing of Same-Sex Unions*, Princeton, NJ: Princeton University Press, pp. 151–64.

Tanis, Justin, 2003, *Trans-Gendered: Theology, Ministry, and Communities of Faith*, Cleveland, OH: Pilgrim Press.

Ward, Keith, 1994, *Religion and Revelation: A Theology of Revelation in the World's Religions*, Oxford: Clarendon Press.

Williams, Rowan, 2002, 'The Body's Grace', in Eugene F. Rogers (ed.), *Theology and Sexuality: Classic and Contemporary Readings*, Oxford: Blackwell, pp. 309–21.

8

An Ascetical Critique of the Concept of 'Gender Complementarity'

RAPHAEL CADENHEAD

Introduction

In the previous chapter Susannah Cornwall persuasively challenged the definition of marriage as a sexually asymmetric union of 'man' and 'woman' – one of the major ripostes against 'gay marriage' (a term that ought to be used advisedly)[1] found in ecclesial pronouncements. Intersex persons, she argued, places a question mark next to the often unquestioned notion of 'binary sex' underpinning such a view. This in turn prompts us to reconsider whether biological complementarity should remain an integral part of the definition of marriage, given that sexual morphology is not always straightforwardly classifiable. Now, in this chapter, I want to consider the moral and spiritual demands attendant upon us as Christians to appropriate various sorts of gendered 'traits' in the virtuous life (generally) and in marriage (specifically), which will, as a secondary aim, challenge the very idea of gender complementarity. This is because recent expostulations against 'gay marriage' not only advance the view that men and women fit together in a genital way (a view whose crudity is rarely spelt out in terms of penile–vaginal penetration by those who subscribe to it), but it is also argued that a man and a woman, joined in holy matrimony, enjoy psychological or affective complementarity: generic traits differentially associated with men and women are said to be congruent with each other in a way that can never be authentically reproduced in the case of two men or two

---

1 The term suggests a difference in species between heterosexual marriage and 'gay' marriage, whereas the argument I wish to advance here is that no categorical distinction can be made between the two: the moral and spiritual challenges remain the same in both. At issue is not whether 'gay' marriage is morally and theologically permissible, I would argue, but whether marriage should in any way be defined according to a certain configuration of sexual morphology.

women (see e.g. Milbank 2012; Gagnon 2001; Wannenwetsch 2000). There are, it seems, two sets of characteristics that readily combine to form a mutually appropriate union: affectionate, intuitive, sensitive, nurturing women are regarded as natural complements to independent, competitive, tough-skinned, rational men.[2] By contrast, two men or two women (perhaps, even more deplorably from this perspective, two intersex or transgender persons) represent a kind of deformed mimicry of a complementary conjugal pattern embedded by God in the affective fabric of humanity.

In this chapter, I want to develop an altogether different kind of conversation around gender and I wish to do so from a surprising perspective, retrieving the ascetical doctrine of a Church Father from the late fourth century, Gregory of Nyssa (c.335–c.395) and his influential ascetic sister, Macrina the Younger (c.330–79). What a most peculiar place to start, some may wonder! Can any good come from the fourth century (to echo Nathaniel's words to Philip in John 1.46)? Indeed, what value can we place on ascetical writings of late antiquity that secular modern sensibilities have regarded for some time now as backward, even repressive? I invite you to withhold judgement for a moment and join me in re-charting territory that has been almost entirely overlooked in contemporary ecclesial and secular discussions on the contentious issues of marriage, gender and sexuality.

The journey begins with that most elemental relationship of all: between humans and God. By exploring Gregory's commentary works we will see how progress in the spiritual life requires us at different moments in spiritual ascent to adopt different gendered postures towards God in prayer. Then we will consider how an individual's moral growth is predicated on gendered transformation. The unending process of moral maturation, we will discover, is possible only through a person's graced capacity to appropriate the full array of virtues over time, whether stereotypically 'masculine' or 'feminine'.

The thesis of this chapter is that the insights of Gregory of Nyssa into personal moral growth and spiritual maturation provide some novel overarching considerations that lead us to regard marriage as an ascetic undertaking in its own right – an ascetic undertaking that overcomes rather than concretizes differentiations in masculinity and femininity, and that therefore places 'gender complementary' in some difficulty as a helpful (or even ethical) concept. The problem with contemporary

---

2 Proponents of 'gender complementarity' include the former Pope in e.g. Wojtyła 2006 [1986] and John Paul II 2006 [1986]; Schumacher 2004; and Allen 2006.

ecclesial discussions on 'gay marriage', as I see it, is that both sides of the debate are so caught up in apologetics that 'sexual ethics' gets reduced to crass adjudications of genital acts, homosexual or hetero-sexual – with questions of gender brought in as an aside, without much thought given to gender's purpose outside genital interactions. This approach distorts and truncates the depth of debate that could be had on the transformative capacity of human erotic intimacy. What is miss-ing, therefore, is a sophisticated and theologically robust understanding of erotic transformation that, as I shall show here, is inexorably linked to the *gendered* practices of contemplative prayer and virtue (both in celibacy and – I shall argue – in marriage).

Before making any headway with the substance of my argument, it is important to clarify some of the terms of the ensuing discussion. In the first instance, the word 'asceticism' (from the Greek, *askesis*, meaning 'practice' or 'training') tends today to conjure up the image of a hermit who performs flamboyant acts of self-mortification in order to restrain unruly sexual passions. Gregory himself does not ever use the substan-tive *askesis* or the verb *askein* with any technical precision or specificity, and prefers instead to speak of 'the life of virtue', 'the perfect life', 'the disciplined life' or 'self-control'. What is more, Gregory adopts somewhat of an integrationist ethic in which the bodily disciplines of the ascetic life (fasting, sexual self-restraint, giving away unnecessary material possessions) are reciprocally interdependent. Asceticism is not, in other words, just about sex. It encompasses a whole approach to life itself that separates greed from need and replaces self-indulgence with service to the poor and to God. While Gregory's ascetical project aims at reorientating *eros* towards its true goal in Christ, ostensibly non-sexual ascetical practices, such as fasting and the renunciation of wealth, help no end with this endeavour. All the virtues are therefore intended to work in concert to facilitate an individual's progress in the moral life, however strange this may at first seem to contemporary ethical sensibilities.

This leads me to issue a second clarification: for Gregory, married persons are able to reach the spiritual and moral goals of the 'virginal life', as he so often calls it, by moderating their sexual appetites and embracing a life of prayer and spiritual devotion. The ascetic life, there-fore, is not a purely solitary endeavour or one necessarily requiring complete sexual abstention. In fact Gregory at one point in his treatise *De virginitate* (*On Virginity*) condemns celibates who are 'unsociable and brutish' because they fail to acknowledge 'the command of love' and have no knowledge of 'the fruit of long-suffering and humility' (*De virginitate* XXIII:3:25–8; Callahan 1999, p. 71). As such, Gregory's deliberations on the ascetic life undercut the conjugal–celibate divide and provide moral insight into both states of life.

Third – and finally – Gregory takes for granted a number of late antique stereotypes about masculinity and femininity, and does not make the political or intellectual manoeuvres that defined the feminist movement of the mid-twentieth century. While a discussion of Gregory's views of gender as such has been a source of immense interest among scholars, my overriding interest here is what Gregory *does* with those gender stereotypes in his theorizations of spiritual and moral maturation. As we will soon see, he does not regard them as concrete absolutes, but labile (i.e. easily altered) characteristics that are open to divine transformation. For the purposes of clarity I have provided a list of Gregory's stereotypical assumptions about gender in the table below:

	Masculinity	*Femininity*
Positive (Moral/ Spiritual) Traits	The steadfast practice of virtue.	Passion (of an ascetically transformed variety); eternal longing for the divine; outpouring of devotion for God in prayer.
	Rational restraint of worldly passions.	
Negative (Sinful) Traits	Excessive sexual drive, especially during one's youth.	A predilection towards jealousy.
		A willingness to be swayed by capricious passions.

With all these definitions and clarifications held firmly in mind, let us now embark upon the first stage of our journey by considering the soul's erotic relationship with God in which gender, for Gregory, plays an important though in contemporary discussion often overlooked role.

Intimacy with God: Shifts in Gendered Identification

Throughout his many writings Gregory of Nyssa consistently portrays the soul's relationship with God in gendered terms, as a conjugal relationship, and insists that different stages of spiritual maturity require us to relate to God differently. Gregory's first port of call in this regard is the so-called Solomonic Corpus.

Following Origen, and before Origen a whole gamut of rabbinic literature, Gregory arranges the books traditionally attributed to Solomon in order of spiritual sophistication to correspond to the steps that the soul needs to take to advance in the spiritual life: Proverbs first, then Ecclesiastes and then – for the spiritually mature – the Song of Songs. A Christian would be expected to gain instruction from the first book in the series then move onwards through prayer and ascetic discipline to the second book and then the third. Intimacy with the divine, for Gregory and indeed many Christians at this time, was thought to require patience in prayer and ongoing moral discipline; it was not something that could be instantly acquired through pure confession of belief.

In some of his commentary works on Ecclesiastes and the Song of Songs, Gregory is alerted to (what comes across to the modern mind as) a rather curious phenomenon: the gendered object of the soul's desires (whether God or Christ) changes in the course of spiritual ascent; so too does the soul's gender. For instance, Gregory observes that in the book of Proverbs the audience is regularly referred to as 'son', which suggests that its moral teaching is designed for more spiritually immature readers. From this, Gregory concludes that the Book of Proverbs elicits human desires for Wisdom (*Sophia* – a feminine noun) in order to persuade the soul to pursue a life of virtue: the 'son', therefore, courts (female) Wisdom, who is rather paradoxically the (male) Christ (1 Cor. 1.24). As immature Christians learn how to live an upright life, putting their former recalcitrant ways behind them, the erotic relationship between 'son' and Wisdom must eventually be relinquished in light of something better.

Discussing what happens when a Christian progresses from Proverbs to the Song of Songs (with Ecclesiastes belonging in the same category as Proverbs), Gregory remarks: 'The one who is called "son" in Proverbs is here called "bride" and Wisdom, correspondingly, is transferred into the role of bridegroom. This is to assure that the human person, once separated from the bridegroom, might be betrothed to God as a holy virgin' (*Gregorii Nysseni Opera* VI 23:1–4; Norris 2012, p. 25). For Gregory, therefore, the Song of Songs compels spiritually advanced Christians to align themselves with the Virgin Bride whose intense erotic desires for the incorruptible Bridegroom are stereotypically 'feminine'. The soul's identity as 'son', therefore, is ultimately displaced by a 'female' identity (the Virgin Bride of Christ); concomitantly, Christ who was Wisdom now becomes 'male', the incorruptible Bridegroom.

Despite these shifts in gendered identity, the imagery here is consistently 'heterosexual' (to use an anachronistic term). It will come as no surprise that we will find no ringing endorsement of 'homosexuality' (so-called) in late antique Christian texts. Nonetheless the implications of what Gregory is saying here are, for our present purposes, quite considerable. Rather than residing in one gender or another, the soul is required to take up and then relinquish various gendered identities: all Christians, whether 'male' or 'female', must be a 'son' first before later becoming the Virgin Bride. The theological backcloth for these progressive displacements of gender is the doctrine of the *imago Dei* ('image of God'): the soul has no fixed gender just as God is not male or female – a point Gregory is frequently wont to make throughout his life on the basis of Galatians 3.28 ('there is no longer male and female ... in Christ Jesus'). Without the restraints of gender to impede the trans-actional spiritual processes between humans and God, the soul is freed up to interact with God with a more expansive erotic repertoire. The end-point of the spiritual life is paradoxically unending. When the soul identifies with the Virgin Bride there are no further shifts in spiritual gender, yet the bride's desires are constantly augmenting and straining forward towards perfection (Phil. 3.13).

So to sum up: desiring a God who transcends male and female (and all their cultural gendered associations) necessitates the taking up of various gender identities that are progressively displaced as the soul makes advancements in the spiritual life. But so far we have spoken only of a kind of *spiritual* gender – what are we to make of the role and worth of gender in the realm of human relationships? There is, as we will now go on to see, considerable overlap between the spiritual life and the moral life: in both, maturity is characterized by flexibility in gender. So let us turn to consider what happens to the soul's gender for Gregory in the process of moral maturation.

Moral Maturation: The Joint Acquisition of Masculine and Feminine Virtues

While Gregory does not summon Christians to abandon gendered stereotypes because they recapitulate the sins of cultural patriarchy (he is not, in this respect, a 'proto-feminist' of any sort), he does develop a sophisticated vision of moral growth that calls on Christians to appro-priate the manifold variety of virtues, whether stereotypically associated with femininity or masculinity, in the pursuit of moral perfection. Two ascetics, Gregory's siblings, managed this feat without succumbing to hubris: Macrina the Younger managed to combine within herself the positive moral and spiritual traits of masculinity and femininity, and

Gregory's brother, Naucratius (whom I shall discuss only briefly) abandoned sinful stereotypical masculinity in the pursuit of virtue.

With regard to Macrina, Gregory at one point seriously questions whether she can still strictly speaking be identified as a 'woman' since she has surpassed her 'nature' (*Vita Sanctae Macrinae* (*Life of St Macrina*) 1:14–17; Silvas 2008, p. 110). He is not here querying her sexed morphology. She was assuredly 'female' in that respect. So if not physically, in what other ways specifically did Macrina surpass her 'nature' as a woman? She did so, I wish to argue here, in three ways: by abandoning all the negative stereotypes of femininity; by transforming worldly feminine traits into spiritual ones; and by taking on board certain positive masculine traits.

In the first instance, Macrina eschews 'the tragic passions – those passions of women' (*Vita Sanctae Macrinae* 3:10–11; Silvas 2008, p. 113) that characterized the literature of the curriculum of classical pedagogy.[3] Macrina preferred instead to devote herself to the reading of the Psalter. Gregory goes to considerable lengths to admonish feminine passion throughout his works and he does so primarily through the lens of grief. This is possibly because grief was regarded by the Stoics as a kind of effeminacy (Cobb 2008, pp. 62–3),[4] and one of the four hardest passions to convert into virtue (Dillon 1983). Xanthippe's weeping, for example, to which men would also succumb, is characterized as feminine in Plato's *Phaedo* (*On the Soul*) (60a; 117d). Therefore just as Macrina dies, Gregory upbraids the virgins for their outpouring of grief and 'disorder', urging them instead to '[l]ook at [Macrina], and remember her instructions, by which she taught [them] to be orderly and seemly at all times'. Excessive outpourings of grief were, in Gregory's time, culturally associated with femininity; for this reason he is determined to show that Macrina overcame such tendencies, which he thought to be linked to worldly distrust in the resurrection, through her resolute faith in God's providence and enduring love.

Another way Macrina overcame her female nature was by adopting spiritually transformed feminine traits otherwise associated with fleshly maternal qualities. She became, for instance, 'a mother in place of [a] mother' (*Epitula* XIV:6:1–2; Silvas 2008, p. 176) to those in her family and especially to Gregory (*Epitula* X:10; Silvas 2008, p. 178) when Emmelia, their mother, died in late 370 or early 371 (Silvas 2007, p. 27). Macrina was also a mother to her own ascetic community at

---

3 It is worth noting Socrates' critique of passionate excess in the Homeric myths of traditional pedagogy. See *Respublica* 377d; 377e; 378b; 379d–e; 386b–387b.

4 For Stoic reactions to the weeping of Odysseus, see Frank 2000, pp. 527–28.

Pontus (*Epitula* XIX:7:2–3; Silvas 2007, pp. 176–7) and identified on her death bed with the Virgin Bride of Christ (*Vita Sanctae Macrinae* 23:2–7; Silvas 2008, p. 133).

A third way Macrina overcame her female nature was by adopting a variety of moral and spiritual masculine roles. She is, for instance, characterized as a 'teacher' (*didaskalos*) (*Epitula* XIX:6:1; Silvas 2007, p. 176), which in Greek has a male title juxtaposed with the feminine definite article. Macrina also acted not only as a spiritual 'mother' to Peter but also as his spiritual 'father' (Silvas 2007, p. 122).

There is, in all this, a twofold appropriation: all that is morally and spiritually redeeming about femininity and masculinity is taken on board by Macrina. But those of us sensitized to feminist values may come to regard Gregory's descriptions of Macrina as generally more negative towards femininity than masculinity. Even the feminine traits she appropriates are transformed from their worldly (stereotypical) associations into superior spiritual characteristics; what is more, there is no evidence that Macrina had to reject negative masculine traits in order to advance in the life of virtue. There is, however, some indication from Gregory that masculine characteristics *do* need to be disavowed; but it is nestled in his account of the life of his brother, Naucratius.

Gregory's admiration of Naucratius stems from the fact that the latter abandoned 'the distractions that come from either military service or the rhetoric of the law courts' as well as 'the din that commonly besets this human life' in order to minister to the elderly people who lived together in poverty and infirmity in the hinterland of society. Naucratius is also described by Gregory as 'taming his own youth … by [ascetical] exercises … subduing his youth both by his toils and by his diligence on his mother's behalf' (*Vita Sanctae Macrinae* 8:17–34; Silvas 2008, p. 119). Throughout Gregory's works the vigour and strength of young men are frequently associated with masculine sexual virility of a sinful, excessive sort. As such, the implication of the *Vita Sanctae Macrinae* – read in the context of Gregory's writings as a whole – seems to be that Naucratius successfully overcame masculine sexual excess by 'subduing his youth' in order to pursue the life of virtue. The stereotypical associations of masculinity, therefore, are not unequivocally positive in Gregory's eyes. They too are tainted by sin and need to be restrained through ascetic discipline to make progress in the moral life.

While Gregory is not a systematic thinker, it is possible, I believe, to join the dots of his thinking on moral maturation. What emerges from his musings is a firm requirement for both 'male' and 'female' ascetics to appropriate and combine the spiritually and morally positive stereotypes of femininity and masculinity, while also rejecting all that is sinful about both. While Gregory does not say this so plainly, the suggestion is clearly that men and women must reject (masculine) sexual excess as well as (feminine) yielding to passion to have any chance of growing in moral stature.

Gregory was thinking primarily of ascetics when developing his doctrine of moral maturation – and he did so, I believe, because of what the ascetic life meant to him in eschatological terms. For him, the ascetic's disavowal of marriage anticipated the life to come in which, as Christ says, human beings will neither marry nor be taken in marriage because we will be 'like the angels' (Matt. 22.30 and parallels). The angelic, 'spiritual' (1 Cor. 15.44) body of the ascetic, completely disentangled from sexual interactions, anticipates the *eschaton* when, for Gregory – following the lead of Galatians 3.28 ('there is no longer male and female ... in Christ Jesus') – the body will no longer be marked by physical sexual differentiation. Gregory's line of argument in this respect can be followed in one of his most famous doctrinal works, the *De hominis opificio* (*On the Making of Humankind*).

The procreative function, Gregory says, belongs not to 'the Divine' but to 'the irrational element' since (or so he reasons) the words 'increase and multiply' (Gen. 1.28) were also used in reference to the irrational creatures (Gen. 1.22). For this reason the 'animal' and 'irrational' form of reproduction 'befits those who had fallen into sin' (*De hominis opificio* XVII:4 PG 189:41–6; NPNF II/5, p. 756); humanity's 'community and kindred with the irrational' is therefore a 'provision for reproduction' (*De hominis opificio* XVII:9 PG 181:40–1; NPNF II/5, p. 752). 'Added' to humanity without relation to time (*De hominis opificio* XVI:18 PG 44 185:53–5; NPNF II/5, p. 754), the procreative faculties guaranteed that 'the multitude of human souls might not be cut short by its fall from the mode by which the angels were increased and multiplied' (*De hominis opificio* XVII:4 PG 189:39–40; NPNF II/5, p. 756). To these protological remarks (concerning human origins), Gregory adds an eschatological point (concerning human destiny) of great importance. The second creation, Gregory says, is manifestly 'a departure from the Prototype'; that is, Jesus Christ, for whom there is 'no longer male and female' (Gal. 3.28; cf. *De hominis opificio* XVI:7 PG 44 181:13–15; NPNF II/5, p. 751). We thus witness here the outworking of Origen's equation of protology and eschatology: the resurrection, therefore, is the 'restoration' (*apokatastasis*) of the first creation, which is in Gregory's mind atemporal (independent of time) and unsexed.

Seen within the arc of creation and resurrection, the ascetic's labile gender characteristics are therefore a prefiguring of a labile resurrected bodily form that is neither male nor female. As I mentioned at the outset, Gregory's ascetic doctrine is not restricted to celibates living in monastic communities. What is not so clear in Gregory's writings, however, is how the lability of gender can be wrought in the conjugal life. After all, Christian wives and husbands would have been compelled – by late antique cultural standards if not by Paul's injunctions – to adopt certain sexual and domestic roles in marriage, primarily governed by notions of (feminine) passivity and (masculine) activity. Gregory says precious little on this topic, perhaps because he thought the gendered dynamics of passivity and activity was somehow unavoidable; perhaps the ascetic, in Gregory's mind, was closest to imitating the divine life, and married persons, while very close, lagged inevitably ever so slightly behind.

The purpose for the rest of this chapter is to draw together the threads of Gregory's ascetic doctrine and offer some speculative thoughts as to how these ideas might open up a different sort of conversation about the role of gender in marriage.

The Ascetic Revival of Marriage

My proposal here, which extends Gregory's theorization of the ascetic life, is that Galatians 3.28 can be realized ascetically in the conjugal life.

The first indication of this may be drawn – perhaps rather unexpectedly – from the imagery of the second creation narrative in Genesis, which is frequently referenced in contemporary ecclesial pronouncements against 'gay marriage' to support the view that gender and biological complementarity belongs intrinsically to the nature of marriage. According to that narrative, God creates Eve out of Adam as a discrete individual so that they can both come together again in the conjugal life; as Christ himself puts it, 'they are no longer two, but one flesh' (Matt. 19.6). This reunification of sexually differentiated bodies refers perhaps primarily to sexual consummation, but it may also be read – within a gendered frame – as an indication of the conjugal *telos* of gender. The purpose of the conjugal life is, in this light, regarded as the at-one-ment of gender differentiation, not its reinstatement or re-entrenchment. This is not to say, as with ascetics, that gender traits are eradicated, but it opens them up to being refashioned so that all their sinful associations can be rejected by the disciplined life. Or – to put it differently – with Christ comes the transformative option that marriage might conquer headship and the fallen stereotypes attributed to masculinity and femininity that have marred erotic relations since the Fall. As such we may then regard 'one flesh' as a hard-won moral goal, not a de facto reality. The conjugal life orientates itself towards the progressive displacement of fixed gendered difference. This now raises the question of *how*, which brings us to the very heart of Gregory's ascetic doctrine.

As stated in the introduction to this chapter, the process of moral maturation, for Gregory, is stunted by fissiparous (i.e. tribalist) forms of individualism. He singles out for particular condemnation a rather self-righteous group of celibates who intentionally cut themselves off from community life out of hubris, fearing its unwelcome exposure of moral faults. For Gregory, living in an ascetic community painfully reveals a person's moral weaknesses. By living beside those more advanced in the life of virtue, a person learns to emulate their example and grow with them towards greater moral rectitude and right living. Gregory regards the relationship between the older ascetic and the fledgling as a transformative central point in ascetic community. The purpose of this relationship is to prevent the enthusiastic younger ascetic from straying from the path of moderation. The older ascetic inducts the younger ascetic into the life of purity so that 'the dignity of this life is distributed by the one who has succeeded in it to those who come near to him' (*De virginitate* XXIII:5:13–14; Callahan 1999, p. 72).

Following this logic, marriage may be regarded as a kind of monastic community in its own right since it too provides countless opportunities for moral development. Each spouse holds up a mirror to the other, exposing their moral vulnerabilities and foibles through the inevitable repetitions of the domestic life. Seen through the eyes of a loving critic, the realization of moral weakness becomes not an opportunity for despair but a chance to grow and develop. Although marriages do not necessarily comprise the differentials in virtue that occur in ascetic communities between more advanced and less advanced celibates, each spouse will nonetheless tend to have greater mastery of certain virtues than the other and vice versa. As such, one spouse can impress upon the other the value of other virtues that the other has not yet mastered simply by living in community together. There is therefore a rich and dynamic sharing of moral strengths between spouses that resembles the kind of exchanges that Gregory cherishes in ascetic communities.

In light of this, the moral regimen of the conjugal life, arguably no less demanding than that of the celibate, is possible only if notions of gender fixity are cast aside in the manner that Gregory advocates. Masculine and feminine characteristics are either rejected or (re-)appropriated *solely on the basis of their moral and spiritual worth, not one's sexual morphology.* Restricting the full complement of virtues to only half (whether stereotypically masculine or feminine), I believe, restricts one's progress in the moral life and staves off criticism of perhaps the most sensitive parts of our moral identity. For this reason – and here is the rub – the notion of gender complementarity is ethically problematic because it summons individuals to hold on to a specific set of very limited virtues and refuses them the fullest opportunity to emulate the God who transcends the limitations of masculinity and femininity. The goal of the moral life is not, therefore, to become passively entrenched on one or other side of the 'gender' divide, clinging proudly to all that is stereotypically associated with masculinity or femininity. Its true goal is to embrace all that is morally beneficial in both and to reject all that is disordered in both.

This is not by any means to advocate a kind of homogenized androgyny in the moral life in which both spouses act and behave identically. On the contrary, the moral challenges that arise equally in ascetic communities and in the conjugal life provide an expansive vision of moral growth. If anything, it diversifies and widens the moral horizon, giving room for virtues that would otherwise be closed off to those who feel more comfortable acquiescing to restrictive and standardized cultural prescriptions of appropriate gender behaviour.

Conclusion

Gregory was not addressing the same dilemmas that we in the twenty-first century are confronted with, so any straightforward transposition of ideals from his era to ours must be met with some hesitation. For this reason, throughout this chapter I have purposefully avoided forms of patristic triumphalism, seeking instead to retrieve Gregory's ascetic doctrine in such a way as to generate new types of conversations around the contentious issue of gender.

In this respect Gregory's writings have provided fascinating conceptual scaffolding for a rich discussion of desire in its various manifestations. I have shown that, for Gregory, the ascetic's graced capacity to overcome the limitations of the fixed stereotypical traits of masculinity and femininity is wrought through a set of progressive displacements. To put it simply: the moral goal is the full appropriation of the virtues, regardless of their associations with gender; the spiritual goal is ever-increasing erotic intimacy with God, which takes on different gender interactions at different stages of maturity in one's prayer life.

In closing, I have sought to argue that the conjugal life itself should be regarded as an ascetic undertaking based not on 'gender complementarity' but a mutual willingness from both spouses to regard the other as a moral instructor in the life of virtue. It does not matter, therefore, whether two men, two women or one of each sex marry. To fixate on this distracts us from the more pressing summons to moral transformation that is almost entirely missing from contemporary discussions on 'gay marriage'. The key challenge in both celibacy and marriage is opening human erotic desire up to the rich possibility of divine refashioning so that its transformative potential may at last be released from the fallen, worldly associations of masculinity and femininity.

References

NPNF II/5 refers to the pagination of Philip Schaff (ed.), 1892, *Gregory of Nyssa: Dogmatic Treatises, etc.: A Select Library of the Nicene and Post-Nicene Fathers of the Christian Church, Second Series*, vol. 5, trans William Moore and Henry Austin Wilson, Grand Rapids, MI: Christian Classics Ethereal Library; New York: Christian Literature Publishing Co.; a pdf is available at www.ccel.org/ccel/schaff/npnf205.pdf.

Allen, Prudence, 2006, 'Man–Woman Complementarity: The Catholic Inspiration', *Logos: A Journal of Catholic Thought and Culture* 9.3, pp. 87–108.

Callahan, Virginia Woods (trans.), 1999 [1967], *Saint Gregory of Nyssa: Ascetical Works*, Washington, DC: Howard University.

Cobb, Stephanie L., 2008, *Dying to be Men: Gender and Language in Early Christian Martyr Texts*, New York; Chichester: Columbia University Press.

Dillon, John M., 1983, '*Metriopatheia* and *Apatheia*: Some Reflections on a Controversy in Later Greek Ethics', in *Essays in Ancient Philosophy: Volume II*, Albany, NY: State University of Albany Press, pp. 508–17.

Frank, Georgia, 2000, 'Macrina's Scar: Homeric Allusion and Heroic Identity in Gregory of Nyssa's *Life of Macrina*', *Journal of Early Christian Studies* 8.4, pp. 511–30.

Gagnon, Robert A. J., 2001, *The Bible and Homosexual Practice: Texts and Hermeneutics*, Nashville, TN: Abingdon Press.

John Paul II (Pope), 2006 [1986], *Man and Woman He Created Them: A Theology of the Body*, Boston, MA: Pauline Books & Media.

Milbank, John, 2012, 'Gay Marriage and the future of human sexuality', *ABC: Religion and Ethics*, 13 March 2012, www.abc.net.au/religion/articles/2012/03/13/3452229.htm.

Norris, Richard A., 2012, *Gregory of Nyssa: Homilies on the Song of Songs*, Atlanta, GA: Society of Biblical Literature.

Schumacher, Michele M., 2004, 'The nature of nature of feminism, old and new: from dualism to complementary unity', in Michele M. Schumacher (ed.), *Women in Christ: Toward a New Feminism*, Grand Rapids, MI: Eerdmans, pp. 17–51.

Silvas, Anna M. (trans.), 2007, *Gregory of Nyssa: The Letters. Introduction, Translation and Commentary*, Leiden: Brill.

Silvas, Anna M. (trans.), 2008, *Macrina the Younger: Philosopher of God*, Turnhout: Brepols.

Wannenwetsch, Bernd, 2000, 'Old Docetism—New Moralism? Questioning a New Direction in the Homosexuality Debate', *Modern Theology* 16.3, pp. 353–64.

Wojtyła, Karol, 2006 [1986], *Love and Responsibility*, London: Collins.

9

Called to Become ... A Vocational Theology of Marriage

JOHN P. BRADBURY

Christian Theology and the Problem of a Theology of Marriage

That there is a Christian theology of marriage is more of a presumption than a reality. That church buildings are the places in Western society where marriages have traditionally been contracted, in the presence of the clergy, makes it a perfectly reasonable assumption that there must be such a thing as a theology of marriage. The reality is that it is rather less obvious than we might presume. First, it presumes that marriage is a 'thing' about which one can have a theology, but as is well illustrated elsewhere in this volume (as in Charlotte Methuen's chapter), marriage has not had a single static definition over time. What is the 'thing' about which we are seeking to develop a theology? Second, while Christians marry, and do so in the context of the Church, and in some traditions this is even considered a sacrament of the Church, plenty of folk who are not Christian get married too. Are we trying to develop a theology of Christian marriage (i.e. a theology of the marriage of two Christians to one another), or a Christian theology of marriage as it happens legally or religiously in all global and religious contexts? It is all too often assumed that a particular Christian understanding of marriage must consist of a universal truth claim that is then embedded in social and legal structures. Is this actually so? The case is perhaps most easily understood with reference to other faiths. Does Christian theology expect a specifically Christian theology of marriage to speak also for a Muslim marriage, say? Or does a Christian theology of marriage make more restricted claims about marriage that concern the institution of marriage within specifically Christian communities?

The question about exactly what a Christian theology of marriage is has recently become far more focused in many Western countries through the introduction of same-sex marriage. In many places Christian churches need to determine whether or not they will conduct these marriages. Many (but not all) churches effectively define marriage differently from the way the state defines it. While churches may want their particular definition of marriage to be the one defined in the public square through the law, by and large it is not. Which version of marriage are we attempting to develop a theology for? It is interesting to note that there are plenty of theologies of sexuality around but relatively few about marriage. Is it the case, perhaps, that secular changes in the understanding of marriage are forcing churches to sit up and think about their theology of marriage seriously? In the first instance this chapter seeks to think through the theology of marriage, from within and for the Christian community of the Church. There are moments, however, where to do this, Christian truth claims about life in the world and God's ways with the world more universally come into play.

Bridegroom and Bride Imagery in Christian Scripture

One biblical understanding that might prove fruitful to our theological endeavour is the fact that, at various points in Scripture, God is described as the 'bridegroom', as is Christ – the 'brides' being the people of Israel and the Church. At first we might recoil from the idea that a human practice of marriage might root itself in the being of God. At first glance we might think that this runs the danger of elevating marriage to such a lofty divine conception that it would be almost useless in the development of a human understanding of marriage that functions within the daily life of the world. But as one stops and contemplates this idea, perhaps one might conclude that it may actually function the other way around. One of the problems that faces any theology of marriage is the temptation to idealize, or even perhaps idolize marriage in the face of the reality that many marriages are broken, abusive and the very opposite of the ideal. In Scripture the brokenness of marriage perhaps comes through even more strongly precisely in the failure of Israel and the Church to be true, faithful and chaste in the marriage to God. Another problematic issue surrounding a theology of marriage is that of gender, which is explored in depth in other chapters of this book (especially that by Raphael Cadenhead). The idea of God or Christ being the bridegroom and Israel and the Church being the bride unsettles our categories of gender. Brides in this metaphor are both female and male.

In the Hebrew Bible prophetic material, the idea of God's marriage to the people Israel mirrors the language of God's covenant with Israel. Seock-Tae Sohn, in his work on the metaphor of marriage, points out the way the marriage formula 'I will be your husband and you will be my wife' is mirrored in the covenant formula 'I will be your God and you will be my people' (Sohn 2002, pp. 44–5). There are various examples in the prophetic literature of the use of the imagery of bridegroom and bride; for example, in Hosea 1—3, Jeremiah 2—3 and Ezekiel 16 and 23.

The first three chapters of Hosea comprise an account of God's command to Hosea to take a wife, Gomer, who is a 'wife of whoredom' (Hos. 1.2–3). This marriage then functions in the text as a parallel to the 'marriage' between YHWH (God) and Israel. The children of Hosea's marriage are given names by God symbolizing the way God will relate to Israel in punishment for their turning away from God. The covenant formula gets inverted ('for you are not my people and I am not your God'), closely followed by the seemingly contradictory claim, which also mixes the metaphors, that 'Yet the number of the people of Israel shall be like the sand of the sea, which can be neither measured nor numbered; and in the place where it was said to them "You are not my people", it shall be said to them, "Children of the living God".' Hosea 2 then offers an extended poetic metaphor of the faithlessness of the wife Israel to her husband, YHWH, and reflecting Israel's confusion over where her good had come from. Despite her faithlessness, YHWH ultimately promises, 'I will take you for my wife in righteousness and in justice, in steadfast love, and in mercy. I will take you for my wife in faithfulness; and you shall know the LORD' (Hos. 2.19–20). This is then paralleled in chapter 3 with the command from YHWH to Hosea to return to Gomer and reclaim her despite her faithlessness. Sohn notes the way the language of covenant and the language of marriage are closely related. Speaking of the Hebrew word for 'faithless', he notes,

> This term is used for both marriage and covenants. In the context of marriage, it is used for the one who breaks the marriage relationship and begins a new relationship with another man. In the context of a covenant, the term is used for the one who has violated the covenantal obligations. (Sohn 2002, p. 93)

Marriage and covenant are clearly parallels for one another and function with the same theological logic. The logic recurs in Jeremiah, particularly in the context of the reflection on the 'new covenant' in chapter 31, where the new covenant is compared with the old. The new covenant is 'not ... like the covenant that I made with their ancestors ... that they broke, though I was their husband' (Jer. 31.32). God is the faithful one in this marriage; humanity, represented in the people Israel, is not the good, faithful marriage partner. This is no idealized or idolized account of marriage, rather one that in human terms is (possibly sadly) strikingly real in its brokenness.

If marriage is a parallel for the covenant between YHWH and the people Israel, then marriage, like the covenant, can be understood as being rooted in some understanding of 'call'. While covenants come in varying forms, unilateral and bilateral in origin, the covenant with Israel cannot be understood theologically other than as rooted in the call of Abraham. The account in Genesis offers no reason for the call of Abraham, and nothing is particularly known of him until the moment of his call. It is a call that brings both blessing for Abraham and the promise that 'in you all the families of the earth shall be blessed' (Gen. 12.3). This then forms the basis of the covenant between God and Abraham, Sarah and their descendants recounted in Genesis 17. The covenant is to bring blessings to those with whom it is made, but significantly also blessings to those outside of the immediate covenant relationship: the families of the earth. Extending the parallel a little further, it might also be interesting to note the observation of the Jewish theologian Michael Wyschogrod that 'the election of Israel is an election that does not exclude the flesh of this people' (Wyschogrod 1996, p. 33). The covenant is a bodily reality – it involves the physicality of human beings, just as marriage does. It would seem that the physical union of God and the people Israel, as they exist for that which is outside of themselves as well as for each other, offers a generative parallel to marriage as we seek after a theology of marriage.

Moving briefly to consider the New Testament, the language of Christ as the bridegroom points us towards some ideas and themes similar to those explored above. There are various direct or indirect moments within the New Testament that suggest that Christ is to be understood as a bridegroom (Matt. 9.15; Mark 2.19–20; Luke 5.34; John 2.1–12; 3.22–30; 2 Cor. 11.1–3; Eph. 5.22–33; Rev. 19.6–9). Perhaps most interesting for our present enquiry is the thought represented in Ephesians. The writer uses marriage as an image for understanding the relationship between Christ and the Church. There is again a sense of mixed metaphors, this time mingling marriage imagery with head and body imagery. We may find the conceptions of gender at play here difficult (and indeed, one might argue, inconsistent with Paul's understanding of being 'in Christ'), along with the hierarchy suggested between husband and wife. Being distracted by these issues possibly takes our attention away from the radical interplay the writer engages in between marriage imagery and head and body imagery. It is worth quoting Ephesians 5.22–33 in full:

> Wives, be subject to your husbands as you are to the Lord. For the husband is the head of the wife just as Christ is the head of the church, the body of which he is the Saviour. Just as the church is subject to Christ, so also wives ought to be, in everything, to their husbands.
> Husbands, love your wives, just as Christ loved the church and gave himself up for her, in order to make her holy by cleansing her with the washing of water by the word, so as to present the church to himself in splendour, without a spot or wrinkle or anything of the kind – yes, so that she may be holy and without blemish. In the same way, husbands should love their wives as they do their own bodies. He who loves his wife loves himself. For no one ever hates his own body, but he nourishes and tenderly cares for it, just as Christ does for the church, because we are members of his body. 'For this reason a man will leave his father and mother and be joined to his wife, and the two will become one flesh.' This is a great mystery, and I am applying it to Christ and the church. Each of you, however, should love his wife as himself, and a wife should respect her husband.

The parallel between marriage and Christ and the Church is striking, and extends even to the sexual act itself. There is the clear extension of the Pauline image of the body of Christ and union with Christ that is found in 1 Corinthians 6.15–17, where Paul speaks about the body of Christ being defiled if a member of the body is 'united with a prostitute'. The husband correlates with Christ and the wife with the Church, but at the same time, Christ is the head and the Church the body. The sexual act between husband and wife is directly applied to 'Christ and the church'. As Michael Tait notes, 'The images husband/wife, head/body are closely interwoven throughout this passage and used sometimes in a literal, sometimes in a metaphorical sense' (Tait 2010, p. 240). Earl Muller notes that 'Our relationship to the Lord is one of loving bodily union and the only significant image we have for that kind of relationship is sexual imagery' (Muller 1990, p. 147). We note here in passing the similarity between Wyschogrod's bodily understanding of the election of Israel and the very bodily imagery Paul uses for the Church.

In light of the above we can say that the primary category for understanding this marital imagery is actually ecclesiology. It is the Church as a social entity that is the bride. But the social entity of the Church contains a variety of different kinds of household within it. There are not just married people but single people too and folk living in a variety of different household combinations.[1]

Being Human: The Christian Understanding of the Person as Social

The Christian doctrine of creation is frequently misunderstood. Detractors of the faith seem intent on insisting that Christians read the six days of creation literally, meaning that if they can disprove this, then the whole of the Christian faith collapses. In reality the Christian doctrine of creation finds its significance in the understanding that God created *ex nihilo*, 'out of nothing'. All that there is is brought into being and sustained in being through the work of God. Without God there would simply be no being. While not a literal account of creation, the opening chapters of Genesis offer rich and fertile theological reflections on what it means to be human.

Within Genesis there are two different accounts of what it is to be human. In chapter 1, God speaks of creating humankind 'in our image, according to our likeness' (Gen. 1.26). The text goes on to say 'God created humankind in his image, in the image of God he created them, male and female he created them.' The question of what, precisely, the 'image' of God is is hotly debated. What is significant for us is that no individual human being alone can fully image God. Humankind, male and female, together image God. Alistair McFadyen proposes that the image may be understood as having two different dimensions. One is vertical, between created humans and the creator God: 'The implication of all this is that human beings cannot stand fully in the image of God by resting in themselves, but only by turning themselves outwards and upwards towards God' (McFadyen 1990, p. 22). The other dimension is horizontal and relational. Humans image the triune God by being persons in relationship, imaging the relationships present in the persons of the Trinity, as well as imaging God in the relationships between and within humanity. Regarding the image of God in God's work in creating humanity male and female:

---

1 I owe the insight that households are a vital unit when considering the relationship between marriage, singleness and ecclesiology to Bennett 2008.

The importance of the connection between human existence in God's image and gender distinction/gender relatedness cannot crudely be exhausted by any understanding of sexuality, marriage or family life. The paradigm's importance lies in the structure of distinction and relation in dialogical encounter which it contains. (McFadyen 1990, p. 38)

In other words, humans exist in relatedness with God and with other humans. Those relationships form us through communicative encounter with one another.

The second chapter of Genesis offers a different account of the creation of humans. This time God is recounted as saying, 'It is not good that the man should be alone; I will make him a helper as his partner' (Gen. 2.18). God then proceeds to make the animals and birds that are named by the man, but in none of those does the man find his helper and partner. God then creates woman from Adam's rib, in whom the man takes great delight. Again, here we see the sense that one human being alone is insufficient. We might also note in passing the way God leaves the choice of partner up to the created man. God offers many possibilities but it is only in the creation of the woman that the man finds his delight. Not only does God create human beings for relatedness, God also gives freedom to creatures to determine in whom they take delight and who should become their partners.

A recent seminal contribution to theological anthropology, the question of what it means in theological terms to be human, is David Kelsey's *Eccentric Existence* (2009) (by which he means, with 'eccentric', that which finds its origins outside of itself). He expresses a reservation about rooting theologies of creation and theological anthropology in these opening chapters of Genesis. He wishes to reserve the 'image' of God more exclusively to Christ. Christians, by virtue of being 'in Christ', 'image the image' of God (Kelsey 2009, pp. 1008ff.). He notes that there are three different ways God relates to humanity: God as God relating to humanity through creation; God relating to humanity through drawing them to eschatological fulfilment; God relating to humanity to reconcile humanity to God when humanity is estranged. For our purposes some of the claims he makes about how God relates to humanity as creator are the most significant.

Kelsey roots his theology of creation most firmly in the Wisdom literature rather than in Genesis. He finds a theology in the books of Proverbs, Ecclesiastes, Song of Solomon and Job concerned with the whole of creation, not humanity in isolation, and observes that the

Wisdom literature concerns itself with our 'everyday finite reality of all sorts – animal, vegetable, and mineral – in the routine networks that are constituted by their ordinary interactions. Taken together, that network of realities defines the spaces and times of our everyday lives and provide us with fellow agents sharing those spaces and times' (2009, p. 190). Kelsey calls this created reality the 'quotidian': 'Human persons are integral to it, as quotidian as everything else' (2009, p. 190). He then goes on to examine the idea that integral to the human engagement with the quotidian are 'practices'. Practices are social forms of engagement that have some defined end but will not necessarily have a product. Kelsey claims that, in the Wisdom literature, human beings are given a standard of excellence with which they are called to engage in these practices. That standard of excellence is wisdom (2009, p. 193). He outlines three different sorts of practices that we engage with: first, practices that are about our engagement with non-humans such as farming; second, practices 'in which human creatures interact with other human creatures', such as 'marriage, child rearing, managing households, preparing meals' and so on (2009, p. 194); third, practices 'in which human creatures interact with social institutions: practices of securing justice and correcting injustice; of borrowing, lending, and managing money; and above all, practices of using language either truthfully or deceptively' (2009, p. 194). With regard to all of these practices, Kelsey develops a Christian theological understanding of vocation that would apply to all created humans. His claim is therefore universal, even if rooted in particular texts of the Christian canon.

> The very context into which we are born has the force of a vocation regarding our practices: human creatures are born into a vocation, called to be wise in their practices ... Because human practices partly make up the quotidian, unwise or foolish practices deform not just individual lives but the quotidian – that is, creation itself. Wise practices yield the well-being of fully human, if dying, life; foolish practices yield a living death. (Kelsey 2009, p. 194)

For Kelsey, all human life is one of vocation, and one that is intrinsically social. Human vocation is to live wisely with one another and wisely within the created order as a whole. Any Christian theology of marriage is also a Christian theology of the practices of wisdom that lead to the flourishing of the quotidian, alongside other social practices that seek to do the same.

The Christian Family *in Christ*

If the universal vocation of humankind is to live wisely for the flourishing of the quotidian, what can be said about specifically Christian
forms of such living? It would be easy at this point to begin to list
different forms of domestic life: marriage, singleness, life in religious
community and so on. The danger of this approach is that these things
become too tightly separated from one another. Jana Bennett observes
this point in her work on marriage and singleness. She explores three
states frequently dichotomized in discussions about marriage: gender
(male and female); married and single; public and private. She argues
that 'Christianity offers a more sane view, which is to see that one's
state of life is not the ultimate question ... I claim that the church
must be determinative for rightly understanding Christian households'
(Bennett 2008, p. 29). This ecclesiological priority given to understanding marriage is rooted in the theology of baptism: '"Water is thicker
than blood" refers to the point that, for Christians, baptism and the
relationships we have with other Christians are more potent than our
blood ties and familial relationships' (2008, p. 31). This point is worth
exploring further.

Intrinsic to God's ways with the world is that there is always a relationship between the individual and the social. God elects Abraham,
Sarah and their offspring – who become the nation of Israel. It is that
group of people who are to be a light to the nations, no one individual
human member of Israel. In Christ and through the work of the Spirit,
God calls into being the Church, the body of Christ. This too is primarily a social reality. The individual is brought into relationship with
God as they are brought into relationship with other people in the life
of the body.

We often find it difficult to get our heads around some of the presuppositions made in Scripture. We live in a world where human identity is
primarily conceived of individually.[2] We take decisions about our identities as individuals: what I'm going to wear, who my friends are, what
I spend my time doing, how I spend my money. We think of ourselves
coming first and the social groups we are part of as secondary. I may
or may not join a church – but if I do I probably join one that I think
suits me and meets my needs (or perhaps the needs of my immediate
family). This is a very long way away from the kind of understanding
of the Church at work in the New Testament, which works almost the

2 For a detailed account of the rise of this sense of the individual, see Taylor 1989.

opposite way around: you are who you are because of the social whole you belong to; you are defined by the 'people' you are from.

When Paul writes, 'As many of you as were baptized into Christ have clothed yourselves with Christ. There is no longer Jew or Greek, there is no longer slave or free, there is no longer male and female; for all of you are one in Christ Jesus' (Gal. 3.27–29), this is something really quite radical. Because one has been baptized into Christ and joins the life of the social reality of the Church as the body of Christ, one's identity is no longer primarily of the social realities that one belonged to before, One is no longer Roman or Israelite, male or female, a slave or free – or at least this is no longer what gives one one's fundamental identity. One's identity comes from being 'in Christ' and not from any ethnic, biological or social distinction that defined one beforehand. This led some in the Roman Empire to begin to talk about a 'third race' – not Jew or pagan, but something else. Denise Buell, in her work on race and ethnicity in early Christian identity, concludes that 'early Christians often developed universalizing arguments using ethnic reasoning, defining themselves as an ethnic or racial whole composed of, in Justin's words, humans "of every race"' (Buell 2005, p. 165). When allegiance to the Empire is what is going to promote social stability, a whole collection of folk turning around and proclaiming clearly that they no longer belonged primarily to the Empire but rather to Christ was indeed socially disturbing and, from the point of view of the Empire, worth persecuting.

A number of things merit our attention in terms of the presumed relationship between the individual and the social in the New Testament context. First, that the individual is indeed a locus of the work of the Spirit of God: a human person can be led into a new social reality that fundamentally changes who they are. In this sense there is an individualizing element to being Christian (which, many have argued, becomes considerably stronger at the time of the Reformation). There is also a very strong socializing element. It is not that I become a Christian alone – I can only be 'in Christ' by being 'in the body of Christ'. I become part of a new social reality that then defines who I am. The radical nature of this new social reality is made clear in Paul's short letter to Philemon, where Paul is requesting Philemon to take back the runaway slave Onesimus and to welcome him back 'no longer as a slave but as more than a slave, a beloved brother' (Philem. 16). N. T. Wright opens his monumental study of Paul's theology with an extended reflection on this request. Commenting on verse 6 he suggests that the Greek normally translated as 'Christ' is better conveyed by the term 'Messiah'.

Paul can speak ... of *Messiah* as a kind of collective noun: *Messiah-and-his-people*. The force of this, frequently, is that because of the Messiah, and particularly because of his death and resurrection and the 'faith/faithless' which that both enacted and evokes, people of all sorts (Jew and Greek, slave and free, male and female) are brought into a single family. Messiah-family. (Wright 2013, p. 17; italics in original)

This status of being in a new family has a concrete and radical effect on the social status that marks out a slave and his owner. Philemon is now to regard Onesimus as a brother, not primarily as his slave. Although Wright also points out later that 'Paul does not ... mean that all ethnic, social and gender distinctions cease to have any meaning at all' (2013, p. 875), it is clear that the biological, sociological and ethnic definitions of humans are radically relativized through their incorporation into the body of Christ (body of Messiah, to follow Wright's usage). Indeed, the social reality of the body of Christ, the Church, becomes one's primary family.

Interestingly, we can begin to see how some of this works itself out in reality by some of the concerns the New Testament has precisely about how one's identity affects the social relationships one is in, and even directly about marriage. Paul sees that the Church has an interest in the relationships between husband and wife. We might find this quite a difficult thing to understand today as we would tend to think that this was nobody's business but our own. Remember, though: social identity precedes individual identity in Paul's world. A question that had arisen is what one should do if one had taken on a new identity 'in Christ' but was married to someone who had not taken on that identity. Which identity was more important? Should one remain married to someone not 'in Christ' or should one leave them? What was being 'in Christ' doing to the married partner who was still a non-Christian? Paul says, 'if any believer has a wife who is an unbeliever, and she consents to live with him, he should not divorce her' (1 Cor. 7.12); likewise for a believing woman and her husband. Even further than this, 'the unbelieving husband is made holy through his wife' (1 Cor. 7.14) and vice versa. This shows the 'power' that social existence in Christ's family has – it reaches out even to the unbeliever.

It sometimes comes as a shock that marriage is considered something of a second-best by Paul: 'To the unmarried and the widows I say that it is well for them to remain unmarried as I am. But if they are not practising self-control, they should marry. For it is better to marry than to be aflame with passion' (1 Cor. 7.8–9). This is a little shocking because marriage here does not seem to be primarily about all the nice things we like to think of it being about today. Rather, it is rather blatantly about sex. If one cannot resist the deep human desire most people experience for sex, one should get married so one can indulge it. Just because this is part of what Scripture says marriage is all about does not mean that marriage is limited to being just about these things (although it is one of the most direct statements Scripture makes about marriage – and certainly a rich theology of marriage cannot ignore sexuality).

The picture that is beginning to emerge is of different states of life within the primary family, or household, of God that is the body of Christ, the Church. The language of 'households' proposed by Jana Bennett is a rich one: 'The particularities of each small household remain. Yet the particularities of all these households find their place in the context of the Household of God, and in that context they bear relationship with each other and undergird each other' (Bennett 2008, p. 158).

Vocation, Marriage, and Life in Christ

We noted above that the Old Testament imagery of YHWH as the bridegroom and Israel as the bride is intrinsically bound up with the idea of the covenant with Israel rooted in the call of Abraham. We also noted the way Paul mixes the metaphors of the Church as the body of Christ, and the Church as the bride of the Christ who is the bridegroom. As the Old Testament image of the bridegroom and bride finds an origin in the notion of 'call' and therefore vocation, so does the New Testament imagery of the body. Ian McFarland quotes a compilation of verses from Paul:

> For just as the body is one and has many members, and all the members of the body, though many, are one body, so it is with Christ ... If the foot were to say, 'Because I am not a hand, I do not belong to the body,' that would not make it any less a part of the body. And if the ear were to say, 'Because I am not an eye, I do not belong to the body,' that would not make it any less a part of the body. If the whole body were an eye, where would the hearing be? If the whole body were hearing, where would the sense of smell be? But as it is, God arranged the members in the body, each one of them as he chose ... that the members may have the same care for one another. If one member suffers, all suffer together with it; if one member is honored,

all rejoice together with it. Now you are the body of Christ and individually members of it. (1 Cor. 12.12, 15–18, 25–26; cf. Rom. 12.4–5). (McFarland 2014, p. 64)

Continuing to mix the Pauline metaphors, the bride is a woman of many members. Within the body of Christ, different individuals are called and chosen for different parts of the body. McFarland spells out the logic of this:

> Living out one's particular place in the body of Christ therefore involves discerning the particular form of that call – one's vocation (literally, 'calling'). And because each person's place in the body is unique, the shape of every vocation is distinctive: however much others may serve as sources of inspiration and insight in discerning one's calling, no one can serve as a template that may simply be copied. (McFarland 2014, p. 65)

McFarland understands human vocation within the body of Christ to have multiple levels and dimensions, which include our different familial relationships and our actions within the public square. Included within this broad and deep conception of vocation as 'working out our salvation' is the question of the kind of household in which we are called to live. He notes that 'entering a monastery might be integral to one person's vocation but the (sinful) rejection of vocation for another. Indeed, even within a single person's life, a particular action (e.g. marriage) may count as fulfilling one's vocation at the age of 30, but not if undertaken at 13' (2014, p. 67).

The universal vocation of humans to wise practices for the flourishing of the quotidian contains within it a kind of subset that is the specifically Christian vocation to be the body of Christ. This is made up of individual Christians, each of whom has a range of particular vocations that shape the part of the body that is theirs to be. One aspect of this last individual vocation is to be a member of a particular household of God, one form of which, which some are called to, is marriage. Bennett cautions us to beware of descriptions of different 'states of life' and to engage them only in such a way that does not 'detract from the unity of Christians in the Household' (Bennett 2008, p. 133). Some brief delineation of such states helps us contextualize the particular vocation within the household of God that is marriage.

Some are called to a life of celibacy. To be celibate is not to be a person without sexual desire but someone who enables and enriches human social life through offering the energy, passion, love and commitment that a sexual relationship might consume to others in the world around them and to God. They are available in a very particular way to other people and God, precisely by not being available in a particular way (that is, sexually). This is not to be understood as some kind of 'lack' but rather as a vocation to be present in a very particular kind of way within life in the world. One of the ways God calls human beings to enrich the flourishing of society as a whole, and the Church in particular, is through the gifts a celibate person has to offer that are particular, and different from the kind of gifts people called into different kinds of human relationship can offer.

It is all too easily presumed within the life of the Church that being single and being celibate are one and the same thing. This is to miss a vital distinction between the two. Single people are open to sexual relationship and the kind of exclusive commitment that might be found within marriage. They therefore enter into relationships with other people within the world in a very different way from people called and committed to celibacy. The Church seems to find singleness very problematic. What does it mean to be open to sexual encounter but not married? The Church often hides this question away in a grey area that it then pretends does not exist. This can be deeply difficult for someone who is single, which may manifest itself in different ways. For single people with the sense that their true vocation lies within a married relationship, it is a source of deep sadness that they are not in such a relationship. Alternatively it can be a source of deep joy that one is available for encounters within the world as someone open to deeply committed, faithful relationships. Human beings, complicated as they are, may experience both of these things simultaneously. The gift of the single person finds expression in their particular networks of relationships and socialities. The gift of friendship is one that many single people offer in a very profound way. They can often 'be there' for others in a way that married couples cannot always be. Equally, the openness of a single person to the possibilities of relationship, and seeing those possibilities of relationship in other people, can be a profound gift to the world, enabling them to see things others miss. Both celibates and single people form households in various ways: sometimes alone, sometimes with friends, sometimes with extended family or elderly relatives. In this way one can see that these vocations are not simply about one's 'state' but contain a related vocation to particular forms of household at any given time.

For some, their vocation is to a particular form of sociality that finds expression in the life of a community. This is sometimes easily recognized, in terms of those who have been called to life within particular religious communities and orders. This often, but perhaps not always, goes hand in hand with celibacy. Equally, there are times when married couples are called to life within community too. We certainly must not think of the different vocations that we have as being mutually exclusive. Those who live within communities, such as the L'Arche communities that form around people with learning difficulties, may have a strong vocation to community life alongside other relationships that may or may not be sexual. There are also forms of religious community life (perhaps such as the Iona Community) in which a profound depth of mutual accountability and communal responsibility is demanded which, again, might run alongside life as either a celibate, single or married person. Again, though, communities exist not simply for the sake of themselves but also for those outside of the particular Christian household that such communities are. This has historically played out through acts of charity and ministry among poor people but may find expression today in all kinds of alternative ways.

Finally we come to marriage. Marriage, like other vocations, exists not primarily for its own sake but for the sake of human flourishing as humans are caught up in the movement of God into the world, returning the world to God. It is one particular form of expression of wise living that seeks the flourishing of the quotidian. Put simply, marriage exists for those outside of it as much as it exists for those within it. Marriage, like all vocations, comes to us as both a gift and a calling. Marriage is certainly not for the sake of the wedding! Marriage is the way certain people are called to their own human flourishing in a way that enables the wider flourishing of human life in the world. This has often been traditionally understood in the sense that marriage is a place that exists for children who are a product of that marriage. This has never been exclusively true. The vocation to marriage is a vocation to a way of serving the human flourishing in the world that God calls us into. That may express itself in becoming parents, of either our own biological children or by adoption (following the divine example of God 'adopting' us as God's children in Christ). It may express its existence for the sake of those outside of it in myriad other social and ecclesial ways too.

The problem with the kind of accounts of different vocations I have offered here is that they are radically idealized. Does the celibate always find the reserves of emotional strength to be radically there for the other? No. Does the person called to celibacy always live up to this call? No. Does the single person always live a life of radical openness to the potential of relationship in all people? Of course not. Does marriage always function in a way that allows us to be drawn into the heart of God? No – marriages are often abusive and deeply broken. The reality of human sin is that we have the inbuilt tendency, as Francis Spufford has put it so nicely recently, to 'fuck things up' (Spufford 2012, p. 27). We do not live in the midst of the kingdom. We live in a penultimate reality: the now and the not yet; the sign and the foretaste. Here the parallel with the divine call to covenant is important: covenants are unbreakable and yet, in the pages of Scripture, frequently broken by humanity. In many ways, idealized accounts of human vocation might be quite damaging. The issue has to be discerned in this penultimate world where we look 'through a glass darkly'. We must be wary of generalizing from particulars: that Jesus was single, does not mean we are all called to be single. Just because some people are called to married life does not mean we all are.

Just because most marriages are between a man and a woman does not mean that they all have to be. It is a very particular vocation. As Bennett puts it, 'Marriage is a specific vocation to be married to a specific person and thus time bound and communally bound. The only general vocation a Christian has is also the only one that is eternal: to be a witness to Christ' (Bennett 2008, p. 174). Marriage understood in this way is not a legal contract, and is not determined by gender or sexuality. It is one of the specific vocations into which the living God calls some human beings, within the broader vocation to be in the household of God and the universal human vocation to seek the well-being of the quotidian. It is a vocation two people are called to as God continually moves through God's creation, drawing us into the inner life of God Godself, such that the kingdom might begin to be realized, even in this penultimate age.

References

Bennett, Jana Marguerite, 2008, *Water is Thicker Than Blood: An Augustinian Theology of Marriage and Singleness*, Oxford: Oxford University Press.

Buell, Denise Kimber, 2005, *Why this new Race: Ethnic Reasoning in Early Christianity*, New York, NY: Columbia University Press.

Kelsey, David, 2009, *Eccentric Existence: A Theological Anthropology*, Louisville, KY: Westminster John Knox Press.

McFadyen, Alistair I., 1990, *The Call to Personhood: A Christian Theory of the Individual in Social Relationships*, Cambridge: Cambridge University Press.

McFarland, Ian, 2014, 'The Saving God', in Kent Eilers and Kyle Strobel (eds), *Sanctified by Grace: A Theology of the Christian Life*, London: Bloomsbury, pp. 61–73.

Muller, Earl C., SJ, 1990, *Trinity and Marriage in Paul: The Establishment of a Communitarian Analogy of the Trinity Grounded in the Theological Shape of Pauline Thought*, New York, NY: Peter Lang.

Sohn, Seock-Tae, 2002, *YHWH, The Husband of Israel: The Metaphor of Marriage between YHWH and Israel*, Eugene, OR: Wipf & Stock.

Spufford, Francis, 2012, *Unapologetic: Why, Despite Everything, Christianity Can Still Make Surprising Emotional Sense*, London: Faber & Faber.

Tait, Michael, 2010, *Jesus, The Divine Bridegroom, in Mark 2:18–22: Mark's Christology Upgraded*, Rome: Gregorian and Biblical Press.

Taylor, Charles, 1989, *Sources of the Self: The Making of the Modern Identity*, Cambridge: Cambridge University Press.

Wright, N. T., 2013, *Paul and the Faithfulness of God: Christian Origins and the Question of God*, London: SPCK.

Wyschogrod, Michael, 1996, *The Body of Faith: God and the People Israel*, Northvale, NJ: Jason Aronson Inc.

Reproduction and the Body's Grace

BRETT GRAY

Introduction

As the Church and individual Christians struggle to come to terms with how we should live in a rapidly changing culture as both baptized and sexual beings, and as the multiple questions around same-sex relationships and marriage press even harder on our thinking, one of *the* seminal texts in this discussion has been Rowan Williams' essay 'The Body's Grace' (Williams 1996). In it is an argument for the theological legitimacy of faithful same-sex partnerships, but it is also more than that. It constitutes what the American theologian Eugene Rogers has called 'the best 10 pages written about sexuality in the twentieth century' (Rogers 2002, p. 309). This compliment probably still holds in the early twenty-*first* century. Yet 'The Body's Grace' is a brief and, now, relatively old document. It is also a text that comes out of a very definite context; it was first given as a lecture to the Lesbian and Gay Christian Movement in 1989, and written while Williams was still an academic in Oxford, before he began his episcopal career in Wales and well before he became Archbishop. It is the work of a thinker less encumbered by responsibilities to the wider institutional Church. In this chapter we will revisit those 10 pages and ask, for all their brilliance and brevity: 'Do they still say enough, and are the right things said?' Specifically, in one of William's primary moves (the relegation of procreation as a theological good within sexual relationships), have more theological costs been incurred than at first realized?

The reader is free at this point to ask: 'Why does this matter to me?' Is this yet another essay by one academic taking a microscope to another's work in order to ask a few pernickety questions? Well, besides the importance and merit of this particular text and its writer, I think the questions to be asked of 'The Body's Grace' are important because they will help us to think through more generally the sorts of questions we ask, and the approaches we take, in formulating our theologies of sex, marriage and same-sex relationships. What is interesting about 'The Body's Grace' isn't just that it is well written and thoughtfully provoking; it also typifies – in its relegation of procreation – a particular theological move often made when arguing for the recognition of same-sex relationships. By querying that move I don't mean to argue against such recognition. Rather, I want to say that if we want to go there we need a better way of arguing for it. I also think that if we cast a wider net in Williams' and others' writings and look beyond 'The Body's Grace', there might be some valuable resources for formulating such a better argument.

'The Body's Grace': What it Actually Says ...

For all that Williams' essay is well known, it is more often referred to than carefully read. So we will start with a brief précis of 'The Body's Grace' and go from there. It begins with an evocation of Paul Scott's sequence of novels, *The Raj Quartet,* and within them the loveless seduction of one Sarah Layton. Despite the misfortunes attendant on this event, Layton discovers that she has nonetheless 'entered her body's grace'. She has gained the knowledge that her body might be 'the cause of happiness to her and to another'. Sexuality, then, even in such an unpromising manifestation as this seduction, is a place where we can discover a sort of transforming knowledge – that we are wanted, that we are potentially an object of delight for another. This literary allusion provides Williams with the dropping-off point for a discussion of grace and sexuality. A Christian understanding of grace comprehends it as 'a transformation that depends in a large part on knowing yourself to be seen in a certain way, as significant, as wanted'. It is, like sexuality, a place of transformative knowledge. We are transformed, by grace, as we discover ourselves to be the objects of *divine* desire; desired by God as if we *were* God, as if *we* were part of the life of the Trinity. This correlation of grace with the discovery of being desired is why, for Williams, sexual desire is so aptly used as a metaphor in the Scriptures. It is a particularly powerful and affecting way of communicating to us that grace involves our intuition of God's ardent desire for us (1996, pp. 58f.).

Williams then turns to a discussion of the nature of human sexual desire and what might be called its *communicative* nature. To be fulfilled, sexual desire must take the risk of communicating, of seeking a response from the other it desires. We have to admit our wants and our needs to another, and therefore – when we are metaphorically, or even literally, at our most naked – we have to risk rejection. This is what Williams calls an 'intense case of the helplessness of the ego alone'. Sexual desire decentres that ego because we are, in our deepest longings, at the mercy of another's response to our communication of those longings. This understanding of sexual desire's communicative, decentring and risky nature allows Williams to speak about what might constitute a malignant form of sexual desire, or perversity. It is a mode of desiring that denies sex's essentially communicative nature and attempts to avoid its implied risk of rejection. Perversity is sexuality in an *incommunicative* mode, one that takes no risks and incurs no vulnerability. It seeks relationships that are asymmetrical, where it can remain in charge through manipulation, threat or control, where it will not be challenged. The real question of sexual ethics then, for Williams, is how communicative, how vulnerable, do we want our sex to be? And since real communication takes time, fidelity becomes central to a Christian sexual ethic: 'Properly understood, sexual faithfulness is not an avoidance of risk, but the creation of a context in which grace can abound because there is a commitment not to run away from the perception of another' (1996, p. 60). Fidelity is good, essentially, because fidelity is good for communication; it is where desire can decentre the desirer's ego in a context of vulnerable conversation through time. It is where we don't *have* to be in control, a context where trust can grow and the risks of speaking and revealing can be undertaken in a growing bond of mutual acceptance.

But human creatures are risk averse and human egos don't like to be at the mercy of others. They often react rather badly when their vulnerability is pushed to the fore. Critically, for Williams, there is something about *same-sex* relationships that precisely pushes these uncomfortable realities to the fore. In such relationships the decentring power of desire, and the threat it poses to a determinedly self-defensive (and thus perverse) ego, is shown up in the sharpest of reliefs. This is because same-sex relationships are not biologically procreative; in a certain sense they are not *for* anything. To put it another way, more often than not different-sexed unions, unless something is done to forestall conception, entail the possibility of children. Heterosexual sex can therefore be understood as *for* something. The desire that surrounds it, and erupts within it, can be placed within an instrumental scheme wherein its unnerving power is contained. It is just something that we have to put up with on the way to something else, a necessary sort of embarrassment in the propagation of the human race. Desire, so contained and orientated towards a procreative goal, may

seem less threatening and decentring. But to Williams, same-sex relationships force the focus *back* on desire's power. Being by definition
biologically non-procreative they are not obviously instrumental to any
other purpose beyond themselves. They force upon us the problem and
the question of 'non-functional joy'. It is this dynamic that helps to
create some of the moral anxiety around homosexuality. It makes us
uncomfortable because, in same-sex relationships, desire's unadulter-
ated promise and threat become all the more visible (1996, p. 67).

This is a line of argument in which *non*-procreative sex and *useless*
desire come to play a vital theological role. Williams, in fact, marks
that the New Testament has very little to say about procreation, and
that more widely in the Scriptures it is desire in its unconstrained
non-functionality that is to the fore when sexual imagery is employed
to speak of God's desire for us. God doesn't want us *for* something;
God just, unnervingly, *wants* us. Thus: 'If we are afraid of facing the
reality of same-sex love because it compels us to think through the
processes of bodily desire and delight in their own right, perhaps we
ought to be more cautious about appealing to Scripture as legitimating
only procreative heterosexuality' (1996, p. 67). A Church that accepts,
as Anglicans do, the legitimacy of contraception, at least implicitly does
not see procreation as necessary for sex to be ethically wholesome.
Thus, to Williams, that Church can only deny the legitimacy of faithful
same-sex relationships by recourse either to a narrow or even 'funda-
mentalist' reading of particular biblical texts, or a problematic theory
of natural gender complementarity. That, in a nutshell, is Williams'
argument for the legitimacy of faithful same-sex love.

The Basic Move

What are we to make of this argument? First of all, Williams too quickly
glosses over Scripture and natural law or gender complementarity. It is
hard to avoid the fact that many generations of Christians have found
arguments against same-sex relationships from these two premises
convincing. And among Evangelicals at least, the motive force for
opposition to same-sex relationships is as much a concern about what
affirming them would imply concerning the authority of Scripture as
it is about a fear of desire and its unnerving potential. There is even,
perhaps, the precursor of a rather unfortunate ad hominem argument
in Williams' essay, in line with the often less than careful use of the
charge of 'homophobia'. But we must also remember that 'The Body's
Grace' is a brief piece, given first to an audience who would have shared

many of its premises, and therefore some hurriedness in its argumentation is inevitable. The issues of natural law and Scripture must also be bracketed in this essay, not because they are unimportant but because they are widely discussed elsewhere.

What, instead, I want to draw attention to is in the background of Williams' argument. It is an almost tectonic supposition that has permeated his thinking over the decades – that the ego's desire to define itself and organize the world according to its own agenda is humanity's fundamental pathology. It is the source, for him, of sexual perversity. It is also a reason why we live in a world where '[p]eople don't seem to be able to move without killing each other' (Williams 1994, p. 89).[1] In the face of such a perversely violent self-centredness the only self worth having, for Williams, is one gained in the risk of vulnerable conversation with God and our fellow human beings, conversation wherein our ego is unsettled. Non-functional desire is *good* because it is part of this unsettling. I do not contest this supposition of Williams', largely because he is probably right. What I do question is Williams' relegation of procreation as a good intrinsic to sex.[2] I want to argue that, in fact, procreation is an important part of sex's theologically vital and unnerving aspect.

As has been already pointed to, the move in 'The Body's Grace' – of relegating the importance of procreation – fits a particular typology or style of argument found among some who wish to affirm the legitimacy of same-sex unions. Another example can be found in the – perhaps similarly influential – argument by Jeffrey John in his *'Permanent, Faithful, Stable': Christian Same-Sex Partnerships* (John 1993). John makes the point that the Church's recognition of the legitimacy of infertile heterosexual marriages is demonstrative of an understanding that procreative possibilities are not intrinsic to the theological good of a covenanted sexual relationship. There are other goods, such as the promotion of faithful commitment, mutual comfort and sexual delight, that are maintained within, and that, in and of themselves, ethically justify non-procreative unions – be they same or differently gendered.

The tendency to engage in this style of argument is also noted by the Catholic theologian and ethicist David Matzko McCarthy. He describes

---

1 Williams is quoting William Golding but the source is not cited.

2 This is a move he replicates in 'Knowing Myself in Christ' (Williams 1997). In that essay he stresses that covenanted relations are a species within the wider genus of Christian vocation, signifying divine faithfulness through living 'under promise', and that because procreation was not necessary for the good of such relationships a way might be found to include same-sex relationships within this genus.

it as a tactic to justify same-sex unions or marriage 'by elevating the unitive end of marriage to the primary position while diminishing the procreative purpose' (Matzko McCarthy 1997, p. 371). Thus the core of a marriage comes to be understood as the interpersonal bond between lovers – a bond that can persist in, and be fulfilled by, both same and differently gendered unions. In these discussions the importance of procreation or family life tends, he notes, to atrophy. What makes Matzko McCarthy so interesting, especially in relation to the sort of argument offered by Williams, is that he is a thinker who wishes to *both* make space for same-sex unions *and* hold on to procreation as an intrinsic good within sexuality. But we will return to that later.

The question I want to provoke first is: 'What, if anything, is lost in this relegation of procreation?' As a theological move it is a relative novelty within Western Christianity, a departure (for good and ill) from a tradition shaped by Augustine.[3] It is Augustine, and his summation of the three theological goods of marriage as procreation, sexual fidelity and the bond (literally *sacramentum*) of unity it entails, that sets the discussion's agenda (Augustine, *On the Good of Marriage*, XXIV.32). The imprint of these three goods is still visible in the modern Church of England's marriage preface, with its talk of 'the delight and tenderness of the sexual union', a 'joyful commitment to the ends of their lives' and marriage as 'the foundation of family life'.[4] It is Augustine's well-known nervousness about unbridled sexual desire cut loose from a procreative intention that is perhaps tacitly behind Williams' critique of such a hesitancy. For that saint the only guiltless sexual act is that which is orientated towards procreation, although non-procreative sex within marriage is a forgivable fault (*venialis culpa*) (Augustine, *On the Good of Marriage*, VI.6). What Williams' argument amounts to is both a (probably necessary) departure from Augustine's anxiety and – following the tendency noted by Matzko McCarthy – a marked shift of theological emphasis towards the unitive goods of marriage over procreation.

---

3 Eugene Rogers, drawing on the work of Paul Evdokimov, argues that procreation never had the same significance in the Christian East. See his *Sexuality and the Christian Body* (Rogers 1999, ch. 3).

4 These words are from the marriage service in *Common Worship: Pastoral Services*, 2nd edn (Archbishops' Council 2005, p. 105). In the older Book of Common Prayer service these goods were also present, if differently ordered and more sternly worded. Procreation coming first, the avoidance of 'fornication' next and 'mutual society, help, and comfort' last of all. See The Book of Common Prayer (Church of England 1969, p. 363).

Yet, interestingly, this shifting of the Augustinian model is a move perhaps only imaginable after the advent of modern contraception. We have a facility for the prevention of conception unimaginable only a few generations ago, one that has allowed us conceptually to decouple sex from babies. Procreation looms less largely in our theological considerations in part because we've brought it under our technological control. This in itself begs some interesting questions about how changes in doctrine work in tandem with changes in the historical and social world in which they are produced. But Williams seems to accept this relegation of procreation as a fait accompli. By doing so the question is, has he also lost an important resource for combating precisely that egoism he finds so problematic – if in the slightly different mode of an *egoism-of-two*?

Marriage these Days

If I can be allowed a brief biographical interlude, before going into academia and higher education chaplaincy I spent seven years as a parish priest. I always served in parishes with attractive medieval, or faux medieval, churches surrounded by lovely green spaces. In my last post there was a remarkably desirable reception venue just up the road. This, among other things, made me a cog in that mighty machine that is the wedding industry – a 'nuptial-industrial complex' worth an estimated £10 billion to the UK economy.[5] It is an industry in which the Church of England is now fully ensconced. Through enterprises such as the Weddings Project (discussed in more detail in Julie Gittoes' chapter in this volume) and the 2008 loosening of restrictions on who can be married where, we aim to compete hotly for our share of the market. Thus on an official Church of England website can be found advice on 'seven steps to a heavenly wedding', accompanied by all the modern consumerist language of 'choice' and 'having it your way'.[6]

This returns me to another contribution made by Matzko McCarthy. He trenchantly critiques modern romantic conceptions of love and marriage in his book *Sex and Love in the Home* (Matzko McCarthy 2001).[7] To him, the modern notion of romantic love assumes it to be a quintessentially private space, outside of the economy's regnant

---

5 http://hitched-wife.org/wedding-facts-economics/summary-stats/each-year-uk-weddings-are-worth-10-billion-pounds.

6 www.yourchurchwedding.org.

7 Perhaps the most embarrassingly titled volume I've ever had to take out of a library.

and reductive market rationality. It is perceived as a shelter from the brutalism of a world where everything, and everyone, is assessed by its marketable value. And yet, perversely, in many of its manifestations modern romantic love reproduces precisely that market rationality it pretends to shelter us from. Love and sex are now 'social and economic currency', used to sell products. They have the 'migratory character of growth capitalism, always dependent upon establishing new markets (or partners and techniques) for their vitality' (2001, p. 3). One of the difficult questions the Church needs to ask itself is: 'In *its* participation in the nuptial-industrial complex, how far does it contribute to this tendency?'

To Matzko McCarthy, consumer capitalism creates its own species of unsettling desire, *consumerist* desire, but its unnerving power is more malignant than that of the desire Williams envisions. Consumerist desire assumes familiarity is an enemy. It always invites us on a nomadic quest for more, for new experiences and products. The self is unsettled, but to the detriment of the routines and practices required for day-to-day fidelity in a marriage and home (Matzko McCarthy 2001, pp. 34ff.). Modern 'romantic' love, for all its denial of economic realities, perversely apes this malignantly mobile desire. To be 'romantic' we must now leave the places where the rest of our life occurs, to find some exotic fantasy. And a 'romantic' wedding is now a fairy-tale event, increasingly in utter disjunction from our day-to-day existence. It is a fairy tale achieved through the technology of consumerism, a purchased magic that these days easily pushes its prince and princess into debt. But when they tire of one another there is always another purchasing opportunity, be it a new product or a new partner.

The reason for this brief digression into modern romance, consumerism and even the Church's potential implication in it is that it raises a question about Williams' treatment of sexual desire. Does he account for, and sufficiently compensate for, the economic and social context of late modernity? Or does he unwittingly create a vision of sexual desire too easily assimilated to a conception of 'romantic love' that, as Matzko McCarthy notes, is surreptitiously disciplined by consumerist capitalism? If Matzko McCarthy is right, there is a type of unsettling desire that is perversely acidic to the faithfulness Williams, rightly, wishes to promote. It is hard to take the risk of communication when both partners have their eye on the next acquisition.

Matzko McCarthy also notes that a common Christian defence mechanism against this acidic environment is simply to speak more loudly about 'family values' and mistakenly emphasize the presumed non-economic and private reserve that is marriage. He is particularly critical of some of the Christian 'personalist' accounts and theologies of transcendent nuptial union that have arisen in his own Roman Catholic tradition. They are, for him, dangerously close to a 'romantic ideal of mutual absorption', which 'threatens to make friendships and other social relations appear as optional or as intrusions' (Matzko McCarthy 2001, pp. 111, 123).[8] Such an approach reifies marriages from their wider social and economic contexts, and thereby presents the possibility of an *egoism-of-two* (2001, pp. 172f.). One wonders if 'The Body's Grace', as well as other arguments for the validity of same-sex unions that emphasize the unitive end of marriage, might also fall into this trap. Williams might be said to 'go vertical' too quickly, and move from the unsettling joy of sexual desire straight to the unsettling joy of God's grace. If so he might prematurely remove sexual relationships from their 'horizontal' contexts in the social and economic world, turning them into an idealized romantic space.

Linda Woodhead, as a sociologist, has also commented on some of the ways of sexuality in modernity, and even on the danger of an *egoism-of-two* (Woodhead 1997). She notes the way that sex in our culture has tended to become, paradigmatically, the private action of individuals seeking their own pleasure. In a sense this makes contemporary sexuality masturbatory in its ethos, even when more than one person is involved (1997, p. 98). This tendency tracks well the concern Williams has about perverse, or incommunicative, sex. It is an ingrown habit of orientation to the self's pleasure that has lost the vision of mutual vulnerability and communication. It is the sexual habit of one whose ego desires to retain its invulnerability. But like Williams, Woodhead sees this masturbatory ego as threatened and destabilized by sex. Drawn (however unwillingly) towards relationship and need, one tends to two. Where Woodhead goes further is in asserting that this two is also destabilized. The confinement of desire and love to a pair bond is hard to maintain. Most obviously, between differently gendered partners, offspring are a possibility. But the socially expansive tendency of sex is wider than biological procreation; enduring pair bonds start to relate to others as a pair, and thereby sexual relationships are embedded into larger social associations (Woodhead 1997, p. 107). Pairs that refuse this expansion beyond themselves become problematically inward looking and even potentially 'demonic'; Wood-

---

8 For a critique of the rise of 'nuptial' theology in Catholic thinking, see the mordant comments in Kerr 2007, pp. 199ff.

head cites the infamous example of Fred and Rosemary West (1997, p. 119). This style of relating might even be called an incommunicative *perversity-of-two*.

What I am gesturing towards in all this is that there is something potentially perverse in even a faithful relationship that has become an *egoism-of-two*. And 'The Body's Grace', while saying much that is good, does not say enough about this. Its emphasis on non-functional desire between two as paradigmatically destabilizing of the ego – and its relegation of procreation – could be used to underwrite a roman-tic apotheosis of the pair, that reified romanticism noted by Matzko McCarthy, which ignores surrounding social and economic realities and, perversely and unintentionally, serves a market capitalism acidic to the very faithfulness sought and held up as an ideal. While possibly communicative within itself, such an ingrown pair does not care to reproduce or expand that communication in such a way as to become a life-giving presence to others. It cannot, to paraphrase the Church of England's marriage preface, 'enrich society' or 'strengthen community'. And yet such an incommunicative result would be deeply contrary to Williams' best instincts. This is evident if we turn to another of his essays concerned with desire, 'The Deflections of Desire' (Williams 2002)[9] – only the desire in focus there is not human and sexual but intra-Trinitarian divine desire. To use theological language in a slightly risky fashion, Williams is speaking about the desire that constitutes God.

Deflections of Desire – two tending to three ...

To Williams, speaking about the Trinity, 'The single life of the God-head is the going-out from self-identity' (the Father) 'into the other' (the Son) 'that cannot be a closed mutuality'. Thus 'the love of one for the other' (the Father for the Son) 'must itself open on to a further otherness if it is not to return to the same'. That further, or third, other-ness is the Spirit. It is this third that keeps the divine life from being read as a 'mutual reinforcement of identity' between the Father and the Son. The Spirit is, in a sense, love's excess, the refusal of the divine life to be a self-satisfied *egoism-of-two*. The Spirit marks, for Williams, that God's is a life where desire is always deflected onwards and outwards, moving from two, to three and then even beyond. Divine desire is thus excessive of, and expanding beyond, any pair. Its ecstasy, its outwards

---

9 This was given first as a conference paper in 1999.

movement, results – among other things – in *our* creation and redemption (Williams 2002, pp. 118f.). It results in that divine desire for us, as if we *too* were God, that is marked in 'The Body's Grace'.

Another way to put this would be to say that divine, intra-Trinitarian desire is intensely communicative and non-perverse, and it is this communicative refusal of perversity that we are called to emulate in our own desiring. To Williams, insofar as the Christian life is the 'transcription into the circumstances of the world of the divine excess and displacements of love', our loves, for God and our fellow creatures, must not be a 'search for a fantasized partner in whom our eros will decisively find its goal and its end'. Rather, our desire must be reconstituted by the excessive nature of God's desire. It *too* must be expansive and outward moving (2002, pp. 119f.). Such a reconstitution would rule out any romantic apotheosis of a pair bond. Thus if 'Deflections of Desire' is used to supplement 'The Body's Grace', a more nuanced theology of desire, divine *and* human, emerges.[10] Such a theology marks the joyful and disruptive nature of a desire that leads the desiring subject away from concerns with the self, or even with their direct object of desire, and out and onwards. One moves to two, then three and then beyond.

Procreation?

But where Williams still, arguably, misses a theological trick is in failing to appropriate procreation as part of his thinking about sexual desire and its expansive nature. Having a baby is, as most parents can testify, the paradigmatic event of love exceeding a pair and moving, rather disruptively and unnervingly, out to a third. Infants are a definite disruption to any self-contained ego, and human children – rather like gay sex – are not all that 'functional'. As Williams himself eloquently expresses it in a sermon on the incarnation – they cry, they clutch and they wordlessly insist, disrupting their parents' world. This is what, to him, makes the Christmas child precisely appropriate as the vehicle for a confrontation 'with the alarming, mysterious, shattering strangeness of God' (Williams 1994, pp. 34–5).

This is not to say that children cannot be put to use, or even become a form of social capital for their parents or a wider society. In the world in which Christianity arose the production of children was a service to

---

10 For Williams there is an appropriateness in connecting 'the nature of divine love with the angularities and failures of created love', and this need not be 'simply appealing to a crude analogy between divine and human "interpersonal" relations' (Williams 2002, p. 127).

the family and the state, part of an ongoing social project, and one that the Church found itself querying.[11] In our current day childbearing is not seen, so much, as a political act, but it can certainly be a consumerist one. There are those who treat their children as an acquisition and an accessory. Situations in which this happens may even look like an *egoism-of-three* (or more), but in reality this is a scenario where the ego of the third, the child, is denied. They are made into a cypher for the parental ego in a perversity where communication, as a decentring interaction, does not extend to encompass them. This is an attempt to stay a one or two and not truly become a three, to deny the clutching disruption and reality of that young third.

But if we theologically reclaim procreation as central to sexuality, how can we move to affirm, if that is what we should do, the possibility of blessing a naturally infertile same-sex union? How do we also not end up painfully relativizing any biologically infertile heterosexual relationship? One recent response to these questions has been that of Robert Song (Song 2014). He has made a move very similar to the one this essay would like to make, reinstating procreation as a central theological good of marriage. To him, however, this implies a scenario where marriage *proper* is still a relation between differently gendered partners, and one that is normatively open to the gift of biological children. However, he also argues for the possibility of a 'third vocation' beyond the traditional Christian options of marriage and celibacy: that of a 'covenanted partnership'. Such a vocation is conceivably open to both same and differently gendered couples. The qualitative difference of such a partnership would be that – in the light of an eschatological trajectory that relativizes both marriage and procreation – biological children are not intended or sought. Procreation is not part of such a relationship's theological *raison d'être*. This is not, it should be stressed, in order to allow a couple to remain a self-satisfied kingdom of two. Rather, such partnerships should in their own way be 'fruitful' within a wider social field, through charity, mission work, adoption, fostering and so on.

A full discussion of the merits or otherwise of Song's proposals is beyond the scope of this essay. Suffice it to say that I think he is right to reinstate procreation as a central good of marriage, but perhaps wrong to then feel the need to establish a 'third vocation'. As well intended as he is in an insistence that a covenant partnership would not be a

11 See for instance Peter Brown's discussion of Chrysostom in Antioch. His teaching deliberately relativized the debt Christians had to the polis to provide future citizens (Brown 2008, pp. 307ff.).

second-class form of marriage (2014, p. 86), it would be almost invariably the case that it would be seen as such. It is also hard to see how
biologically infertile marriages would not, somehow, come to be seen
as more a 'covenanted relationship' than a marriage proper, or at least
only a 'marriage' in a very etiolated sense. Perhaps the better choice,
instead of establishing a novel third option within the Christian tradition, would be a careful expansion of what we understand as marriage's
procreative good, an expansion beyond a purely biological register.
Childbearing may be the paradigmatic human case of the outwards and
excessive movement of love from two to a third and onwards, but it is
not the *only* mode of such movement. And such an expansion of the
linguistic register of procreation is not a novelty within the Christian
tradition.

Advocates of 'traditional' family values may be surprised at just how
'non-traditional' Christianity can be on the subject. To take, for example, John Chrysostom, in the light of the resurrection of Christ – and
the coming resurrection of all – the impetus to procreate *biologically*
in order to ensure the human future is gone. Instead, there is another
possibility, of having *spiritual* children through mentoring, discipleship and mission: 'If you desire children, you can get better children
now, a nobler childbirth and better help in your old age, if you give
birth by spiritual labour.'[12] Thus even a monk can have offspring, more
rewarding in their own way than natural offspring.[13] There is a similar
move in Augustine. He too notes the change in priorities within the
Christian dispensation and argues that: 'in our day no one who is perfect in piety seeks to have children except in a spiritual way, whereas in
the past to have children in a carnal way was itself an act of piety.'[14] So
if we expand the language of procreation beyond the biological, it is a
metaphorical expansion that has already happened in different places
within the tradition.

To reclaim procreation, within such an expanded register, as an
intrinsic good for marriage is to say that while not all relationships can
and should be genetically fecund, they can and should be spiritually
and socially fecund. They can 're-produce' their love in wider contexts,
deflecting their desire for one another outwards in life-giving ecstasy
in various ways – through adoption, mentoring, hospitality, mission,

---

12 'Homily on Marriage I', in Eugene Rogers (ed.), *Theology and Sexuality* (2002,
p. 90).

13 'Against Opponents of the Monastic Life' in ibid., pp. 93f.

14 *The Good of Marriage*, XVII.19

service and so on.[15] These are all actions that can fulfil the (expanded) procreative good of marriage. This is the fruitfulness Song envisioned in covenant partnerships, but here it can be had without recourse to a new category of vocation. This expansion is something like what Matzko McCarthy calls 'social reproduction'. For him such 'social reproduction' resists individualistic egoism as well as the romantic mythology of relationships reified from their wider contexts. Such social reproduction can even, because it engages wittingly with the economic realities that modern romantic love seeks to deny, be the beginning of thoughtful resistance to the regnant market model in all its undermining of fidelity (Matzko McCarthy 2001).

In the end, Williams' argument in 'The Body's Grace', and other arguments that employ the move of relegating procreation to make space for same-sex relationships and marriages, are in danger of reducing our vocabulary. They lose, in losing procreation, a whole semantic field wherein desire's true decentring power is brought to the fore and egoisms of one or two are challenged. By creatively reclaiming the language of procreation – if in an expanded register – we can keep an important and remarkably versatile theological tool in play. We can have all of Augustine's theological goods without perhaps the Augustinian anxiety about the non-*biologically* procreative aspects of sex, because the good of procreation finds expression in a whole raft of creative possibilities beyond simply making and raising babies. And in this expanded register a same-sex relationship might be judged, in its own way, as procreative as any heterosexual one as it reproduces the flourishing and joy it has brought to two in a wider context.

References

Archbishops' Council of the Church of England, 2005, *Common Worship: Pastoral Services*, 2nd edn, London: Church House Publishing.
Augustine, *The Good of Marriage*.
Brown, Peter, 2008, *The Body and Society: Men, Women, and Sexual Renunciation in Early Christianity*, new edn, New York, NY: Columbia University Press.
Church of England, 1969, The Book of Common Prayer, Oxford: Oxford University Press.

---

15 See Eugene Rogers' eloquent argument for adoption as a Christian practice that more faithfully replicates God's relation to the believer than biological procreation in *Sexuality and the Christian Body* (1999), especially chapter 12 *passim*.

John Chrysostom, 'Homily on Marriage I', in Eugene F. Rogers (ed.), *Theology and Sexuality: Classic and Contemporary Readings*, Oxford: Blackwell, p. 90.

John Chrysostom, 'Against Opponents of the Monastic Life', in Eugene F. Rogers (ed.), *Theology and Sexuality: Classic and Contemporary Readings*, Oxford: Blackwell, p. 93.

John, Jeffrey, 1993, *'Permanent, Faithful, Stable': Christian Same-Sex Partnerships*, London: Darton, Longman & Todd.

Kerr, Fergus, 2007, *Twentieth-Century Catholic Theologians*, Oxford: Blackwell.

Matzko McCarthy, David, 1997, 'Homosexuality and the Practices of Marriage', *Modern Theology* 13.3, pp. 371–97.

Matzko McCarthy, David, 2001, *Sex and Love in the Home: A Theology of the Household*, London: SCM Press.

Rogers, Eugene, 1999, *Sexuality and the Christian Body: Their Way Into the Triune God*, Oxford: Blackwell.

Rogers, Eugene F. (ed.), 2002, *Theology and Sexuality: Classic and Contemporary Readings*, Oxford: Blackwell.

Song, Robert, 2014, *Covenant and Calling: Towards a Theology of Same-Sex Relationships*, London: SCM Press.

Williams, Rowan, 1994, *Open to Judgement: Sermons and Addresses*, London: Darton, Longman & Todd.

Williams, Rowan, 1996, 'The Body's Grace', in C. Hefling (ed.), *Our Selves, Our Souls and Bodies: Sexuality and the Household of God*, Boston: Cowley, pp. 58–67

Williams, Rowan, 1997, 'Knowing Myself in Christ', in Timothy Bradshaw (ed.), *The Way Forward? Christian Voices on Homosexuality and the Church*, London: Hodder & Stoughton, pp. 12–19.

Williams, Rowan, 2002, 'The Deflections of Desire: Negative Theology in Trinitarian Disclosure', in Oliver Davies and Denys Turner (eds), *Silence and the Word: Negative Theology and Incarnation*, Cambridge: Cambridge University Press, pp. 115–35.

Woodhead, Linda, 1997, 'Sex in a Wider Context', in Jon Davies and Gerard Loughlin (eds), *Sex These Days: Essays on Theology, Sexuality and Society*, Sheffield: Sheffield Academic Press, pp. 98–120.

Marriage and English Law

AUGUR PEARCE

Introduction

Marriage is a matter of theological interest – hence this book. The pairing or grouping of individuals and the formation of domestic units are also of interest to wider society. Both happened well before the time of Christ and in regions unfamiliar with the Christian Scriptures. In many societies these phenomena are regulated by law, which may be wholly independent of religion, give effect to a religious understanding or abdicate its role in this area to a separate religious authority.

The recent discussions of marriage reform in England proceeded with considerable religious input. Religious groups and individuals responded to consultations. Some were consulted directly on the proposed reforms generally, as well as on the implications for themselves. In Parliament religious considerations were voiced by the Lords spiritual and many other legislators.

In the eyes of some there was altogether too much religious input into a question that should have been decided on utilitarian or libertarian principles; while for others the whole project was an instance of state presumption, intruding into an area governed by divine law where human decision-makers had no standing. Not for the first time, it was suggested that the law of England and the laws of God had parted company.

The 2013 marriage question belongs within a wider debate as to the religious character of English law. It was recently stated by a senior judge:

> The general law may of course protect a particular social or moral position which is espoused by Christianity, not because of its religious *imprimatur*, but on the footing that in reason its merits commend themselves ... The Judaeo-Christian tradition, stretching over many centuries, has no doubt exerted a profound influence upon the

judgment of lawmakers as to the objective merits of this or that social policy ... But the conferment of any legal protection or preference upon a particular substantive moral position on the ground only that it is espoused by the adherents of a particular faith, however long its tradition, however rich its culture, is deeply unprincipled ... In the eye of everyone save the believer religious faith is necessarily subjective, being incommunicable by any kind of proof or evidence. It may of course be *true*; but the ascertainment of such a truth lies beyond the means by which laws are made in a reasonable society.[1]

The history of English marriage law throws light on the truth or otherwise of this opinion. For most of that history, Christianity dominated the English landscape. Religion loomed large and was uncontestedly the business of government. The links between marriage law and marriage theology were explicit: the core of marriage with legal effect being 'marriage in the sight of God'. At the Reformation any authority in this area enjoyed by the clergy as of right was repudiated; gradually their factual control also waned. But the laity can do theology as well. It is hard to imagine Tudor, or even Hanoverian, legislators concerned only with 'objective merits'. Much more recent reform, in particular of marriage impediments, has paid careful attention to theology: the sponsor of the measure to widen divorce grounds in 1937 concluded that 'In the finest sense of the word, this is a Christian Bill.'[2]

It has been a long time since the beliefs underlying English law were universally shared. Since Archbishop Cranmer determined 'the King's great matter' on 23 May 1533, Roman Catholics have held views on marriage validity contradicting the official English position. Each major reform has produced new dissenters. The arrival of Jewish and other non-Christian faiths, with unfamiliar formation rites and rules of their own, made new contrasts between religious practices and marriage before the law. Their acceptance (and that of the non-religious) into English society meant it could no longer be claimed that the national religion was the religion of the population.

But demographic changes do not by themselves change existing law or its basis. Nor do notions of separation as introduced elsewhere by revolution or codified constitutions. What has happened in England, this chapter suggests, is *not* that marriage law has lost its Christian

---

1 *Macfarlane v. Relate Avon Ltd.* [2010] EWCA Civ 880, *per* Laws LJ at [23]; italics in original.

2 Hansard (Commons), col. 644.

character but that those who dissent from it have been accommodated: by freedom to voice their views, by the absence of any obligation to solemnize marriages of which they disapprove and by legal effect conditionally given to their own marriage formation practice. Whether this is 'deeply unprincipled' or an acceptable compromise between continuity and modernity, the reader must decide.

Our appeal to history must also, however, take account of the Tudor constitutional developments without which the first marriage reforms would not have been possible. The lawmaking authority of the medieval clergy – domestic as well as foreign – was repudiated as usurped. In the realm's ecclesiastical as well as its temporal causes, the monarch was supreme and laws were made or adopted only by the concurrence of prince and people.[3] In relation to its *official* religion therefore (as opposed to the voluntary rules of Dissent), England has never recognized a separate 'law of the Church'. Hence, it will be suggested, recent appeals to 'the canon law of the Church of England' are misconceived; and it must be asked whether the accommodation of dissent from marriage law within the national religious establishment has struck the correct balance between officials' scruples and public rights.

The Early and Medieval Background

English marriage law did not begin with Christian theology. Its roots lay in an institution already well developed in the Roman Empire where the first Christians lived. But Christians' beliefs influenced how they acted within that law; and when they gained the opportunity to influence the law (for example, on divorce), they took it. The legal tradition that the Christian episcopate preserved, after the fall of the Empire in the West, was thus coloured by Christian ideas and already largely in the bishops' hands. The distinction made in AD 494 by Bishop Gelasius I of Rome between 'the sacred authority of the priests and the royal power', respectively concerning 'the reception and proper disposition of the heavenly mysteries' and 'matters affecting the public order',[4] gained ground; and the idea that marriage was a 'spiritual' matter seemed to be confirmed by Peter Lombard's *Four Books of the Sentences* (c.1150), numbering it among his seven sacraments.

---

3 Act of Supremacy 1558 s.9; Ecclesiastical Licences Act 1533, Preamble.
4 Letter to Emperor Anastasius; Fordham University collection at http://legacy. fordham.edu/halsall/source/gelasius1.asp.

The Elements of Marriage Formation to 1753

Before statute intervened, the formation of marriage comprised three stages of varying importance: preliminaries, contract and solemnization. For a time consummation was believed a further essential; but ultimately scholars reasoned that Mary, who conceived Jesus while 'espoused to Joseph, [but] before they came together' (Matt. 1.18, AV), must nevertheless have been fully married at that time. After the Reformation registration was directed,[5] but merely to record an already accomplished fact.

1 Contract

The contract was itself a significant advance over some pre-Christian formation modes in which the decision of a bride's father, rather than the bride herself, was conclusive. It required the mutual agreement of two people, each with the requisite capacity, to take one another as spouse: either with immediate effect (*per verba de præsenti*) or on conditions that were later fulfilled or waived.

A contract of marriage was distinguished from a contract to marry in the future (*per verba de futuro*), today called engagement, from which either party could release the other. But carnal copulation was treated as waiver of any condition or an agreement to convert a future into a present contract.

Law's intimate correlation with theology was illustrated by language about the internal and external fora of divine action. The internal forum was the realm of conscience, of sin and forgiveness, where God worked directly. Here no proof of a contract was required, for God 'knoweth the secrets of the heart' (Ps. 44.21, AV). The parties to a marriage contract no longer carried the moral guilt of fornication if they consummated their union. However, sex thereafter with an outsider carried the greater guilt of adultery; and any marriage with another was morally void.

The law acknowledged the internal forum. Judges acknowledged the simple marriage contract as 'marriage in the sight of God'.[6] They accepted that a contracted couple could not be fornicators, and if the

---

5 By royal injunction from 1538, by canon from 1598.

6 *Collins v. Jessot* (1705) 6 Mod 155; Solicitor-General William Murray, introducing Lord Hardwicke's Bill in the House of Commons, Hansard XV, 78 (1753: 'A good marriage by the laws of God and nature').

contract was proved could not be punished as such.[7] But the external forum, where God's authority was mediated through human law-makers and judges, needed proof and had to balance morality with other considerations.

Without corroborated proof – not merely by the parties' word – a court could make no order flowing from the contract. It might even make orders inconsistent with it, making the parties choose between obedience to authority and fidelity to the contract they alone knew to have been made. And if a contracted party purported to enter another such contract in the first partner's lifetime, any judgment risked prejudicing one set of innocent parties. So if the second contract were solemnized and one party to it then died, evidence of the first contract would no longer be received and the second would be legally impregnable. In the external forum, therefore, the second contract came to be called not void but 'voidable' during the time when it still remained at risk.

2 Solemnization

While 'marriage in the sight of God' was conclusive in the internal forum, many of the legal effects of marriage – especially those that the temporal courts administered – flowed only from a *solemnized* contract.

Without solemnization a husband did not take over the administration of his wife's property, leaving her free to conduct her own transactions and make her own will. Nor were offspring able to inherit as legitimate heirs.[8] A Dean of the Arches in 1796, considering the effect of a Jewish wedding interrupted before the equivalent stage (which would give property rights) had been reached, asked:

> Is it possible then for this Court to ... say that this person is now the wife of Mr. Belisario as he has claimed her to be, when it is proved that he has not a right to a penny of her fortune, and that she has a right to dispose of it? ... A man cannot be the husband of a woman by the law of England, without having the civil rights, which he has not.[9]

---

7 *Wigmore's case* (1707) Holt KB 460.

8 *Foxcroft's case* (1282) 1 Rolle's Abridg. 359; John Perkins, *A Profitable Book treating of the Laws of England, principally as they relate to Conveyancing*, 1532, pp. 74–5; *Paine's case* (1661) 1 Sid 13.

9 *Lindo v. Belisario* (1796) 1 Hagg Con App 7, *per* Wynne DA.

Solemnization served four purposes: publicity, blessing, instruction and solidarity. It shared the first aim with banns but was much older. William Lyndwood, editor of the English domestic canons in his *Provinciale* of *c.*1432, explained solemnization 'in the face of the church', *in facie ecclesiæ*, as 'in the sight of the people congregated in the church building'. Making the couple's neighbours witnesses to the contract itself ensured there would be no scandal in cohabitation thereafter, and no likelihood of either party denying the contract had been made.

Blessings were part of the Jewish marriage rite and there is evidence of very early nuptial blessings among Christians. In medieval times the Lord's Supper was often celebrated on the occasion. Family and friends could pray with the bridal pair; and for the Reformers, the opportunity for moral instruction was not to be missed.

Sources before 1753 are contradictory as to which of these requirements was essential to convert a marriage contract into a marriage for all legal purposes.

It seems fairly clear that a liturgical rite was not essential. If a couple contracted in the church building before a clerk and witnesses, this produced the desired legal effects.[10] A consecrated building was also not essential at common law, despite Canon 62 of 1603–5 demanding it. Lord Hardwicke's Act[11] recited that 'many Persons do solemnize Matrimony in Prisons and other Places' and went on to declare such marriages void; but it would not have been needed if they were void already.

The attendance of a clerk in holy orders was a more difficult question, particularly after Toleration. If protestant Dissenters married in their own congregations before a minister not in such orders, all the purposes of public solemnization were satisfied. The setting was considerably more respectable than the Fleet Prison; and though before 1753 such marriages were far from rare, Dissenters' offspring inherited their parents' land without challenge for illegitimacy.[12] But there were

---

10 John de Burgh, *Pupilla Oculi*, 1385; Rolle, *Abridgment des plusieurs cases*, 1668, 341; *Welde v Chamberlaine* (1684) 2 Shower KB 301; Salmon, *Critical Essay concerning Marriage*, 1724. The Act 3 Jac I c.5 (1606), depriving marriage before Roman Catholic clergy of property consequences, would not have been necessary if the Prayer Book rite had anyhow been essential.

11 s.8.

12 Quaker husbands were sometimes treated as married: one was held liable for a wife's debts (in 1696; Burnet, *Life and Death of Sir Matthew Hale*, p. 73), another entitled to seek criminal conversation damages (*Deane v. Thomas* (1829) 1 Moo & Malk 361).

cases where a widow was refused dower (an interest in her husband's estate)[13] or a widower administration of his wife's estate[14] because the officiant at their marriage had not been a clerk. This might also determine which parent's parish was charged with a pauper's relief under the Poor Law.[15] A controversial decision of the House of Lords in 1844, well after the question had been resolved by statute, held the common law had required the presence of a clerk for solemnization to have any legal effect.[16] But it seems clear from later decisions that this was not a provision adapted to conditions overseas; so where the common law governed marriages outside England, no clerk was required.[17]

3 Timing of the contract

A marriage contract might be made separately from solemnization by accident because the parties did not understand the law's solemnization requirements. It might be deliberate because the parties wished to contract within the family circle, possibly executing property settlements at the same time, and proceed later to the ceremony in church. Whether an earlier 'betrothal' was in fact a marriage contract or merely an engagement (a contract *de futuro*, with future effect) depended on the language used.

A contract might also be deliberately unsolemnized in order to keep it secret. In this situation an ecclesiastical court could, before 1753, order solemnization *in facie ecclesiæ* and punish the parties if they had copulated without waiting for the ceremony.[18]

4 Preliminaries

A banns requirement only entered the adoptive common law after the Fourth Lateran Council in 1215,[19] though there is evidence of some earlier English practice. Advance publicity gave an opportunity for

---

13 *Wigmore's case* (1707) Holt KB 460.

14 *Haydon v. Gould* (1711) 1 Salk 119.

15 *R. v. Inhabitants of Luffington* (1744) Burr Sett C 232.

16 *R. v. Millis (1844)* 10 Cl & F 534. It was accepted in this case that a deacon could officiate (see Watson, *Clergyman's Law*, 1701, p. 99), though many of the authorities taken to support the House's conclusion referred only to a priest.

17 E.g. because there was no local form that could practically be observed by an English couple; *Caterall v. Caterall* (1847) Rob Ecc 580, *Maclean v. Cristall* (1849) Perry's Oriental Cases 75.

18 *Matingley v. Martyn* (1632) Jones W 257.

19 Can. 51.

impediments to be declared, preventing a void marriage being (perhaps inadvertently) contracted or consummated. If the marriage was unsuitable it gave parents or guardians a chance to intervene. The alternative preliminary, an episcopal dispensation from banns or 'marriage licence', speeded the process but was not intended to defeat its aim, so applicants for a licence had to swear to parental consent and the absence of impediments.

Before 1753, if preliminaries were omitted but no impediment in fact existed, the couple could be punished but the marriage remained valid for all purposes.

Gelasius and Cromwell – The Unity of the Law and the Role of Parliament

The Gelasian dichotomy between temporal and spiritual authority was rejected by the Reformation Parliament in 1533, largely in the language of Thomas Cromwell, and by the Accession Parliament of Elizabeth I. It followed that marriage was neither a 'worldly thing' as Luther taught, nor the province of the clergy as Rome continued to believe. It was one of the realm's concerns or 'causes' which, whatever their subject matter, was regulated by a single authority: the monarch was 'supreme governor of this realm, as well in spiritual or ecclesiastical causes as temporal'.[20] Though jurisdiction as to the enforcement or dispensation of marriage rules remained divided, as it had been since 1070, the allocation of marriage was a question of expediency:

> All ... causes of matrimony and divorces ... the knowledge whereof *by the goodness of the princes of this realm* appertaineth to the spiritual jurisdiction of this realm ... shall be from henceforth heard examined discussed clearly finally and definitively adjudged and determined within the King's jurisdiction and authority and not elsewhere, in such courts *spiritual and temporal* of the same as the natures conditions and qualities of the causes and matters aforesaid in contention ... shall require.[21]

However, in amending the law the monarch was expected to act with Parliament, and sixteenth-century reforms concerning impediments,

---

20 Act of Supremacy 1558 s.9.
21 Ecclesiastical Appeals Act 1532 s.1 (italics added).

dispensations, the solemnization liturgy and matrimonial jurisdiction[22] showed Parliament took its oversight of marriage seriously.

The Adoptive Common Law

Rules on marriage that had emanated from episcopal councils, supplemented by papal decrees and developed by commentators, continued to provide the bulk of England's marriage law after the Reformation. But Parliament was emphatic this was not because of any authority inherent in the clergy.

Rules from the Continent and Asia Minor, so Parliament declared, bound Englishmen only if, 'at their free liberty, by their own consent' and with royal sufferance they had 'bound themselves by long use and custom to the observance of the same, not as to the observance of the laws of any foreign prince, potentate or prelate, but as to the accustomed and ancient laws of this realm, originally established as laws of the same by the said suffrance, consents and custom'.[23]

A rule on marriage therefore applied not because it was part of the 'canon law' but because it had been adopted into the customary or common law of England. As Mr Justice Vaughan observed in 1660, 'If the canon law be made part of the law of this land, then is it as much the law of the land, and as well, *and by the same authority*, as any other part of the law of the land. And if it be not made the law of the land, then hath it no more effect than a law of Utopia.'[24]

A rule of the Continental canon law was rejected, for example, in 1235, when legitimation by subsequent marriage was declared not to apply to inheritance in England. Instead the indigenous common law was restated in statute: 'He is a bastard who is born before the marriage of his parents.'[25] The controversial ruling in 1844 that a clerk was required to attend solemnization to give a marriage full validity would,

---

22 E.g. Submission of the Clergy Act 1533 (final appeal), Ecclesiastical Licences Act 1533 (dispensations), Succession to the Crown Act 1533, Marriage Act 1540, Clergy Marriage Act 1548 (all impediments), Acts of Uniformity 1548–1551 (liturgy); also the Acts 37 Hen VIII c.7 (1545), which conditionally confirmed Elene Barr's marriage to a third party in her first husband's lifetime, and 5 & 6 Ed VI st.4 (1552) confirming the further marriage of the Marquess of Northampton following his divorce *a mensa et thoro* from his first wife ('from bed and board', today termed judicial separation). The effect of both Acts was to dispense from the impediment of a prior solemnized marriage.

23 Ecclesiastical Licences Act 1533, Preamble.

24 *Edes v. Bishop of Oxford* (1667) Vaughan 18 (italics added).

25 Statute of Merton (20 Hen III) c.9.

if correct, provide another example of an indigenous rule preferred to those developed on the Continent.

Lord Blackburn summed up the post-Reformation understanding when he spoke of the common law in narrower and wider senses: meaning respectively the indigenous rules, applied in what had until shortly before been the courts of Westminster Hall, and the adoptive rules that the ecclesiastical courts had applied in marriage cases.[26]

The Domestic Canons

England's bishops also met in council during the middle ages and, with other clergy, made canons to supplement the Continental rules. In 1532 they admitted they had done so without right, and an Act of the following year accepted their submission, reminded them no canon could contravene the general law but allowed canons to be made thenceforth with royal licence and assent. Earlier canons might 'be used and executed as they were afore the making of this Act'.[27]

Several sets of canons, including provisions on marriage, were made in the reign of Elizabeth I but superseded by the more comprehensive provision of 1603 (Canterbury) and 1605 (York). The relevant canons of 1603 concerned preliminaries to marriage,[28] the place and time,[29] parental consent,[30] prohibited degrees of kindred and affinity,[31] registration,[32] evidence in matrimonial causes[33] and the bar to further marriage that continued despite a divorce 'from bed and board'.[34]

Middleton v. Crofts[35]

The limited reach of domestic canons, and the adoption test to be applied to the Continental canon law, were both illustrated in 1736 when a Herefordshire couple, who had been through a ceremony of marriage conducted in the local parsonage in the early morning, without banns called, and been summoned before the local ecclesiastical

---

26 *Mackonochie v. Lord Penzance* (1881) L.R. 6 AppCas 424, 446.
27 Submission of the Clergy Act 1533 ss. 1, 3, 7.
28 Canon 62 and 101–4.
29 Canon 62.
30 Canons 62 and 100.
31 Canon 99.
32 Canon 70.
33 Canon 105.
34 Canon 107.
35 (1736) 2 Atk 650.

court for irregular solemnization, challenged the validity of the rules alleged against them in the Court of King's Bench. All three rules – the requirement of banns, the requirement of a 'church or chapel where one of them dwelleth' and the requirement that solemnization take place 'between the hours of eight and twelve in the forenoon … and likewise in time of divine service' – could be found in Canon 62 of 1603. Though worded as prohibitions on ministers solemnizing marriages, their indirect effect on laypeople seeking to marry was obvious.

The unanimous King's Bench decision was, first, that none of the three requirements was binding on the couple merely by virtue of approval in convocations of the clergy. The provincial convocations bind only the clerics represented in them, and cannot make law for the whole English Church. The second question was, therefore, whether the three rules could be found in the adoptive common law; for if so, the couple were undoubtedly bound. It was held that banns and solemnization in church had both become common law requirements, which the couple could be punished for disregarding. But the so-called 'canonical hours' had never been adopted in England except by the convocations, so no censure could be passed for the early timing of the ceremony. The canonical requirement of parental consent might well have been viewed in a similar light if ever challenged, since this too was unknown before the Reformation.

Solemnization Reforms from 1753

Parliament returned to the regulation of marriage in 1753, to address the problem of clandestine solemnization. Mavericks in holy orders were held responsible for the unsuitable and unrecorded unions that took place outside church buildings without families' knowledge, but nevertheless had full legal effect. The remedy was to set out certain elements of solemnization as mandatory and invalidate ceremonies failing to conform. Seventy years on, a replacement Act added additional requirements but removed the draconian sanction of nullity except when both parties knew of a defect. Minor modifications followed in 1856.

Lord Hardwicke's Act provided that unless banns had been duly published (or a licence obtained), a solemnized marriage would be null and void 'to all intents and purposes'.[36] Parental consent was no longer to rely on a doubtfully effective provision in the canons: either parent

---

36 Clandestine Marriages Act 1753 s.8.

could 'forbid the banns' of a minor, making publication void, but if no objection were raised at publication, solemnization could proceed.[37] For licences a stricter rule prevailed: a minor's licence would be void if the appropriate consent was factually lacking.[38] Solemnization was to take place in 'a church or chapel where banns have been usually published', non-compliance again resulting in nullity. Requirements of two witnesses and registration (its first appearance in statute) carried no sanction.

The 1823 Act added to the requirements, but nullity was only to ensue if the parties 'knowingly and wilfully intermarried' in violation. The 'canonical hours' that had been held non-binding in *Middleton v. Crofts* became a statutory requirement, and knowing acquiescence in solemnization by a person not in holy orders was finally stated to render the marriage void.[39] Rules were further tightened by the Act of 1856, which required 'a duly qualified clergyman of the United Church of England and Ireland' and that only the forms and ceremonies of that Church (that is, the Prayer Book Order) should be used.[40] No sanction of nullity was attached by the 1856 Act, but from this time onwards it was possible to assume all parish church marriages would be 'according to the rites of the Church of England', and the 1949 consolidation described them by reference to rite rather than location.

More far-reaching changes were made by Lord John Russell's Marriage Act 1836, passed simultaneously with the Act introducing central marriage registration. Together these Acts created a new public office of superintendent registrar, with no religious connotations, and allowed trustees of buildings used for alternative public worship to seek their registration for marriages.[41] Two options were then given to couples not wishing to marry in the parish church. They could marry in a registered building 'by such form and ceremony as they see fit to adopt',[42] or in the office of the registrar with no religious service at all.[43] The essential words of the marriage contract were set out in the Act and required to be used in either venue.[44] In lieu of banns published in

---

37 Ibid. s.3.

38 Ibid. s.11.

39 Marriage Act 1823 s.22. Successive relaxations extended the times when marriage might take place, until the Protection of Freedoms Act 2012 s.114 abolished the restriction entirely.

40 Marriage and Registration Act 1856 s.11.

41 Births and Deaths Registration Act 1836 s.7; Marriage Act 1836 s.18.

42 Marriage Act 1836 s.20.

43 Ibid. s.21.

44 Ibid. s.20.

the parish church there would be a notice of (intended) marriage, given and displayed at the register office, after which a certificate would be issued as authority for the marriage to proceed.[45] There was no need for a clergyman at such solemnization: the registrar's presence would validate it,[46] though a later amendment allowed the 'governing body' of a registered building to authorize a person of their choice as validator instead.[47] At no stage was any role given to a Dissenting minister as such: if he officiated it would only be as a feature of the 'form and ceremony' that the parties had chosen.

The Act of 1836 relegated three long-standing canonical requirements (building, clerk and rite) from being the general expectation to being elements of one formation alternative. Even for parish church marriages, it allowed the new notice and certificate in lieu of banns. As clergy began, not long afterwards, to make high claims for the authority of the convocations, some found the non-canonical certificate procedure objectionable, and the Act of 1856 allowed couples to marry by it in a parish church only with the minister's consent.[48]

The Acts of 1823, 1836, 1856 and 1898, now consolidated with provisions for special cases in the Marriage Act 1949, contained between them the principal marriage formation requirements of today.[49]

The Marriage Contract since Solemnization Reform

The Acts just mentioned reformed solemnization and penalized non-compliance. With one exception they left the marriage contract untouched. The exception was that courts could no longer order solemnization on proof of a contract *de præsenti*.[50]

From one viewpoint this stripped the unsolemnized contract of its greatest significance. If it could no longer be 'specifically performed', what was it worth? The temporal courts might award damages for breach but this merely placed it on a par with engagement *de futuro*. However, the legislation said nothing about the internal forum, in which the contract retained the moral force it had always enjoyed.

---

45 Ibid. ss. 4 and 7.

46 Ibid. s.20.

47 Marriage Act 1898.

48 Marriage and Registration Act 1856 s.11.

49 E.g. marriage in armed forces chapels, of detained and housebound persons and of the terminally ill. The Marriage Act 1994 provided for local authority approval of premises as marriage venues for non-religious solemnization only.

50 Marriage Act 1753 s.13; Marriage Act 1823 s.27.

Nor did it expressly abolish the impediment of prior contract; and for a long time afterwards doubts persisted whether a contracted party's later marriage could still be annulled on that basis.[51]

The reason why this remained untested was that unsolemnized contracts *de præsenti* virtually disappeared after 1753. Lord Hardwicke's Act gave notice to all those previously ignorant that solemnization was indispensable; so they contracted their marriages in the course of solemnization rather than before it. Rather than speculate about the hypothetical unsolemnized contract, therefore, it is helpful to focus on the fact that the contract still remains part of every solemnized marriage. The public liturgy contains words of contract; the 'form or ceremony' used in registered buildings, register offices and approved places and in any solemnization for the detained or housebound must contain words of contract.[52] Quaker marriage practice requires each party, during the meeting in which they marry, to declare he or she takes the other party as spouse. The giving of a ring at the *kedushim*, the first part of a Jewish marriage ceremony, is only effective if the ring is willingly accepted.

Lord Chancellor Campbell remarked in 1861, 'I deprecate the expression of parties being "married in the sight of God" if the marriage is not recognized by the law of the country in which they live.'[53] But human fallibility had driven a wedge between the internal and external fora long before the Reformation, with the requirement that a contract must be proved to be judicially acted on. That did not stop the external forum recognizing the rule of the internal as an ideal. Much more recently the High Court has reiterated that 'the essence of marriage is the formal exchange of voluntary consents to take one another for husband and wife.'[54]

Controversial Reforms

1 Divorce

In permitting divorce with the freedom to remarry, the Matrimonial Causes Act 1857 opened an era of religious controversy over marriage unparalleled since the 1530s. The Act required proof of one party's

---

51 Late-nineteenth-century treatises express this doubt, which was only finally laid to rest when the Matrimonial Causes Act 1973 declared its lists of grounds of nullity and voidability to be exhaustive.

52 Marriage Act 1949 ss. 44(3)–(3A), 45(1), 45A(3), 46B(3).

53 *Beamish v. Beamish* (1861) 9 HLC 274, 338.

54 *Collett v Collett* [1968] P 482, *per* Ormrod J.

adultery, which had always been accepted[55] as justification for the wronged spouse to separate; but unlike most personal Divorce Acts, it also allowed remarriage by the 'guilty' party.

Much greater controversy was generated by the Matrimonial Causes Act 1937 which, following broadly the recommendations of a Royal Commission in 1912 but in the climate of heightened sensitivity following the abdication of Edward VIII, extended divorce grounds to cover desertion, cruelty and incurable insanity.

Abolition of collusion as a bar to divorce in 1963 indicated an openness to allow the spouses themselves to judge whether their marriage remained viable, but collusive divorces depended on a fiction of fault and were never satisfactory. The Divorce Law Reform Act 1969 moved concepts of 'guilt' into the background by making irretrievable breakdown the primary test, though an updated version of the 1937 grounds remained as 'facts' to be shown before irrevocable breakdown could be found. Consensual separation for an adequate period, however, was added to those facts.

2 Affinity

The Marriage Act 1540 declared it lawful for 'all persons that be not prohibited by God's law to marry' to do so. This abrogated any Continental rules imposing bars of merely human origin; but the Act made no attempt to list the unions remaining forbidden. In 1563 Archbishop Matthew Parker produced a 'table of kindred and affinity', an interpretation of the laws of God which, if correct, stated the effect of the 1540 Act.

Parker's table was incorporated into Canon 99 of 1603–5, but as already noted this could give it no greater force as regards the laity than it already possessed. Lord Lyndhurst's Matrimonial Causes Act 1835 not only gave the prohibited degrees statutory force but also declared offending marriages void, when they had long been merely voidable. This heightened the controversy surrounding three of Parker's relationships (wife's sister and wife's brother's or sister's daughter) that were not in fact forbidden in Leviticus 18, unless the general words of 18.6 were taken to go beyond the specific cases enumerated in 18.7–17. Victorian parliaments began to consider this question, and in 1907 an Act was passed to legalize marriage to a deceased wife's sister. Subsequent affinity legislation allowed additional contentious unions,

---

55 On the basis of Matthew 19.9.

including the one that had led to Princess Catherine's annulment in 1533; clearly Parliament's assessment of the laws of God had changed.

3 Marriageable age and parental consent

The adoptive common law set the age of marital capacity at 12 for a bride and 14 for a groom. Between those ages and 21 the only restrictions on marriage were the parental rights in relation to marriage preliminaries introduced by the Act of 1753. The 'age of consent' was raised to 16 for both genders in 1929[56] and the 'age of majority' lowered to 18 from 1970.[57]

4 Characteristics ascertained after marriage

The 1937 Act allowed a marriage to be annulled, on petition within a year by a party who discovered in the other party certain characteristics of which he or she had up to then been ignorant: certain mental conditions, communicable venereal disease or pregnancy by another. Consummation, once aware of the condition, was to act as a waiver. Each of these grounds could be argued to derive from the notion of consent, which ignorance on such a key point invalidated. But it was more difficult to argue this for wilful refusal to consummate, which some viewed as divorce by the will of the parties.

5 Gender issues

The impediment of like sex had existed since Roman times. Roman society had been more open to same-sex relationships than their medieval successors, but had never seen the need to attach the legal consequences of marriage to such unions. Under the bishops' influence, Theodosius I decreed the death penalty for any same-sex couple who used a conventional marriage rite.

In England, neither statute nor canon spelt out this impediment (perhaps considering it self-evident)[58] until the phenomenon of intersex partners called for clarity.[59] The Matrimonial Causes Act 1973 added it to the list of factors rendering a marriage void.

---

56 Age of Marriage Act 1929.
57 Family Law Reform Act 1969.
58 *Corbett v. Corbett* [1970] 2 WLR 1306.
59 Law Commission Report 33 *Nullity of Marriage*, 1970, para 33.

However, growing awareness that gender identity went beyond physical characteristics meant that, by the early twenty-first century, transgender individuals were seeking to marry people of the opposite sex to that which they perceived themselves to be. Under pressure from the European Court of Human Rights, Parliament legislated to allow a person to marry in their assigned gender.[60] To some who believed that physical attributes indicated the gender unalterably bestowed by God, the marriages allowed by the Act were same-sex marriages.

Actual same-sex marriage was recognized by law in 2013, following a period in which same-sex partners had been able to gain many of the material benefits of marriage from a new legal institution introduced by the Civil Partnership Act 2004. But civil partnership, it was stressed at the outset, was not marriage. Not only did it lack marriage's name and accompanying respectability, it lacked the core of marriage – the contract to take one another as spouse with immediate effect. Religious solemnization was also excluded.[61] Instead parties declared on paper their wish to become each other's civil partner[62] – a status with no historically understood content, which could therefore only be interpreted according to the benefits spelt out in the Act creating it. Whether this could be considered to bestow married status in the internal forum was therefore highly uncertain – certainly many civil partners considered themselves married in conscience, but many did not, and continued the pressure for the law to allow them to contract and hence to marry 'in the sight of God'. That aspiration was not met until the 2013 Marriage (Same Sex Couples) Act took effect.

6 The legal effects of marriage

Given the tendency in past centuries to determine whether a relationship was marriage by examining its external forum effects,[63] it is striking how far those effects have changed since the Hanoverian era. Damages for criminal conversation were abolished in 1857.[64] Many of the effects of coverture (the husband's right to administer his wife's property) disappeared in 1870,[65] dower and curtesy (interests in a deceased spouse's

---

60 Gender Recognition Act 2004 s.9(1).

61 Civil Partnership Act 2004 s.2(5).

62 Civil Partnership Act 2004 ss.2(1), 7(1).

63 See remarks of Wynne DA in *Lindo v. Belisario*, quoted above, and of Lord Cottenham in *R. v. Millis*, above, at 878.

64 Matrimonial Causes Act 1857 s.59.

65 Married Women's Property Act 1870.

estate) were replaced by new inheritance rights in 1925.[66] Marriage was a factor in the definitions of adultery and fornication, but the ecclesiastical courts' jurisdiction to censure laymen for these offences ended in 1963.[67] In 1970 the order for restitution of conjugal rights was abolished.[68] Many of the legal disadvantages of illegitimacy for offspring were ended in 1988.[69] And in 1991 the notion that a wife gave on marriage an irrevocable consent to intercourse was held to have been a misunderstanding of the common law.[70] On the other hand, marriage has gained importance in new fields, such as social provision, pensions, equality law and immigration.

The Accommodation of Dissent

1 Alternative believers and non-believers

Since many of the reforms described in the last section were controversial on religious grounds, we must now consider how far the law has moved to accommodate disparate beliefs in this area.

To hold, and even voice, divergent understandings of marriage was lawful long before the freedom of religion and its manifestation were guaranteed by the European Convention.[71] Apart from special cases like challenges to a monarch's right to the Crown, expression of a view about marriage is covered by the general common law freedom to do whatever is not prohibited.

The toleration of alternative religion has extended this freedom to religious groups who feel the need to establish tribunals to rule on religious validity of marriage, and possibly also religious divorce, for their own purposes. Such bodies and their rulings have significance only within the community concerned: if a Roman Catholic diocesan tribunal adjudges a marriage null, its status in the eyes of the law (as extant or dissolved) is unaffected. If a *Beth Din* authorizes the delivery of a *get* or Jewish divorce, the affected marriage may be ended in Jewish eyes but again its English status remains unchanged.[72]

---

66 Administration of Estates Act 1925 s.45.

67 Ecclesiastical Jurisdiction Measure 1963.

68 Matrimonial Proceedings and Property Act 1970 s.20.

69 Family Law Reform Act 1987 s.1.

70 *R. v. R* [1991] 3 WLR 767.

71 European Convention on Human Rights, Art 9; Human Rights Act 1998.

72 But see Matrimonial Causes Act 1973 s.10A, introduced in 2002 to address the problem of Jewish husbands divorcing Orthodox wives only at law without following Jewish custom.

Attempts to form marriage within a religious group and following its usages have received varying treatment. Any consensual marriage among alternative believers was likely to amount to a marriage contract that, as already observed, required no formalities. Roman Catholic rites constituted full solemnization since their priests were in orders.

The 1844 Lords' decision that the indigenous common law had required an attendant clerk in orders for solemnization to be valid did, on the other hand, retrospectively invalidate many unions of Dissenting protestants who, prior to 1753, had seen no great necessity to attend the parish church to marry. The saving factor was that most affected couples were by then dead. Their bastardized offspring were vulnerable to claims against their inherited property but very few were brought.

The pressure brought by the 1753 Act itself to marry in the parish church – and so, almost inevitably, by the Prayer Book liturgy – bore lightly on most Dissenters. It was moderated towards Quakers and Jews, the groups most likely to object when the Act was passed. The legal status of their marriages remained in doubt, but no more than before the Act, and gained full recognition in the Act of 1836. Unitarians and non-believers, however, found the obligation to marry by a Trinitarian religious rite a serious burden.

The 1837 Act allowed religious rites of all sorts to be used in registered buildings, not in their own right but as 'the form and ceremony [the parties] see fit to adopt'.[73] Non-believers and those with no buildings could contract marriage before a registrar and follow their own rites subsequently.

Problems remained in newly settled communities not fully integrated into English society. One example flowed from the influx of Russian and Polish Jews after 1880. Guided by strictly observant rabbis, they married by Jewish usages, divorced by Jewish usages (both of which were legally unobjectionable) and then married again (which was bigamy, since the Jewish marriage had legal effect but the *get* did not). Leaders of England's integrated Jewish community, who had long adopted the principle that a legal marriage must be ended by a legal divorce, even if a religious divorce accompanied it, were incensed at the reputational damage and recommended criminal sanctions against the 'foreign rabbis'.[74]

Closely comparable examples arise today where Muslim, Sikh, Hindu and Oriental Christian (e.g. Coptic) arrivals in England move mainly

---

73 Marriage Act 1836 ss.2, 20.
74 Evidence to the Royal Commission on Divorce and Matrimonial Causes, PP 1912–13, xx [Cd 6481] qq. 41384 and 41477.

in their own circles, many unaware of the registered building regime. If a non-compliant ceremony is meant to effect a legal marriage, the officiant risks prosecution for solemnization contrary to the Marriage Acts; but if not, it lies outside the nullity (and therefore the financial provision) jurisdiction of the courts. Varying conclusions have been reached on the facts, and reliance placed in some cases on legal presumptions of validity or compliance.[75]

Registered buildings, Friends' meeting houses and the venues where Jews marry are all in principle private property. The trustees' or owners' freedom to refuse access is usually enough to allow them to stand aloof from marriages of which they disapprove. An express requirement of hosts' permission was nevertheless imposed by the Marriage and Registration Act 1856. The Roman Catholic hierarchy achieved a special requirement for consent by the parish priest, an officer more easily controlled than lay trustees.[76]

Since 1965 discrimination law has qualified freedom to refuse services offered to the general public, but dissent from marriage reforms never touched protected 'equality strands' until the Gender Recognition Act. Recent legislation has given express exemptions to alternative religious groups that decline to host marriage for religious reasons.[77]

2 The religious establishment and the registration service

A crucial contrast between alternative religious groups on the one hand, and the religious establishment and the registration service on the other, is that both the latter exist to serve the public. Parish churches are not private property but held for the use of the parishioners.[78] Solemnization of parishioners' marriages is one of the duties of a parish minister.[79] Register offices are provided and registrars employed at public expense for a statutory purpose.

Registrars and parish ministers have consciences, and not all of them agree with every aspect of English marriage law as reformed. But

---

75 *R. v. Mohamed Ali* [1964] 2 QB 352, *R. v Bham* [1966] 1 QB 159, *Gereis v Yagoub* [1997] 1 FLR 854, *A-M v A-M* [2001] 2 FLR 6, *Gandhi v Patel* [2002] 1 FLR 603, *A v. A* [2012] EWHC 2219 (Fam). The 1973 Law Commission Report on *Solemnization of Marriage in England and Wales* described 'the deliberate solemnisation of invalid marriages' as a 'growing mischief'.

76 s.11.

77 Equality Act 2010 Sch 3 paras 24(2)–(4) and 25A; Marriage (Same Sex Couples) Act 2013 s.2

78 *Griffin v. Dighton* (1864) 5 B&S 103.

79 *Argar v. Holdsworth* (1758) 2 Lee 516.

(unlike officers of Dissenting groups) neither can distinguish the rules by which they operate from the law of the land. In the case of parish ministers this is a consequence of the unity of the law as declared at the Reformation, and was confirmed by the House of Lords in a celebrated case arising out of the first affinity reform: 'there can be no duality in marriage'.[80]

Religious freedom, in such a situation, is the freedom to resign.[81] Ministers have won respect in the past by transferring denomination to avoid legal expectations with which they could not comply. But in 1857 Parliament set a precedent of offering an exemption from parish ministers' duty to solemnize the further marriage of a divorced 'guilty party'. No comparable exemption was offered to a registrar who might have to do this: registrars' interests were not represented by a body of Lords spiritual in Parliament.

This precedent was followed at the twentieth-century affinity reforms and in relation to divorce in the Act of 1937; but with one significant difference. In 1857 a balance was struck between clerical scruples and parishioners' rights: a minister declining to officiate was to permit another minister from the same diocese to do so in his place.[82] In 1907 this was optional: a permission refusal would prevent parishioners marrying in their parish church at all.[83] The 1907 approach was taken in the later statutes and in 1937 extended also to divorce for adultery.[84]

3 Conscience clause or 'law of the church'? The revised canons

Though a parish minister was accorded in 1857 the right to decline to officiate, he was clearly under no duty to do so. The Act protected him against discipline for *solemnizing or* refusing to solemnize.[85] Ministers who believed the Act consistent with Christian principle could therefore freely act under it, whatever their brethren believed. The language of the 1907 Act was more opaque but did not prevent ministers acting under the reformed law if they felt it right. The parishioner's right to marry in the parish church existed at common law and therefore prevailed over the canon forbidding such marriages, except where the conscience clause was invoked. What the clergy could not do with impunity was to

---

80 *Thompson v. Dibdin* [1912] AC 533 at 543, *per* Lord Ashbourne.

81 *X v. Denmark* EComHR application 7374, 8 March 1976.

82 Matrimonial Causes Act 1857 s.58.

83 Deceased Wife's Sister Marriage Act 1907 s.1.

84 Matrimonial Causes Act 1937 s.11. See now Marriage Act 1949 ss.5A–5B, Matrimonial Causes Act 1965 s.8(2).

85 Matrimonial Causes Act 1857 s.57.

marry under the new law themselves: another concession won by Archbishop Davidson allowed them to be disciplined for so doing as 'if this Act had not been passed'.[86] However, in 1946 the clergy convocations accepted the inevitable and amended the canon on affinity.

The episcopal hierarchy was as divided on these questions as were worshippers. By 1937, Archbishop Temple of York among others was starting to advocate an ideal for 'the church's members' distinct from 'what the State imposes under penalty'.[87] In line with this the convocations passed resolutions calling for punishment of lay people who divorced under that year's Act and remarried. (This was, of course, quite beyond their powers as explained in *Middleton v. Crofts*.) Bishop Barnes of Birmingham, though, objected to a bill harmonizing marriage law with 'the opinion [of] the overwhelming majority of enlightened Christian people in this country' being treated as 'a concession to a semi-pagan community'.[88]

An ambitious project to replace the Jacobean canons began before the Second World War and gathered pace after it. In 1949 draft canons reflecting a rigorist approach to marriage came for consideration. One sought to forbid all remarriage in church after divorce, another to forbid the marriage of the unbaptized. Legal advice that there was in fact no distinct 'church law' in these areas and that legislation would be difficult to achieve caused the proposals to be dropped in 1956;[89] while a separate Archbishops' Commission argued against nullity tribunals on the Roman Catholic model.[90] Ordinands were an easier target: legislation to exclude the remarried from ordination was passed in 1964.[91]

The marriage canons given royal assent in 1964 were a damp squib compared to the original proposals. Canon B40 combined language from the Prayer Book solemnization rite with the definition of marriage offered in 1886, during a nullity suit based on polygamy.[92] The remaining canons to see the light of day did no more than reiterate the law. So far as remarriage after divorce was concerned, the convocations and later the General Synod ultimately took the more realistic path of guidance and persuasion rather than purporting to legislate.

86 Deceased Wife's Sister Marriage Act 1907 s.4.

87 Hansard (Lords) col. 782; 1 June 1937.

88 Ibid. cols. 812 and 818.

89 *York Journal of Convocation*, May 1956, 60–3; *Chronicle of Convocation*, May 1956, pp. 49–50, 81.

90 Archbishops' Commission, *The Church and the Law of Nullity of Marriage*, London: SPCK, 1955, pp. 42–4.

91 Clergy (Ordination and Miscellaneous Provisions) Measure 1964 s.9.

92 *Hyde v. Hyde & Woodmansee* (1866) LR 1 P & D 130.

4 Same-sex marriage

The Act opening marriage to all couples became law in 2013 after a surprisingly smooth passage through both Houses. Bishops who spoke against its passage before Second Reading appeared to revert to William Temple's line when the bill received overwhelming support in the House of Lords. But already as introduced, the bill contained provisions quite unlike those in any earlier marriage reform. Instead of a conscience clause, even on the minister-friendly 1907 model, parish church solemnization was excluded and parishioners' rights confined to opposite-sex marriage.[93] The opinions of the episcopate and the General Synod electorate were allowed to trump the consciences of those clergy and parishioners who believed the reform was another 'Christian bill'.[94]

Strangest of all, it was declared that Canon B40, with its opposite-sex definition of marriage, was not contrary to the requirement for canons to be consistent with statute.[95] Since the statute declares same-sex marriage lawful, this is nonsense. A possible meaning is that the canon was *exempted* from the requirement and therefore not abrogated automatically as was, for example, Canon B35 para. 3 when the time of marriage was deregulated in 2012. But if the canon continues in being, what is its effect? Normally canons either restate the law or impose additional obligations on the clergy, but this canon contradicts the law and the relevant paragraph is not worded as imposing clerical duties. Hopefully litigation to test the meaning of this provision can be avoided.

Conclusion

Lord Justice Laws considered a law rooted in religion 'deeply unprincipled'.[96] This survey of the development of marriage law in England suggests it does indeed have the Christian character one would expect from its age in the light of English religious history. But the freedom given to those who reject its underlying theology to hold and voice their own opinions, to marry in their own ways and to refrain from participating in forming unions of which they disapprove suggests there is now a principled respect for alternative views.

---

93 Marriage (Same Sex Couples) Act 2013 s.1(2) and (4).
94 See text to n. 2 above.
95 Ibid. s.1(3).
96 See text to n. 1 above.

The institution of marriage in English law has no necessary connection with the clergy. They have no lawmaking authority in this area except to regulate themselves, and episcopally appointed judges have lost the jurisdiction in matrimonial causes they once had. A clerk's presence was never essential to concluding a marriage contract and it is doubtful whether it was ever essential to solemnization (save that in England between 1823 and 1836 couples could not knowingly acquiesce in solemnization by a non-clerk). Since 1836 a clerk has only been required in one of several alternative formation procedures.

But an institution can be religious in a Protestant country without the need for clerical involvement. Despite its pre-Christian origins, England recognized in marriage a divinely instituted status with moral implications, the core of which was the contract. That contract remains an essential part of English marriage today, while solemnization requirements come and go. Though capacity to make the contract, in other words an absence of impediments, is equally essential, Parliament has regulated impediments for most of its history with careful attention to theological arguments.[97] Even in today's utilitarian political climate there has been no deliberate divergence, no statutory renunciation of the Christian claims made earlier for marriage, in the courts and indeed by Parliament itself. If the conclusions Parliament has reached are disputed by many believers or the bulk of the clergy, that does not necessarily make them wrong.

Reference

Pearce, C. C. A., 2002, 'The Christian Claims of the English Law of Marriage', in Adrian Thatcher (ed.), *Celebrating Christian Marriage*, Edinburgh: T&T Clark, pp. 403–20.

---

97 For a fuller treatment, see Pearce 2002.

Afterword: Setting Marriage in Context

RACHEL MUERS

Rereading Hannah's Story

I begin, following the example of several of the contributors to this
volume, by taking an unusual scriptural way into the theology of
marriage – the story of Hannah (1 Samuel 1—2). Ordinarily this is not
read as a story about marriage at all but as a story about the pain of
childlessness, the abundant joy of prayers answered. Thinking about
marriage, however, and in particular about the ways marriage makes
intimacy shareable and gives rise to fruitfulness, we might pause earlier
in Hannah's story – at the first point at which the expected proprieties
of the family are interrupted:

> On the day when Elkanah sacrificed, he would give portions to his
> wife Peninnah and to all her sons and daughters; but to Hannah
> he gave a double portion, because he loved her ... [he] said to her,
> 'Hannah, why do you weep? Why do you not eat? Why is your heart
> sad? Am I not more to you than ten sons?' (1 Sam. 1.4–5, 8)

Elkanah is excessively devoted to Hannah, we might think, just because
of who she is and irrespective of what she can do for him; he longs for
her to find the same joy in him as he finds in her. His excessive love –
which is over and above what the maintenance of his status as patriarch
requires, and which indeed threatens to destabilize it – is not restricted
to the private sphere. It overflows into the public and the liturgical
realm and becomes visible in the 'double portion' ceremonially allo-
cated to her in defiance of expectations. Love pushes against the limits
of what is supposed to be fitting, appropriate or reasonable. It makes its
own reason; Elkanah gave Hannah a double portion *because* he loved
her.

Stopping here, making this a story about Elkanah – as the beginning of 1 Samuel might lead us to believe it is[1] – would present a touching and rather familiar picture of romantic love, the couple who are everything to each other and need nothing more, appropriate enough to some contemporary visions of marriage. This reading would helpfully interrupt any attempt to make 'biblical' marriage mostly about reproduction; but it would also leave us – as Brett Gray suggests, in relation to a well-known essay by Rowan Williams – without a full appreciation of the social *or* the theological significance of marriage.

However, 1 Samuel 1—2 turns out not to be (mainly) Elkanah's story, and the ideal of self-sufficient coupledom proves unsustainable; perhaps it always does. As the story progresses, Hannah's own desire for a child of her own also moves her into a public liturgical space. Her desire, like her husband's love, is 'excessive', disruptive, generative; it first disturbs the peace of the sanctuary and then gives rise to a blessing. Perhaps when Hannah first refuses food and then takes her anxiety 'before the LORD' she is struggling with the intolerable tensions between the different dimensions of her marriage – her inability to fulfil a woman's one essential role in a patriarchal system, the intensity of her husband's love, the daily struggle of co-existing with her 'rival'. None of this, it seems, can be resolved behind the scenes; she has to set her love and suffering 'before the LORD'; they have to break out at the heart of the social, liturgical and theological systems she inhabits.

The blessing she receives in answer to her prayer seems not to resolve the tensions – it certainly fails to put the patriarchal structure neatly back together again. Samuel himself, Hannah's longed-for son, is surplus to the family's reproductive requirements (and we are allowed to wonder whether Elkanah would have been quite so sanguine about Hannah's childlessness if he had not already had plenty of children). Hannah's desire and vow moves the boy Samuel out from Elkanah's household to the temple, and out from the temple to the service of 'all Israel'.

At the heart of the story, Hannah's song of praise proclaims both her own 'victory' and the cosmic, political and social transformation brought about by the reign of God, the same God who established the 'pillars of the earth'. A bittersweet and complicated love-and-marriage story, as the new relationships and new questions it generates move outwards through the temple and towards the people, becomes visible as the story of God as creator, judge and redeemer – without ceasing

---

1 1 Samuel 1.1: 'There was a certain man of Ramathaim, a Zuphite from the hill country of Ephraim, whose name was Elkanah son of Jeroham son of Elihu ...'

to be this particular story about devotion and promise and longings fulfilled and unfulfilled.

Hannah's story, reflected in her song, is a story of individual and social transformation – with the gift of God and a confluence of human loves at its heart. It is an embodied promise of the kingdom of God, without ever ceasing to be this one particular story. The challenge – as always with Hannah's song and with its re-citation in the Magnificat – is to read it as something other than a temporary interruption to business as usual, a little outbreak of difference within a pattern of sameness (to use Frances Clemson's terms). I shall return later to the question of the disruptive and transformative character of theologies of marriage – but first I look at the ways this volume of essays takes marriage, and the theology of marriage, outwards.

Thinking Outwards from Marriage

This collection of essays has sought to demonstrate the potential breadth and depth of a theology of marriage, and the range of resources – scriptural, traditional, historical, scientific, artistic – that can go towards developing such a theology. On the face of it it should not be surprising that, beginning with marriage, theologians are compelled to engage not only with a full range of doctrinal loci but also with questions about the nature of doctrine itself. For one thing, as Ben Fulford and others point out, the biblical and traditional sources place images of marriage at the heart of the narratives within which Christian theology locates itself – narratives of redemption, reconciliation and eschatological consummation. For another, theological reflection on marriage is inevitably directly related to, and informed by, everyday life – related not only to the core commitments and formative relationships between individuals but also to the churches and to a wide range of other institutions, and to economic and social and familial systems.

We might ask, though, whether there is any reason why *marriage* should be a particularly inclusive or generative theological topic. After all, we might think, in systematic theology it should be possible to start anywhere; or at least it should be possible to speak about anything as it relates to God as origin and *telos*, and thus to locate any significant feature of natural and social life within a larger story of creation, revelation and redemption. Alternatively or additionally we might think that marriage is one of many very important human phenomena, about which theology has much to say – and then assume that developing a theology of marriage is a matter of applying the right set of broad principles and claims to this specific phenomenon, checking that the result is not obviously ridiculous, and moving on to the next one.

In putting this volume of essays together the authors have chosen not to assume that we – theologians, or the churches – already have all the right theories, texts or concepts at the ready for solving (what seems often today to be) the 'problem' of marriage. Nor on the other hand have they attempted simply to generate a theological understanding of marriage that would be relevant to – in the sense of fully congruent with – a specific set of contemporary experiences and concerns. These essays start from marriage as the crossing point, the node or knot, of numerous strands of theology and anthropology – and work outwards from it in order better to understand the network of connections around it.

As a project in constructive theology, however, these essays also seek to *repair* the theological connections around marriage, and in doing so to repair some of the disconnections in wider thought and practice around marriage. A good theology of marriage, as these essays demonstrate, challenges the setting-apart and idealization of romantic love, as well as the reluctance to critique the modern marriage industry; it challenges the theological reading of marriage through a narrow account of gender complementarity, as well as the reduction of marriage to sexual encounter; it challenges the separation of (thinking about) marriage from (thinking about) other vocations, as well as the neglect of ecclesiology in theologies of marriage. Part of the point of this volume is to show what can go wrong, and what we can lose, when we do not connect up our theological thinking about marriage. The more important point, however, is to show what can be gained by following the threads and repairing the connections.

It is also important to say that the theology of marriage is worth attending to now, in particular, just because of contemporary anxieties about marriage. Tensions within and around marriage – like those that animate Hannah's story – enter the public and liturgical space and disrupt it. Theologians can choose to suppress these tensions and anxieties with ready-made answers (as Eli the priest initially tries to do) – or, given enough time and resources, to wait a little longer, listen a little more carefully and receive whatever gift or blessing might emerge from the anxiety. The essays in this volume begin in the middle of things, surrounded by and involved in practices and institutions that are both life-giving and broken – just where theologies of marriage (Charlotte Methuen's article reminds us) have always begun.

As the essays here show, the theology of marriage is not a private, a marginal or a 'niche' interest. Like Hannah it does not (or should not) remain in-house and does not limit itself to domestic concerns. It poses political and economic questions, not least to the 'nuptial-industrial complex' and the commodification of romantic love. It opens up liturgical and ecclesiological reflection by directing us to the mutual implication of claims about marriage and claims about the Church; and it raises questions about the nature and sources of theology itself.

Inclusive Exclusivity as a Challenge for Theologies of Marriage

Where does theological reflection on marriage take us? One obvious starting point is with Julie Gittoes' account of inclusive exclusivity. Marriage, Gittoes writes in her account of the Church of England liturgy, is a seal upon the heart *and* a crown upon the head, neither without the other. It is personal but not private. The love expressed and enjoined in marriage 'goes public'; it radiates to and is reflected in the community that celebrates it. The 'inclusive exclusivity' of the love between Christ and the Church is imaged in marriage – a profound mutual love that just as such becomes a gift to the world, drawing others into its light. John Bradbury articulates the connection between the Christ–Church relationship and the marriage relationship in terms of the social vocation of humanity in Christ – being called into particular intense relationships that bless and reshape wider networks of social relations.

Good theologies of marriage, we might want to say, would display and spread this core story of 'inclusive exclusivity'. To look closely at marriage – with an 'exclusive' focus on this specific relationship and this specific vocation – sheds light on the wider, dynamic and unbounded network of social relations and the diversity and complexity of vocations, and the way all of them are held together in and transformed by the particular intensity of divine love in Christ. A theology of marriage is particularly well suited to bring together – in generative ways – specific issues that are often held apart: basic questions in theological anthropology (for example, around gender and sexuality) with basic questions in theological method (for example, around tradition and authority); theologies of creation with rich accounts of individual and social vocation.

The worry raised by many of the essays in this collection, though, is that theologies of marriage often seem to start from a sweepingly *in*clusive claim – that marriage construed in a certain way is culturally universal, unequivocally affirmed throughout Christian history or the unshakeable foundation of society – and then use this as a basis for various *ex*clusive moves; for example, excluding certain voices and experiences from the theology of marriage or from the goods of marriage itself.

As Rowan Williams explores in the well-known piece discussed by Brett Gray, sexual encounter and sexual desire entail vulnerability. Making an intimate relationship public through marriage – connecting it to the wider community and offering it as the basis for shared visions of the future – adds new levels of risk and vulnerability. But as many of the authors in this book show as they analyse the contexts in which theologies of marriage emerge, the 'vulnerability' involved in marriage is unevenly distributed. It is unevenly distributed within marriage itself – so, for example, in Hannah's story, *she* carries both the social vulnerability of childlessness and the physical risk of childbearing. It is also unevenly distributed across society. The respectability and public recognition accorded to my marriage sets limits to the 'vulnerability' I take on. With my marriage unquestioned, my relationship is not vulnerable to social opprobrium nor my family to the threat of dissolution.

In working on the theology of marriage, then, we need to face difficult questions about the 'gatekeeper' role of the churches and of theologies – the power to declare certain relationships, or certain ways of marriage, orthodox, respectable, traditional and theologically appropriate, and hence to marginalize others. These are some of the questions put by Mike Higton's rereading of recent Church of England statements on marriage, in which he attends inter alia to the risks bound up with making claims about (in particular) 'natural' roles of men and women or natural expressions of sexuality. Higton's observation that Christian theology – alongside other powerful cultural forces – makes a world in which 'toxic myths ... are used to exclude and to demean', and in which 'violent abuse can hide', demonstrates that theological thinking about marriage raises questions about the ethics and politics of theology itself.

Theologies of marriage are rather obviously theologies of vulnerable bodies – but it is also useful to be reminded, following the strands of a theology of marriage, that *all* theologies have the potential to affect bodies: which bodies matter and are valued, which are fed and welcomed, which are recognized or heard in their suffering, which cannot be recognized at all. Susannah Cornwall's chapter highlights the 'hiddenness', in the churches and far more widely, of people whose bodily experience of sex and gender does not fit a dominant (and itself historically contingent) account of how human sex 'ought' to work.

And as Brett Gray observes, the social and ideological power of the churches, embedded in the respectability and recognition accorded to marriage and (in at least some recent documents) in the reaffirmation of normative heterosexuality, is closely linked to other kinds of power – such as the immense profitability of the 'nuptial-industrial complex' and various new and not-so-new manifestations of the sexual double standard. We need to recognize the extent to which the institution of marriage is not only – as in the marriage liturgies quoted by several contributors – a remedy for sin but itself always implicated in sinful structures. In Hannah's story, Elkanah's excessive and (possibly) self-sacrificing love for Hannah was still love offered by a patriarch with the power to determine the lives and 'portions' of his wives and children, who is accorded a genealogy of his own while his wives' stories are determined by their relationships to him. Hannah and Peninnah still fight over status and profit at each other's expense – not to mention at the expense of the sexually 'deviant' women who appear elsewhere in the biblical narrative and who suffer as a result of not being given a secure place within the familial system.

Prophetic Theologies of Marriage

Theologies of marriage and gender, as these essays describe them, are also doctrines of power in/over bodies. They are ways of declaring which bodies matter and how they matter; which bodies and which relationships are honoured and crowned; which are consigned to oblivion. How do our theologies of marriage proclaim the reign of the God who raises up the poor and lifts the needy from the ash-heap into a seat of honour? In our theologies of marriage, on whose heads are crowns being set?

Charlotte Methuen, in her tracing of the history of marriage, displays among other things the critical and prophetic dynamics of a theology of marriage – how Christian theologies of marriage have historically challenged the unbridled exercise of patriarchal power, demanded attention to the voices of women (as consenting, or not, to marriage) and called into question the power of marriage to perpetuate the concentration of wealth and power. A 'traditional' theology of marriage that followed *this* tradition would be wary of giving an unqualified affirmation to (any set of) existing ways of doing marriage – particularly as regards how they apportion wealth and status, honour and shame, crowns and ashes. It would recognize, in fact, that marriage is not *created* by theology – it is found, celebrated, critiqued and reshaped. Theologies of marriage need to involve critical reflection on how theology treats the social realities it 'finds' – how it bears faithful witness both to the prophetic critique of existing orders and to the blessing of bodily life.

Every theological account of marriage recognizes that the churches did not invent marriage. As Methuen shows in detail, the relationship between ecclesial and liturgical marriage on the one hand and the public recognition and celebration of marriages on the other has been complex. The churches have not, historically, simply taken marriage 'as they found it' but nor have they reinvented it from scratch. The history of marriage in Christian contexts is, among other things, the history of conversations with and about wider cultural assumptions about marriage and sexuality – in which there is prophetic challenge both from and to the churches, and also the need in every case for wisdom and discernment.

It is for this reason, among others, that many of the authors in this collection are nervous of the predominance of appeals to Genesis 1—3 for theologies of marriage. Ben Fulford, following a cue from David Kelsey, proposes rooting theologies of marriage in a reading of Scripture that begins in the middle – in the double story of reconciliation and eschatological fulfilment, centred on the story of Jesus, and in a theological anthropology centred on the Wisdom tradition. This way of reading Scripture, and in particular this way of doing theological anthropology, tends to make marriage both less and more important, theologically speaking. Marriage becomes less important because we do not try to make it refer back to a pre-lapsarian ideal duality and complementarity, bearing some significant proportion of the burden of our accounts of the good human life. At the same time, marriage becomes more important because sexuality, love and familial relationships – present throughout the biblical tradition – are recognized in their ubiquity and their quotidian complexity, a strand of our lives always tangled in with other strands.

Our essays draw attention to the ways the commitment of marriage is undertaken and lived out, as Julie Gittoes puts it, 'in the face of the penultimate contingencies of life and death'. Theologies of marriage are, we might suggest, properly located in the 'penultimate' – or as Frances Clemson sees it, in the 'while' before the eschaton. Arguably, good theologies of marriage will lead directly into theological anthropologies that speak to all aspects of life in the 'penultimate'.

With and Beyond the Given: The Fruitfulness of Theologies of Marriage

Theologies of marriage are, to be sure, always also going to be theologies of creation – responsive, as Mike Higton puts it, to the 'natures we have been given in creation'. There is nothing in these essays that seeks to deny either the fact or the specific forms of human creatureliness. The argument of this book, however, is that theologies of marriage can and should address all aspects of our situation as human creatures. It is, for example, proper to our 'natures' to be desiring, time-taking, community-forming, linguistic and sign-making, orientated towards God as our origin and end – and all of these aspects of the 'natures we have been given in creation' are relevant both to marriage and to the theology of marriage.

All of this seems to suggest a marginalization of gender and sexuality in theologies of marriage. However, a key move made in this volume, specifically in relation to the sexuate character of created human life, is to understand the 'givenness' of sex and sexuality in terms of vocation. As Susannah Cornwall's chapter demonstrates, this entails being more attentive to the various *specific* ways sexed nature is 'given' to human beings – not trying to make each person's sex and sexuality fit a pre-given (and on numerous grounds unsustainable) exclusive binary of sexed identity, nor a compulsory heterosexuality orientated towards reproduction. The main point is not, however, that the 'given' forms of sexuate nature are diverse but rather that sexuate nature is 'given', to humanity generally and to human beings specifically, as an integral dimension of their vocation towards God and towards others.

While it is not particularly new to speak of marriage in terms of vocation, it is striking that so few recent theological discussions of marriage – those arising specifically in response to debates over same-sex marriage – draw on this central idea of vocation. Perhaps, as John Bradbury's chapter highlights, part of the problem is that discussions of marriage have become overly dominated by sets of static identity-defining binaries – male and female, married and single, public and private – and hence have failed to appreciate the ways the biblical and traditional witness on marriage relativizes not only marriage itself but more importantly the various binaries that structure it. Recognizing the integral human vocation – into and as community, with God and with one another – recognizes everything that marriage marks and celebrates, but sets marriage in a wider context as a 'vocation to a way of serving the human flourishing', a way of being present to and for others. As Raphael Cadenhead demonstrates through his reading of Gregory, moreover, attention to this integral human vocation does not only enable but arguably *requires* the 'displacement' of the stereotypes of (binary) gender on which certain influential accounts of complementarity in marriage are based.

The essays draw repeatedly on the insight that the marriage relationship exists for the sake of a wider network of relationships – for the family, for the Church, for the whole human community. This 'for the sake of', however, needs to be understood in time-taking and vocational terms – marriage is 'for the sake of' the human community's calling into the kingdom of God. Christian marriage, we have suggested, is not for the sake of reproducing a present social order indefinitely, just as it is.

What is revealed here is the fruitfulness of a *theology* of marriage – and how this fruitfulness goes beyond the simple reproduction of a tradition, the maintenance of existing theological conditions. Thinking theologically about marriage is important, not just because it keeps the privileges of marriage or of the churches in place by placing them on a secure theological footing but also because it challenges how we think theologically about other things. Theologies of marriage developed reactively, in the context of wider social changes to which the churches 'respond', may miss the generative potential of thinking about marriage. As I have suggested, there are many reasons in the present context why marriage might be seen as a theological *problem*; in which case, the aim of a theology of marriage would be to fix the problem and allow things to carry on (having secured the continuing respectability of theology). The essays here suggest that this is not the only or the best way to approach a theology of marriage.

The 'problems' surrounding marriage are easy to recognize. Several authors in this volume observe that marriage, and human sexuality more generally, entails vulnerability – and the inevitable recognition of our deep implication in the human propensity to 'fuck things up' (to repeat John Bradbury's reference to Francis Spufford's elegant summary of the doctrine of sin). Susannah Cornwall writes of sexed persons as not only fragile but 'damaged' and caught up in patterns of action and response that risk repeating and passing on the damage. More widely, as I have already noted, the institution of marriage – historically and to the present – is constructed and lived in various ways that are systematically damaging.

However, all the essays reflect the intuition that treating marriage mainly in terms of the problems of human relationships and their possible solutions – as a 'remedy for sin' or as a way of completing the incompleteness of a person – misses the heart of the matter. Marriage, as celebrated liturgically and as lived day to day, precedes and exceeds any lack or need. It is the crown on people's heads, the delightful and perfectly fitting gift that makes them both 'more themselves' and more *than* themselves.

Good theologies of marriage, we might suggest, should be 'crowns' for theology. We should not just grasp for theologies of marriage because we – society or the churches – have a problem with marriage; we should receive the unexpected theological gifts that reflection on marriage can bring. We should allow the theology of marriage to be fruitful, by freeing it from the requirement to fix our problems with gender and sexuality – or, for that matter, with ecclesial authority or Church–state relations. In the final section of this afterword, I suggest one way theologies of marriage might be fruitful in future.

Final Thoughts: The Extraordinariness of Weddings and the Ordinariness of Marriage

It is a frustration shared by many teachers of theological ethics – perhaps of ethics more generally – that our students prefer to see and discuss ethical issues only in a few well-defined limit situations, often situations that they themselves have never encountered directly. (This tendency – to think that ethics is mainly about euthanasia and whether to push the nuclear button – seems, unfortunately, to have survived the sustained critique of 'decision' ethics in recent decades.) It is difficult to persuade anybody to be really interested in the ethical freight of everyday situations – interested enough, that is, to want to stop and think about what they mean for theological anthropology or how they might be read from the perspective of Christian texts and traditions and narratives. Students of theological ethics often want to study marriage and sexuality, and textbooks on ethics usually contain chapters on marriage and sexuality. However, discussion of marriage tends to be focused on weddings – who is 'allowed' to marry whom; and discussion of sexuality tends to be focused on sexual intercourse – who is 'allowed' to have sex with whom. The questions asked in ethics are about extraordinary events rather than ordinary time-taking life – about weddings rather than marriage and about 'having sex' rather than sexual or erotic life.

I used to think that the preference for well-defined limit situations and extraordinary events, in the study of ethics, was partly about the reluctance of students – and indeed of ethicists – to expose the material of their daily lives to critical scrutiny, to risk turning ethical judgements on to themselves or on to their peers. Thinking about marriage (and in particular Raphael Cadenhead's reflections on marriage as ascetical training in the virtues pertaining to gendered and sexuate life), I now wonder whether there is another explanation. Are we – as theologians and theological ethicists, teachers as well as students – sometimes reluctant to acknowledge how much, on our own terms, our daily lives might *matter*? Is it sometimes too difficult to think through the implications of the claim that theology refers to us and the world we inhabit – that the *anthropos* of theological anthropology (graciously called and redeemed and drawn towards the kingdom of God) is the particular human being each of us is (complete with body, soul and human propensity to fuck things up)? Perhaps the interest in limit situations in theological ethics is not so much about not wanting to admit failures as about not wanting to do the work of understanding the theological claims embodied and embedded in daily life.

As we see in the beginning of 1 Samuel, it is impossible to get away either from the smallness of the story of marriage or from its connections to the entire scope of God's story with humanity; every strand from this little knot of a story can be followed into eternity. Marriage is one place where we cannot avoid making enormous, indeed extraordinary, theological claims about the stuff of ordinary life – and then living, day by day, with and into the claims that we make. Marriage is a space of lived theology. It strikes me as surprising that so little attention has been paid to marriage – as opposed to weddings – in theological ethics or in theological work that seeks to attend closely to ecclesial practice and mission. Particularly if we were to stop thinking of marriage in terms of an ideal to be 'lived *up* to' (and thus, inevitably, 'fallen short of'), and instead to see it more as a vocation to be lived *in* to, we might be able to recognize and celebrate more of the gifts that real marriages offer to theology. This volume is, its authors hope, the beginning of a renewed conversation in which such possibilities can be explored.

Bibliography

Aitken, Jo, 2007, '"The Horrors of Matrimony among the Masses": Feminist Representations of Wife Beating in England and Australia, 1870–1914', *Journal of Women's History* 19.4, pp. 107–31.

Allen, Prudence, 2006, 'Man–Woman Complementarity: The Catholic Inspiration', *Logos: A Journal of Catholic Thought and Culture* 9.3, pp. 87–108.

Archbishop's Commission, 1971, *Marriage, Divorce and the Church: The Report of a Commission Appointed by the Archbishop of Canterbury to Prepare a Statement on the Christian Doctrine of Marriage*, London: SPCK.

Archbishops' Council of the Church of England, 2000, *Common Worship: Pastoral Services*, 2nd edn, London: Church House Publishing.

Archbishops' Council of the Church of England, 2005, *Common Worship Pastoral Services*, London: Church House Publishing.

Archbishops' Council of the Church of England, 2013, *Men and Women in Marriage: A Document from the Faith and Order Commission Published with the Agreement of the House of Bishops of the Church of England and Approved for Study*, GS Misc 1046, London: Church House Publishing.

Augustine, *Confessions* I.11.17, trans. and ed. Albert C. Outler, London: SCM Press, 1955, p. 21, online at www.ccel.org/ccel/augustine/confessions.pdf.

Augustine, *The Good of Marriage*.

Barth, Karl, 1961, *Church Dogmatics* III.4: *The Doctrine of Creation*, trans G. W. Bromiley and T. F. Torrance, Edinburgh: T&T Clark.

Barth, Karl, 2002 [1946], 'No!', in Emil Brunner and Karl Barth, *Natural Theology: Comprising 'Nature and Grace' by Professor Dr Emil Brunner and the Reply 'No!' by Dr Karl Barth*, London: Geoffrey Bles/Centenary Press, pp. 67–128.

Barton, John, 1999, 'New Testament as Performance', *Scottish Journal of Theology* 52.2, pp. 179–208.

Barton, John, 2014, *Ethics in Ancient Israel*, Oxford: Oxford University Press,

Bennett, Jana Marguerite, 2008, *Water is Thicker Than Blood: An Augustinian Theology of Marriage and Singleness*, Oxford: Oxford University Press.

Billings, Alan, 2004, *Secular Lives, Sacred Hearts*, London: SPCK.

Bonner, Gerald, 1963, *St Augustine of Hippo: Life and Controversies*, Norwich: Canterbury Press.

Book of Common Prayer 1549, www.justus.anglican.org/resources/bcp/1549/Marriage_1549.htm.

Book of Common Prayer 1928, www.justus.anglican.org/resources/bcp/CofE1928/CofE1928_Confirmation&Marriage.htm#Marriage.

Brink, Leendert, 1982, 'Ehe/Eherecht/Eheschliessung VI: Mittelalter', in Gerhard Krause and Gerhard Müller (eds), *Theologische Realenzyklopädie*, vol. 9, Berlin: De Gruyter, pp. 330–6.

Brown, Peter, 2008, *The Body and Society: Men, Women, and Sexual Renunciation in Early Christianity*, new edn, New York, NY: Columbia University Press.

Brownson, James, 2013, *Bible, Gender, Sexuality. Reframing the Church's Debate on Same-Sex Relationships*, Grand Rapids, MI: Eerdmans.

Brunner, Emil, 2002 [1946], 'Nature and Grace', in Emil Brunner and Karl Barth, *Natural Theology: Comprising 'Nature and Grace' by Professor Dr Emil Brunner and the Reply 'No!' by Dr Karl Barth*, London: Geoffrey Bles/ Centenary Press, pp. 15–64.

Buell, Denise Kimber, 2005, *Why this new Race: Ethnic Reasoning in Early Christianity*, New York, NY: Columbia University Press.

Butler, Judith, 1990, *Gender Trouble: Feminism and the Subversion of Identity*. New York, NY: Routledge.

Cahill, Lisa Sowle, 1996, *Sex, Gender, and Christian Ethics*, Cambridge: Cambridge University Press.

Callahan, Virginia Woods (trans.), 1999 [1967], *Saint Gregory of Nyssa: Ascetical Works*, Washington, DC: Howard University.

Candler, Peter M., 2006, *Theology, Rhetoric, Manuduction, or Reading Scripture Together on the Path to God*, Grand Rapids, MI: Eerdmans.

Catholic Bishops Conference of England and Wales, 2013, 'Statement on the Passing of the Marriage (Same Sex Couples) Act', www.catholic-ew.org.uk/ Home/News/Marriage-Same-Sex-Couples-Act.

Central Board of Finance of the Church of England, 1980, *Alternative Service Book*, London: Church House Publishing.

Central Board of Finance of the Church of England, 1988, *The Ordination of Women to the Priesthood: A Second Report by the House of Bishops of the General Synod of the Church of England*, London: General Synod of the Church of England.

Church Growth Research Programme, 2014, 'Statistics – Age Profile', www. churchgrowthresearch.org.uk/statistics_age_profile.

Church of England, 1969, The Book of Common Prayer, Oxford: Oxford University Press.

Church of England, 2012, 'A Response to the Government Equalities Office Consultation – "Equal Civil Marriage" – from the Church of England', www. churchofengland.org/media/1475149/s-s%20marriage.pdf.

Cleugh, Hannah, 2014, 'Marriage, the Reformation and the BCP', paper given at the Affirming Catholicism conference 'Thinking About Marriage? Theological and Historical Perspectives' on 25 January 2014, available at www.youtube. com/watch?v=jCs7S3FMuls.

Coakley, Sarah, 2013, *God, Sexuality, and the Self: An Essay 'On the Trinity'*, Cambridge: Cambridge University Press.

Cobb, M., 2012, 'An Amazing 10 Years: The Discovery of Egg and Sperm in the 17th Century', *Reproduction in Domestic Animals* 47 Suppl. 4, pp. 2–6.

Cobb, Stephanie L., 2008, *Dying to be Men: Gender and Language in Early Christian Martyr Texts*, New York; Chichester: Columbia University Press.

Coleman, Peter, 2004, *Christian Attitudes to Marriage: From Ancient Times to the Third Millennium*, London: SCM Press.

Combs, Mary Beth, 2006, 'Cui bono? The 1870 British Married Women's Property Act, Bargaining Power, and the Distribution of Resources Within Marriage', *Feminist Economics* 12.1–2, pp. 51–83.

Congar, Yves OP, 2004 [1964], *The Meaning of Tradition*, San Francisco, CA: Ignatius Press.

Cooper, Kate, 2007, *The Fall of the Roman Household*, Cambridge: Cambridge University Press.

Cornwall, Susannah, 2010, *Sex and Uncertainty in the Body of Christ: Intersex Conditions and Christian Theology*, London: Routledge.

Cornwall, Susannah, 2012, 'Intersex and Ontology: A Response to *The Church, Women Bishops and Provision*', University of Manchester: Lincoln Theological Institute.

Countryman, L. William, 2001, *Dirt, Greed and Sex: Sexual Ethics in the New Testament and their Implications for Today*, London: SCM Press.

Crouzel, Henri, 1982, 'Ehe/Eherecht/Ehescheidung V: Alte Kirche', in Gerhard Krause and Gerhard Müller (eds), *Theologische Realenzyklopädie*, vol. 9, Berlin: De Gruyter, pp. 325–30.

Cumming, Laura, 2014, 'Rembrandt: The Late Works Review: Dark, Impassioned, Magnificently Defiant', *The Observer*, 19 October, www.theguardian.com/artanddesign/2014/oct/19/rembrandt-late-works-review-national-gallery-magnificently-defiant.

Dillon, John M., 1983, '*Metriopatheia* and *Apatheia*: Some Reflections on a Controversy in Later Greek Ethics', in *Essays in Ancient Philosophy: Volume II*, Albany, NY: State University of Albany Press, pp. 508–17.

Doctrine Committee of the Scottish Episcopal Church, 2012, *Marriage and Human Intimacy: Perspectives on Same-Sex Relationships and the Life of the Church*, Grosvenor Essay No 8. Edinburgh: General Synod Office.

Farley, Margaret, 2013, rev. edn, *Personal Commitments: Beginning, Keeping, Changing*, Maryknoll, NY: Orbis Books.

Fausto-Sterling, Anne, 2012, *Sex/Gender: Biology in a Social World*, London: Routledge.

Ford, David F., 2015, 'Theology at Full Stretch', Bampton Lectures, University Church of St Mary the Virgin, Oxford, 20 January 2015.

Frank, Georgia, 2000, 'Macrina's Scar: Homeric Allusion and Heroic Identity in Gregory of Nyssa's *Life of Macrina*', *Journal of Early Christian Studies* 8.4, pp. 511–30.

Frei, Hans, 1975, *The Identity of Jesus Christ*, Philadelphia, PA: Fortress Press.

Frei, Hans, 1990, *Types of Christian Theology*, New Haven, CT: Yale University Press.

Frei, Hans, 1993, 'The Literal Reading of Biblical Narrative: Will it Stretch or Will it Break?', in George Hunsinger and William C. Placher (eds), *Theology and Narrative: Selected Essays*, New York, NY: Oxford University Press, pp. 117–52.

Gagnon, Robert, 2002, *The Bible and Homosexual Practice: Texts and Hermeneutics*, Nashville, TN: Abingdon Press.

Gillis, John R., 1985, *For Better, For Worse: British Marriages, 1600 to the Present*, Oxford: Oxford University Press.

Gittoes, Julie, Brutus Green and James Heard (eds), 2013, *Generous Ecclesiology: Church, World, and the Kingdom of God*, London: SCM Press.

Government Equalities Office, 2012, *Equal Civil Marriage: A Consultation*, www.gov.uk/government/uploads/system/uploads/attachment_data/file/133258/consultation-document_1_.pdf.

Hammond, Cally, 2014, 'Augustine and Early Church Understandings of Marriage', paper given at the Affirming Catholicism conference 'Thinking About Marriage? Theological and Historical Perspectives' on 25 January 2014, available at www.youtube.com/watch?v=suD2iFiKtZQ.

Hardy, Daniel W., 2001, *Finding the Church: The Dynamic Truth of Anglicanism*, London: SCM Press.

Hardy, Daniel W., 2002, 'Worship and the Formation of a Holy People', in Stephen Barton (ed.), *Holiness Past and Present*, London: T&T Clark, pp. 477–98.

Hardy, Daniel W., 2010, *Wording a Radiance: Parting Conversations on God and the Church*, London: SCM Press.

Hays, Richard B., 1997, *The Moral Vision of the New Testament: A Contemporary Introduction to New Testament Ethics*, Edinburgh: T&T Clark.

Higton, Mike, forthcoming 2016, 'Christian Doctrine and the Discipline of Reading Scripture', in Angus Paddison (ed.), *Theologians on Scripture*, London: T&T Clark.

House of Bishops of the Church of England, 1999, *Marriage: A Teaching Document from the House of Bishops of the Church of England*, London: Church House Publishing, www.churchofengland.org/media/45645/marriage.pdf.

House of Bishops of the Church of England, 2005, 'Civil Partnerships – A Pastoral Statement from the House of Bishops of the Church of England', www.churchofengland.org/media-centre/news/2005/07/pr5605.aspx.

House of Bishops of the Church of England, 15 February 2014, 'Pastoral Guidance on Same-Sex Marriage', www.churchofengland.org/media-centre/news/2014/02/house-of-bishops-pastoral-guidance-on-same-sex-marriage.aspx.

Jerome, letter 22: *To Eustochium*, 2, www.fordham.edu/halsall/basis/jerome-letter22.asp.

John Chrysostom, 'Against Opponents of the Monastic Life', in Eugene F. Rogers (ed.), *Theology and Sexuality: Classic and Contemporary Readings*, Oxford: Blackwell, p. 93.

John Chrysostom, 'Homily on Marriage I', in Eugene F. Rogers (ed.), *Theology and Sexuality: Classic and Contemporary Readings*, Oxford: Blackwell, p. 90.

John Paul II (Pope), 1988, '*Mulieris Dignitatem* (On the Dignity and Vocation of Women)', www.vatican.va/holy_father/john_paul_ii/apost_letters/documents/hf_jp-ii_apl_15081988_mulieris-dignitatem_en.html.

John Paul II (Pope), 2006, *Man and Woman He Created Them: A Theology of the Body*, Boston, MA: Pauline Books and Media.

John Paul II (Pope), 1997, *The Theology of the Body: Human Love in the Divine Plan*, Boston, MA: Pauline Books.

John Paul II, 2006 [1986]), *Man and Woman He Created Them: A Theology of the Body*, Boston, MA: Pauline Books & Media,

John, Jeffrey, 1993, 'Permanent, Faithful, Stable': Christian Same-Sex Partnerships, London: Darton, Longman & Todd.

John, Jeffrey, 2012, Permanent, Faithful, Stable: Christian Same-Sex Marriage, London: Darton, Longman & Todd.

Johnson, William Stacy, 2012, A Time to Embrace: Same-Sex Relationships in Religion, Law and Politics, 2nd edn, Grand Rapids, MI: Eerdmans.

Jones, Timothy Willem, 2013, Sexual Politics in the Church of England, 1857–1957, Oxford: Oxford University Press.

Jordan, Mark D. (ed.), 2006, Authorizing Marriage? Canon, Tradition, and Critique in the Blessing of Same-Sex Unions, Princeton, NJ: Princeton University Press.

Jordan, Mark D., 2002, The Ethics of Sex, Oxford: Blackwell.

Jordan, Mark D., 2005, Blessing Same-Sex Unions: The Perils of Queer Romance and the Confusions of Christian Marriage, Chicago, IL: University of Chicago Press.

Jordan, Mark D., 2006, 'Arguing Liturgical Genealogies, or, the Ghosts of Weddings Past', in Mark D. Jordan with Meghan T. Sweeney and David M. Mellott (eds), Authorizing Marriage? Canon, Tradition, and Critique in the Blessing of Same-Sex Unions, Princeton, NJ: Princeton University Press, pp. 102–20.

Kärkkäinen, Veli-Matti, 2014, Trinity and Revelation, Grand Rapids, MI: Eerdmans.

Kelsey, David, 2009, Eccentric Existence: A Theological Anthropology, Louisville, KY: Westminster John Knox Press.

Kerr, Fergus, 2007, Twentieth-Century Catholic Theologians, Oxford: Blackwell.

Laqueur, Thomas, 1990, Making Sex: Body and Gender from the Greeks to Freud, Cambridge, MA: Harvard University Press.

Loughlin, Gerard, 2004, 'Sex after Natural Law', in Marcella Althaus-Reid and Lisa Isherwood (eds), The Sexual Theologian: Essays on Sex, God and Politics, London: T&T Clark, pp. 86–98.

Luther, Martin, 1519 (1966), 'A Sermon on the Estate of Marriage', in Jaroslav Pelikan (ed.), Luther's Works, vol. 44: The Christian in Society I, Minneapolis, MN: Fortress Press, pp. 7–14.

Luther, Martin, 1522 (1962), 'The Estate of Marriage', in Jaroslav Pelikan (ed.), Luther's Works, vol. 45: The Christian in Society II, Minneapolis, MN: Fortress Press, pp. 13–51.

Luther, Martin, 1535a (1958), 'Lectures on Genesis' (part 1), in Jaroslav Pelikan (ed.), Luther's Works, vol. 1: Lectures on Genesis Chapters 1 – 5, Minneapolis, MN: Fortress Press.

Luther, Martin, 1535b (1963), 'Lectures on Galatians, 1535' (part 1), in Jaroslav Pelikan (ed.), Luther's Works, vol. 26: Lectures on Galatians, 1535, Chapters 1 – 4, Minneapolis, MN: Fortress Press.

Macdonald, Lesley Orr, 2001, Out of the Shadows: Christianity and Violence against Women in Scotland, Edinburgh: Centre for Theology and Public Issues.

MacLean, Ian, 1980, The Renaissance Notion of Woman, Cambridge: Cambridge University Press.

Martin, Emily, 1991, 'The Egg and the Sperm: How Science Has Constructed a Romance Based on Stereotypical Male–Female Roles', Signs: Journal of Women in Culture and Society 16.3, pp. 485–501.

Martin, Francis, 2001, 'Marriage in the Old Testament and Intertestamental Periods', in Glenn W. Olson (ed.), *Christian Marriage: A Historical Study*, New York, NY: Crossroad, pp. 1–49.

Martin, Jessica, 2013, 'Living with Holiness and Desire', in *Report of the House of Bishops Working Group on Human Sexuality*, Archbishops', Council, pp. ix–xvi. London: Church House Publishing.

Matzko McCarthy, David, 1997, 'Homosexuality and the Practices of Marriage', *Modern Theology* 13.3, pp. 371–97.

Matzko McCarthy, David, 2001, *Sex and Love in the Home: A Theology of the Household*, London: SCM Press.

McCluskey, Colleen, 2007, 'An Unequal Relationship between Equals: Thomas Aquinas on Marriage', *History of Philosophy Quarterly* 24.1, pp. 1–18.

McFadyen, Alistair I., 1990, *The Call to Personhood: A Christian Theory of the Individual in Social Relationships*, Cambridge: Cambridge University Press.

McFarland, Ian., 2014, 'The Saving God', in Kent Eilers and Kyle Strobel (eds), *Sanctified by Grace: A Theology of the Christian Life*, London: Bloomsbury, pp. 61–73.

Methuen, Charlotte, 2008, '"Denke an dein Kind, das ohne dich nicht leben kann!" Mütter in der Nachfolge Christi', in Annette Esser and Andrea Günther (eds), *Kinder haben – KindSein – Geboren sein*, Königstein: Ulrike Helmer Verlag, pp. 47–60.

Methuen, Charlotte, 2013a, 'Marriage: One Man and One Woman?', www.opendemocracy.net/ourkingdom/charlotte-methuen/marriage-one-man-and-one-woman.

Methuen, Charlotte, 2013b, '"And your Daughters shall Prophesy!" Reforming Women and the Construction of Authority', *Archiv für Reformationsgeschichte* 104.1, pp. 82–109.

Methuen, Charlotte, 2014, 'Thinking About Marriage: An Excursion Through Christian History', *Modern Believing* 55.2, pp. 149–62.

Milbank, John, 2012, 'Gay Marriage and the future of human sexuality', *ABC: Religion and Ethics*, 13 March, www.abc.net.au/religion/articles/2012/03/13/3452229.htm.

Morris, Jeremy, 2014, 'Marriage and the Church of England in the Nineteenth Century', paper given at the Affirming Catholicism conference 'Thinking About Marriage? Theological and Historical Perspectives' on 25 January 2014; available at www.youtube.com/watch?v=RE5NRB_W5MY.

Muers, Rachel, 2008, *Living for the Future: Theological Ethics for Coming Generations*, London: T&T Clark.

Muller, Earl C., SJ, 1990, *Trinity and Marriage in Paul: The Establishment of a Communitarian Analogy of the Trinity Grounded in the Theological Shape of Pauline Thought*, New York, NY: Peter Lang.

Nissinen, Martti, 1998, *Homoeroticism in the Biblical World: A Historical Perspective*, Minneapolis, MN: Fortress Press.

Norris, Richard A., 2012, *Gregory of Nyssa: Homilies on the Song of Songs*, Atlanta, GA: Society of Biblical Literature.

Office for National Statistics, 2013, 'What Percentage of Marriages End in Divorce?', www.ons.gov.uk/ons/rel/vsob1/divorces-in-england-and-wales/2011/sty-what-percentage-of-marriages-end-in-divorce.html.

Office for National Statistics, 2013, 'Trends in Civil and Religious Marriages, 1966–2011', www.ons.gov.uk/ons/rel/vsob1/marriages-in-england-and-wales--provisional-/2011/sty-marriages.html.

Office for National Statistics, 2014, 'Live Births Within Marriage / Civil Partnership', www.ons.gov.uk/ons/rel/vsob1/birth-summary-tables--england-and-wales/2013/stb-births-in-england-and-wales-2013.html#tab-Live-Births-Within-Marriage-Civil-Partnership.

Økland, Jorunn, 2014, 'Paul, Marriage and the New Testament', paper given at the Affirming Catholicism conference 'Thinking About Marriage? Theological and Historical Perspectives' on 25 January 2014; available at www.youtube.com/watch?v=eh8Zv-A2Ti4.

Oliver, Gillian, 2012, *The Church Weddings Handbook: The Seven Pastoral Moments that Matter*, London: Church House Publishing.

Paoletti, Jo, 2012, *Pink and Blue: Telling the Boys from the Girls in America*, Bloomington, IN: Indiana University Press.

Pearce, C. C. A., 2002, 'The Christian Claims of the English Law of Marriage', in Adrian Thatcher (ed.), *Celebrating Christian Marriage*, Edinburgh: T&T Clark, pp. 403–20.

Péguy, Charles, 2005, *The Portal of the Mystery of Hope*, trans. David Louis Schindler Jr., London: Continuum.

Perkin, Joan, 1989, *Women and Marriage in Nineteenth-Century England*, London: Taylor & Francis.

Porter, Muriel, 1996, *Sex, Marriage, and the Church: Patterns of Change*, North Blackburn, Victoria: HarperCollinsReligious.

Pritchard, John, 2013, *Living Faithfully: Following Christ in Everyday Life*, London: SPCK.

Probert, Rebecca, 2008, 'Examining Law through the Lens of Literature: The Formation of Marriage in Eighteenth-century England', *Law and Humanities* 2.1, pp. 29–48.

Probert, Rebecca, 2009, *Marriage Law and Practice in the Long Eighteenth Century: A Reassessment*, Cambridge: Cambridge University Press.

Quash, Ben, 2002, 'Making the Most of the Time: Liturgy, Ethics and Time', *Studies in Christian Ethics* 15.1, pp. 97–114.

Quash, Ben, 2005, *Theology and the Drama of History*, Cambridge: Cambridge University Press.

Quash, Ben, 2012, *Abiding*, London: Bloomsbury.

Quash, Ben, 2013, *Found Theology: History, Imagination and the Holy Spirit*, London: Bloomsbury.

Roberts, Christopher Chenault, 2009, *Creation and Covenant: The Significance of Sexual Difference in the Moral Theology of Marriage*, New York, NY: T&T Clark International.

Rogers, Eugene F., 1999, *Sexuality and the Christian Body: Their Way into the Triune God*, Oxford: Blackwell.

Rogers, Eugene F. (ed.), 2002, *Theology and Sexuality: Classic and Contemporary Readings*, Oxford: Blackwell.

Rogers, Eugene F., 2005, *After the Spirit: A Constructive Pneumatology from Resources Outside the Modern West*, Grand Rapids, MI: Eerdmans.

Rogers, Eugene F., 2006, 'Trinity, Marriage and Homosexuality', in Mark D. Jordan with Meghan T. Sweeney and David M. Mellott (eds), *Authorizing Marriage? Canon, Tradition, and Critique in the Blessing of Same-Sex Unions*, Princeton, NJ: Princeton University Press, pp. 151–64.

Rowe, Kavin, 2009, *World Upside Down: Reading Acts in the Graeco-Roman Age*, New York, NY: Oxford University Press.

Rowe, Kavin, 2009, *Early Narrative Christology: The Lord in the Gospel of Luke*, Grand Rapids, MI: Baker Academic.

Sachs, William L., 2009, *Homosexuality and the Crisis of Anglicanism*, Cambridge: Cambridge University Press.

Salzman, Todd A. and Michael G. Lawler, 2008, *The Sexual Person: Toward a Renewed Catholic Anthropology*, Washington, DC: Georgetown University Press.

Sayers, Dorothy L., 1994 [1941], *The Mind of the Maker*, London: Mowbray.

Sayers, Dorothy L. and Barbara Reynolds (trans.), 2004, *Dante Alighieri, The Divine Comedy: Paradise*, rev. edn, London: Penguin.

Schaff, Philip (ed.), 1892, *Gregory of Nyssa: Dogmatic Treatises, etc.: A Select Library of the Nicene and Post-Nicene Fathers of the Christian Church, Second Series*, vol. 5, trans. William Moore and Henry Austin Wilson, Grand Rapids, MI: Christian Classics Ethereal Library; New York: Christian Literature Publishing Co., www.ccel.org/ccel/schaff/npnf205.pdf.

Schmidt, Thomas E., 1995, *Straight and Narrow? Compassion and Clarity in the Homosexuality Debate*, Leicester: IVP.

Schoedel, William R., 2000, 'Same-Sex Eros: Paul and the Greco-Roman Tradition', in David L., Balch (ed.), *Homosexuality, Science, and the 'Plain Sense' of Scripture*, Grand Rapids, MI: Eerdmans, pp. 43–72.

Schumacher, Michele M., 2004, *Women in Christ: Toward a New Feminism*, Grand Rapids, MI: Eerdmans.

Seitz, Christopher, 2000, 'Sexuality and Scripture's Plain Sense: The Christian Community and the Law of God', in David L. Balch (ed.), *Homosexuality, Science, and the 'Plain Sense' of Scripture*, Grand Rapids, MI: Eerdmans, pp. 177–96.

Silvas, Anna M. (trans.), 2007, *Gregory of Nyssa: The Letters. Introduction, Translation and Commentary*, Leiden: Brill.

Silvas, Anna M. (trans.), 2008, *Macrina the Younger: Philosopher of God*, Turnhout: Brepols.

Sohn, Seock-Tae, 2002, *YHWH, The Husband of Israel: The Metaphor of Marriage between YHWH and Israel*, Eugene, OR: Wipf & Stock.

Song, Robert, 2014, *Covenant and Calling: Towards a Theology of Same-Sex Relationships*, London: SCM Press.

Spufford, Francis, 2012, *Unapologetic: Why, Despite Everything, Christianity Can Still Make Surprising Emotional Sense*, London: Faber & Faber.

Stone, Lawrence, 1977, *The Family, Sex and Marriage in England 1500–1800*, London: Weidenfeld & Nicolson.

Tait, Michael, 2010, *Jesus, The Divine Bridegroom, in Mark 2:18–22: Mark's Christology Upgraded*, Rome: Gregorian and Biblical Press.

Tanis, Justin, 2003, *Trans-Gendered: Theology, Ministry, and Communities of Faith*, Cleveland, OH: Pilgrim Press.

Taylor, Charles, 1989, *Sources of the Self: The Making of the Modern Identity*, Cambridge: Cambridge University Press.

Taylor, Diane, 2013, 'Sperm Donors who Know Parents can Apply to see Children, Court Rules', *The Guardian*, 31 January 2013, www.guardian.co.uk/lifeandstyle/2013/jan/31/sperm-donors-parents-apply-contact-children.

Thatcher, Adrian, 1999, *Marriage After Modernity: Christian Marriage in Postmodern Times*, Sheffield: Sheffield Academic Press.

Vanier, Jean, 2004, *Drawn into the Mystery of Jesus through the Gospel of John*, London: Darton, Longman & Todd.

Vines, Matthew, 2014, *God and the Gay Christian: The Biblical Case in Support of Same-Sex Relationships*, New York, NY: Convergent Books.

Wannenwetsch, Bernd, 2000, 'Old Docetism—New Moralism? Questioning a New Direction in the Homosexuality Debate', *Modern Theology* 16.3, pp. 353–64.

Ward, Graham, 2005, *Christ and Culture*, Malden, MA: Blackwell.

Ward, Graham, 2006, 'Tradition and Traditions: Scripture, Christian Praxes and Politics', in Justin S. Holcomb (ed.), *Christian Theologies of Scripture: A Comparative Introduction*, New York, NY: New York University Press, pp. 243–60.

Ward, Keith, 1994, *Religion and Revelation: A Theology of Revelation in the World's Religions*, Oxford: Clarendon Press.

Westermann, Claus, 1994, *Genesis 1–11*, Minneapolis, MN: Fortress Press.

Wiesner, Merry E., 2008, *Women and Gender in Early Modern Europe*, Cambridge: Cambridge University Press.

Wiesner-Hanks, Merry E., 2000, *Christianity and Sexuality in the Early Modern World*, London: Routledge.

Williams, Rowan, 1989, reprinted 2003, *The Body's Grace*, London: Lesbian and Gay Christian Movement.

Williams, Rowan, 1994, *Open to Judgement: Sermons and Addresses*, London: Darton, Longman & Todd.

Williams, Rowan, 1996, 'The Body's Grace', in C. Hefling (ed.), *Our Selves, Our Souls and Bodies: Sexuality and the Household of God*, Boston: Cowley, pp. 58–67.

Williams, Rowan, 1997, 'Knowing Myself in Christ', in Timothy Bradshaw (ed.), *The Way Forward? Christian Voices on Homosexuality and the Church*, London: Hodder & Stoughton, pp. 12–19.

Williams, Rowan, 2002, 'The Deflections of Desire: Negative Theology in Trinitarian Disclosure', in Oliver Davies and Denys Turner (eds), *Silence and the Word: Negative Theology and Incarnation*, Cambridge: Cambridge University Press, pp. 115–35.

Williams, Rowan, 2002, 'The Body's Grace', in Eugene F. Rogers (ed.), *Theology and Sexuality: Classic and Contemporary Readings*, Oxford: Blackwell, pp. 309–21.

Williams, Rowan, 2002, *Resurrection: Interpreting the Easter Gospel*, 2nd edn, London: Darton, Longman & Todd.

Williams, Rowan, 2014, *The Other Mountain*, Manchester: Carcanet.

Wilson, Alan, 2014, *More Perfect Union? Understanding Same-Sex Marriage*, London: Darton, Longman & Todd.

Witte, John Jr, 1997, *From Sacrament to Contract: Marriage, Religion, and Law in the Western Tradition*, Louisville, KY: Westminster John Knox Press.

Wojtyła, Karol, 2006 [1986], *Love and Responsibility*, London: Collins.

Woodhead, Linda, 1997, 'Sex in a Wider Context', in Jon Davies and Gerard Loughlin (eds), *Sex These Days: Essays on Theology, Sexuality and Society*, Sheffield: Sheffield Academic Press, pp. 98–120.

Woodhead, Linda, 2013, 'Do Christians Really Oppose Gay Marriage?', www.religionandsociety.org.uk/events/programme_events/show/press_release_do_christians_really_oppose_gay_marriage.

Woodhead, Linda, 2014, 'What People Really Think About Same-Sex Marriage', *Modern Believing* 55.2, pp. 27–38.

Woodhead, Linda, 2014, 'Questioning the Guidance', *Modern Believing* 55.3, pp. 286–91.

Wright, N. T., 2013, *Paul and the Faithfulness of God: Christian Origins and the Question of God*, London: SPCK.

Wyschogrod, Michael, 1996, *The Body of Faith: God and the People of Israel*, Northvale, NJ: Jason Aronson Inc.

Index of Biblical References

Genesis 1	26, 31, 140	1 Samuel 1.1	192n.
Genesis 1–2	45, 56	1 Samuel 1–2	191–2
Genesis 1–3	198	1 Samuel 1.4–5,	8 191
Genesis 1–11	55	1 Samuel 1.8	56
Genesis 1–26	140		
Genesis 1.26–28	30	Job 10.8–19	55
Genesis 1.28	129		
Genesis 1.27–28	56–7	Psalm 44	21
Genesis 1.31	30	Psalm 104.10–28	54
Genesis 2	57	Psalm 104.29–30	54
Genesis 2.18	141		
Genesis 2.24	66	Proverbs	54
Genesis 2.4b–3.24	55	Proverbs 5.15–20	57
Genesis 3	55	Proverbs 8.11	58
Genesis 12.3	138	Proverbs 8.22–31	59
Genesis 17	138		
Genesis 19	45	Ecclesiastes	125
Genesis 29	31	Ecclesiastes 9.7–10	57n.
Exodus 21.7–11	31	Song of Songs	57–8, 84,
Exodus 22.16–17	31		125
		Song of Songs 3.3	57n.
Leviticus 18	45, 181	Song of Songs	
Leviticus 18.22	60	4.9–12	57n.
Leviticus 18.6	181	Song of Songs 5.1–2	57n.
Leviticus 20	45	Song of Songs 6.3	58
Leviticus 20.13	60	Song of Songs	
		6.8–10	58
Deuteronomy		Song of Songs 8.1–2	57n.
22.28–29	31	Song of Songs 8.5	57n.
		Song of Songs 8.6	84

Isaiah	54
Jeremiah 2–3	137
Jeremiah 31	158–9
Ezekiel 16	137
Ezekiel 23	137
Hosea 1–3	137
Hosea 1.2–3	137
Hosea 2.19–20	137
Matthew 1.18	170
Matthew 19.6	130
Matthew 19.7–9	34
Matthew 19.9	181
Matthew 5.31–2	34
Matthew 9.5	138
Matthew 22.30	129
Mark 2.19–20	138
Mark 10	45, 54
Luke	47
Luke 1.1–4	52
Luke 5.34	138
John 1 (Johannine Prologue)	54
John 1.56	122
John 2.1–12	138
John 3.22–30	138
John 16.13	75
John 16.16	75
John 20.27	64
John 20.28	64
John 20.29	64
Acts	48
Acts 2	48, 50
Acts 2.16–36	51
Acts 2.20	51
Acts 2.36	48
Acts 2.40	49
Acts 2.42–47	50
Acts 2.47	50
Acts 3.12–26	51
Acts 4.18	49
Acts 6.2	49
Acts 6.7	49
Acts 7.1–53	51
Acts 8.30–35	51
Acts 11.21	50
Acts 13.16–41	51
Acts 13.44	49
Acts 13.48	49
Acts 14.14–17	51
Acts 14.16–17	51, 54
Acts 17.22–28	51
Acts 17.26	50, 54
Acts 22.26	50
Romans 1.17	50n.
Romans 1.18	54n.
Romans 1.18–32	45, 60
Romans 5	54
Romans 12.2	53
Romans 12.4–5	147
1 Corinthians 1.24	125
1 Corinthians 2.2	26
1 Corinthians 2.4–5	50n.
1 Corinthians 6.15–17	139
1 Corinthians 7	45
1 Corinthians 7.1–16	33
1 Corinthians 7.12	145
1 Corinthians 7.14	33, 145
1 Corinthians 7.8–9	34, 146
1 Corinthians 10.1	53
1 Corinthians 11.2–16	52
1 Corinthians 11.23	65
1 Corinthians 12.12	147

1 Corinthians 12.15–18   147
1 Corinthians 12.25–26   147
1 Corinthians 13   32, 88
1 Corinthians 15   54
1 Corinthians 15.44   129

2 Corinthians 2.17   50
2 Corinthians 5.18–21   50
2 Corinthians 11.1–3   138

Galatians 1.1   49n.
Galatians 1.11   49n.
Galatians 3.27–29   144
Galatians 3.28   126, 129–30

Ephesians 3.20   76
Ephesians 5.22–25   32
Ephesian 5.22–33   45, 138–9
Ephesian 5.32   34

Philippians 3.13   126

Colossians 1.15   54
Colossians 3.18–4.1   32

2 Timothy 3.16   53

Titus 2.1–10   32

Philemon 6   144
Philemon 16   144

1 Peter 2.18–3.7   32
1 Peter 33.1–2   39n.

1 John 4.16   88

Revelation 19.17, 20   92
Revelation 19.6–9   138

Index of Names and subjects

Abraham (biblical figure) 138, 143, 146

Act of Supremacy 1558 169n., 174n.

Acts of the Apostles 48–52, 54

Acts of Uniformity 1548–1551 175n.

Adam (biblical figure) 35, 54–5, 104, 130, 141

Administration of Estates Act 1925 184

Affection 33, 94, 96, 99

Affinity 34, 176, 181–2, 187–8

Age of consent 4, 182

Age of Marriage Act 1929 182n.

Alighieri, Dante 79

Alternative Service Book 1980 39

Annulment 182

Another Year (Leigh) 97

Asceticism 10, 34, 35n., 122–33

Augustine 33–4, 39n., 105, 157, 164

Banns 9, 172–4, 176–9

Baptism 48–50, 143

Barth, Karl 7, 8, 108–10

Betrothal 173

Bible 3, 4, 30, 44–5, 47, 137

Bigamy 185

Births and Deaths Registration Act 1836 178

Book of Common Prayer 18, 37, 157n.

Bride price 31

Brunner, Emil 7, 8

Butler, Judith 106–7

Canon law 18n., 39, 169, 175–6

Celibacy 32, 34–6, 38, 123, 133, 147–9, 163

Children 2, 3, 4, 15, 19, 29, 31, 33, 35–40, 66–7, 71, 84, 90–1, 97, 101–6, 110, 112–13, 118, 137, 149, 154, 162–4, 192, 197

Christ as a Bridegroom 23, 136, 138, 146

Christ as a Head 138–9, 126

Church as a Bride 23, 31, 90, 92, 94, 108, 125, 136–7, 140, 146–7

Church Dogmatics (Barth) 8, 109

Civil Partnership Act 2004 183

Clandestine Marriages Act 1753 (Hardwicke) 36

Clergy (Ordination and Miscellaneous Provisions) Measure 1964 188

Clergy Marriage Act 1548 175

Commitment 11, 12, 18, 27, 31, 55, 59, 71, 78n., 82, 84–99, 113–14, 118, 147–8, 154, 156–7

Common Worship 15, 18, 23, 37, 66n, 82n., 84, 87n., 157

Complementarity 10, 14, 15, 16, 17, 20, 31, 40n., 62, 71–4, 101, 103–4, 121, 130, 132, 155, 194, 198, 20

Concubine 31, 58

Congar, Yves 63–4, 66, 76

Consanguinity 34

Consent 1, 34, 73, 94–5, 174, 176–9, 182, 184, 186

Consummation 73, 130, 170, 182

Eschatological 44, 85, 193

Contraception 39, 103, 118, 155, 158

Contract (legal) 89, 92, 97, 150, 170–3, 178–80, 183, 185, 190

Covenant 23, 58, 85, 90, 92, 95, 97, 137, 138, 146, 150, 163, 165

Covenant and Calling (Song) 3, 45, 56, 60n., 85, 90, 163, 165

Creation 5, 7, 8, 9, 14, 18, 19, 23–4, 26, 30–1, 40, 44, 51, 54–6, 67, 71, 74n., 78–9, 87–90, 97, 111, 129–130, 140–2, 150, 154, 162, 193, 195, 199

Creator 7, 23, 26, 48, 51, 54, 140–1, 192

Creatureliness 23, 78

Cromwell, Thomas 174

Crown (theological) 83–4, 87, 90, 93, 96–7, 98–9, 195, 201 (head)175n., 184

David (biblical figure) 31

Deceased Wife's Sister Marriage Act 1907 181, 188n.

Declarations 1, 88, 94

Divorce 1, 4, 36, 40, 45, 54, 69, 72, 98, 145, 168–9, 175–6, 180–2, 184–5, 187–8

Divorce Law Reform Act 1969 181

Eccentric Existence (Kelsey) 54–5, 57–8, 141–2, 198

Ecclesiastical Appeals Act 1532 174n.

Ecclesiastical Jurisdiction Measure 1963 184

Ecclesiastical Licences Act 1533 169, 175

Elizabeth I 174, 176

Elkanah (biblical figure) 56, 191, 192

Engagement 170, 173

English Reformation 37

'Equal Civil Marriage' (Church of England) 15

Equality Act 2010 186

European Convention on Human Rights 182

Eve (biblical figure) 55, 104, 130

Faithfulness (within marriage) 11, 80, 85, 89, 90, 92, 96, 98, 137, 154, 159, 162 (God's) 85, 92, 95–6, 156n.

Fall 35–6, 55, 131

Family Law Reform Act 1969 182n.

Family Law Reform Act 1987 184n.

Fecundity 4, 117

Female nature 127–8

Fidelity 10, 16, 57, 92, 113, 154, 157, 159, 165, 171

Found Theology (Quash) 75–6, 78n.

Fourth Lateran Council 34, 173
Friendship 33, 148
Fruitfulness 89–90, 95, 97, 103, 117, 165, 191, 199–200

Gender Recognition Act 2004 183n., 186
Generativity 102
Gentiles 45n., 48, 51
Gregory of Nyssa 101, 121–34, 200

Hannah (biblical figure) 191–4, 197
Henry VIII 34n.
Holy Spirit 8n., 27, 36, 48–50, 53, 63, 71, 75, 76–7, 79, 88, 92, 97, 99, 115, 143–4, 161
Human Rights Act 1998 184n.
Hymns 1

Image of God 109, 140, 126
Inheritance 33, 35, 175, 184
Intersex 9, 56, 103, 110, 112, 121–2, 182
Israel 47–8, 51–2, 136–9, 143, 146

Jacob (biblical figure) 31
Jerome 33, 35
Jesus 23–4, 26–7, 44, 47–54, 60, 63–65, 92, 102–3, 108, 129, 150, 170, 198
Jewish Marriage 32, 172, 180, 185
Job (biblical figure) 55–6, 141
John Chrysostom 162n., 164
John Paul II (Pope) 73, 104–6, 122n.
Jordan, Mark D. 62, 68, 70–1, 104

Katherine of Aragon 34n.

Laqueur, Thomas 35, 57, 72, 74n.
Leah (biblical figure) 31
Legal Contract 92, 97, 150
Liturgy 3, 15, 18n., 19, 63, 66, 70n., 83–93, 98–9, 175, 180, 185, 195
Lord 26, 48–52, 54, 80, 85, 92, 139
Luther, Martin 36–7, 174

Macrina the Younger 122, 126–8
Marriage (Same Sex Couples) Act 2013 69, 86n., 183
Marriage Act 1540 175, 181
Marriage Act 1823 178n., 179n.
Marriage Act 1836 178, 185n.
Marriage Act 1898 179
Marriage Act 1949 179, 180n., 187n.
Marriage Act 1994 179
Marriage and Registration Act 1856 178n., 179n., 186
Marriage: A Teaching Document (Church of England) 18n.
Married Women's Property Act 1870 38, 183n.
Married Women's Property Act 1882 38
Martin, Jessica 82, 90–1, 95, 97, 99
Matrimonial Causes Act 1835 181
Matrimonial Causes Act 1857 180, 183n., 187
Matrimonial Causes Act 1937 181, 187n.
Matrimonial Causes Act 1965 187n.

Matrimonial Causes Act 1973
180n., 187n., 182, 184
Matrimonial Proceedings and
Property Act 1970 184n.
Matzko McCarthy, David 113,
156–61, 165
Men and Women in Marriage
(Faith and Order Commission)
17, 23, 25, 30–1, 35, 66, 68–9,
71–2, 74, 86n.
Monogamy 31

Natural Law 7, 8, 52, 74, 155–6
Naucratius 127–8
Nuptial mass 2

Onesimus (biblical figure) 144–5

Paul (biblical figure) 32–3, 50n.,
52–3, 65, 139, 144–6
Péguy, Charles 63
Pentecost 48–50
Permanence 28, 85, 90
Permanent, Faithful, Stable (John)
156
Polygamy 31, 188
Prayer 1, 25, 70, 88, 92, 95–6,
122–5, 191, 192
Pregnancy 35, 116, 132
Procreation 4, 15, 19–21, 31, 33,
35–7, 39, 66–7, 69, 85, 88–90,
102, 106, 115, 152–3, 155–8,
160–5
Property 5, 31, 33, 38, 171,
172n., 173, 183, 184n., 185–6
Protestant Reformation 36–8,
144, 168, 170, 174–7, 180,
187
Public ceremony 1, 2, 38, 67, 69,
173, 176–8, 180, 185–6

Quaker Marriage 180

Rachel (biblical figure) 31
Redemption 23, 26–7, 80, 87–8,
162, 193
Registrar 178, 185, 187
Reproduction 19, 31, 56–7, 59,
103–4, 117–18, 129, 152–165,
192, 199–200
Roman Empire 144, 169

Sacrament 2, 33, 135
Same-sex marriage 3, 5, 7 9,
18, 25, 30, 44, 45, 63, 68, 70,
86–7, 136, 183, 189
Samuel (biblical figure) 192
Sarah (biblical figure) 138, 143
Sayers, Dorothy L. 67, 79
Singleness 140, 143, 148
Solomon (biblical figure) 31, 58,
124
Song, Robert 3, 45n., 56, 60n.,
85, 90, 163, 165
Submission of the Clergy Act
1533 175n., 176n.
Succession of the Crown Act
1533 175n.

Table of Kindred Affinity 181
'The Body's Grace' (Williams)
152
The Identity of Jesus Christ
(Frei) 47
The Incredulity of Saint Thomas
(Caravaggio) 64
The Jewish Bride (Rembrandt)
83–4, 97
Thirty-Nine Articles 37
Thomas (biblical figure) 64–5,
67

Tradition 4, 5, 7, 9, 10, 26–7, 46, 62–81, 87, 106, 108, 113, 157, 160, 164, 167, 195, 197, 200

Transgender 107–8, 112, 114, 122, 183

Trinity 36n, 85, 88–9, 97, 140, 153, 161

Virginity 35, 123

Vocation 4, 35–6, 44, 74, 82, 91, 101–2, 112, 114, 142–3, 146–50, 156n., 163, 165, 195, 199–200

Vows 86, 94–6

Wedding at Cana 86, 91, 93, 97

Weddings Project (Church of England) 83, 85–6, 93, 99, 158

Wisdom 31, 53–4, 56–9, 125, 141–2, 198

Witness (legal) 1, 89, 172, 178

'Woman Wisdom' 58